THE
MIDDLE EASTERN
KITCHEN

GHILLIE BAŞAN

THE
MIDDLE EASTERN
KITCHEN

GHILLIE BAŞAN

WITH SPECIAL PHOTOGRAPHY BY
JONATHAN BAŞAN

KYLE CATHIE LIMITED

**This book is dedicated to our friend
Monica von Habsburg, who has
a passionate appetite for life**

Previous page: View of the Bosphorus from the Süleymaniye mosque, Istanbul, Turkey
Right: The Friday mosque, Isfahan, Iran

First published in 2001 by Kyle Cathie Limited, 122 Arlington Road, London NW1 7HP
www.kylecathie.com

This paperback edition published in 2005

ISBN 978 1 85626 608 6 (13-digit)

Text Copyright © Ghillie Başan 2001
Photography Copyright © Jonathan Başan 2001
(for further copyright acknowledgements, see page 240)

Editor: Sheila Davies   Copy-editor: Robina Pelham-Burn   Editorial assistant: Georgina Burns
Designer: Geoff Hayes   Production: Lorraine Baird and Sha Huxtable

Ghillie Başan is hereby identified as the author of this work in accordance with Section 77 of the Copyright, Designs and Patents Act 1988.

A Cataloguing in Publication record for this title is available from the British Library.

Printed and bound in Singapore by Craft Print International Ltd.

CONTENTS

INTRODUCTION

There's something incredibly sumptuous about the food of the Middle East. It is steeped in history and mystery, teasing the palate with exotic and tantalising flavours. Delicate and spicy, aromatic and fragrant, scented and syrupy – these are some of the words that come to mind. The tastes are rich and pleasing, the images romantic, airy and ancient. Rose petals and orange blossom, tamarind and dates, figs and apricots, mulberries and melons, saffron and orchid root, almonds and pistachios, olives, coriander and cumin – a myriad of flavours and dishes that are intricately entwined in the fascinating history of this vast, diverse and exciting region.

Every village, town, valley or hillside tells a story. There are the ancient Pyramids of Egypt and the Hanging Gardens of Babylon; the last route walked by Christ and the tomb of the Virgin Mary; the desert where John the Baptist survived off locusts and King Herod's fortress where the dancing Salome was given a gift of the unfortunate John's head. There is the place where Cleopatra bathed and the site where Alexander the Great sought the Oracle's advice; the Mount of Olives, the Temple of Artemis and the Gate of Hercules; the desert where Lawrence of Arabia was based during the Great Arab Revolt; Roman amphitheatres and the castles built by the Crusaders. There are the ancient cities, the holy cities, the ghostly, ruined cities, the desert cities, the towering mud cities and the exquisite Nabataean fortress city carved out of sandstone; the Bedouin camps, the troglodite cave dwellings and the reed huts in the marshes; the Black Sea, the Red Sea and the Dead Sea. There are early Christian and Byzantine churches, Jewish synagogues and magnificent domed, tiled mosques. And there is the splendid Topkapı Palace, from where the

Ottomans ruled for almost five centuries and held lavish feasts. The history of the region drips like rain off every branch of the trees, it flows through the meandering rivers and breathes through the pores of the land. As a visitor you can't fail to be impressed, tripping over relics of antiquity like the raised roots of a wizened old olive tree. For the peoples who live there, the history has had a profound effect on their lives, shaping their beliefs, their customs and their culinary traditions.

Historically, the lands of the Middle East have always been turbulent. They have seen civilisations and empires come and go. It is where Africa, Europe and Asia have always met, traded and fused. It is the birthplace of the three principal monotheistic religions – Christianity, Judaism and Islam. So, for centuries, it has witnessed clashes between cultures and religions, forcing peoples and their traditions to merge or move. This is particularly evident in the culinary cultures of the region, where ingredients have been adopted and dishes have been adapted with the movement of peoples, the conquering of territories and the might of religion. In the minds of many in the West, the Middle East strikes a discordant note. It is often regarded as one land, full of rich Arabs with multiple wives concealed behind veils and as a breeder of Islamic fundamentalism and fanaticism. This, of course, is not true. Beneath the simmering surface of this ancient region inhabited by Arabs, Turks, Persians, Assyrians, Armenians, Kurds, Muslims, Jews and Christians there is a gentler side too, a world where they are all clearly united in two things – their hospitality and food.

For this book, I have selected loose boundaries, based on the modern definition of the Middle East, to

Herding goats in the mountains around Petra, Jordan

include Iran, Turkey, Iraq, Syria, Lebanon and the Palestinian Territories, Jordan, Egypt, Yemen, Qatar, Kuwait, Oman, Saudi Arabia and the United Arab Emirates. It is a difficult region to tie together for a book on food. There are so many blurred areas, where one culture claims a dish over another, so the pieces of the jigsaw don't always slot neatly into place, at times requiring a great deal more explanation than is permitted here. But if there is a single, modern Middle Eastern culinary tradition to be identified, it is one that has been influenced and united by the Persian, Islamic and Ottoman empires, with a sprinkling of the Byzantine and Roman empires thrown in. Like the spices of a dish, these influences can be added with a light or heavy hand, for the

cooking of the Middle East is not academic. Two families living next door to each other might cook the same dish in different ways. A devout Muslim might reserve the dish for a religious feast, a Christian might eat it for supper with a glass of wine. Whatever the culture or faith, the culinary traditions are based on custom and lore passed down from mother to daughter. As a vociferous champion of Middle Eastern food and a grateful recipient of all the hospitality I have ever received, I hope this book will go some way towards making this monumental movable feast both accessible and enjoyable. But first, in order to get an understanding of the cooking of the Middle East today, we need to disentangle some of the elements of its fascinating culinary history.

A BRIEF HISTORY

Through the discoveries of archaeologists, we now know that as early as 12,000 BC, agriculture was first practised by the earliest organised societies in the valley of the Nile and later, around 8,000 BC, in the Fertile Crescent of Mesopotamia (ancient Iraq). Known as the 'Cradle of Civilisation', Mesopotamia could also be considered the birthplace of Middle Eastern food. The meat of domestic and wild animals was roasted whole over an open flame. Wheat and barley were the principal grains. Vegetables were stewed with herbs or meat. Honey and date juice were used as sweeteners. Milk was turned into cheese and butter, which was clarified so that it kept. Archeological evidence suggests that there were about three hundred kinds of bread, some of them baked in a clay oven. Apart from the early desert inhabitants, who probably ate much the same food as the Bedouin today, little is known about the other ancient peoples of the Middle East, like the Syrians,

The temple of Philae, Egypt

Cappadocians and Babylonians. As they invaded and conquered, the Persian, Greek and Roman empires would have contributed to the character of the region's food.

Around the twelfth century BC, it was the Phoenicians, the intrepid seafarers and craftsmen who inhabited the eastern Mediterranean coast, who influenced the region with their articles of trade. Their ships carried shrubs, herbs, dried fish and fruit, nuts, exotic spices and perfumes. The lucrative spice trade was almost entirely controlled by the Phoenicians, until Alexander the Great set up his own entrepôt at the mouth of the Nile. The Persian Empire of 558–330 BC, which stretched from Russia to Egypt and from Greece to India, wielded a strong influence on the culinary practices of the region. Believers in pleasing the eye as well as the palate, the Persians spread their skills and their own produce, such as pomegranates and saffron. With the ancient Silk Route from China to Syria travelling through its northern regions and the trade routes in the south, the location of Persia in the ancient world meant that it served as a conduit for many products, such as lemons and aubergines, coming from the east. The Romans, whose sea power enabled them to send ships directly to India, took over from the Greeks and, at the same time, the Silk Routes across Central Asia, linking China and Rome, were regulated by Han emperors, who, in their drive to secure their borders, displaced the Mongol and Central Asian pastoral tribes, forcing them to invade new territories. This led to the severing of overland routes and, eventually, to the fall of the Roman Empire in the fifth century, but the sea trade routes survived.

With the split of the Roman Empire in AD 395, the eastern half became the Byzantine Empire, which governed Greater Syria until the early seventh century. During the reign of Justinian I and the empress Theodora in the sixth century, great feasts, comprising dishes from India, Armenia, Persia, Greece, Cyprus and Syria, were held at the Byzantine court. Soups and vegetable stews were popular. Meatballs, grilled fish, duck, or whole baby lamb appeared as main courses and roasted suckling pig, cold hams and spicy pork sausages were also consumed. However, the most sophisticated and lavish cuisine at this period came from the other great power, the Sassanids, a dynasty that ruled Persia from the third to the seventh centuries. With the decline of the Byzantine Empire and the influence of India, for Alexander the Great and his successors had made parts of India and Persia Hellenic strongholds, there was an exciting mix of well-developed culinary traditions and philosophies. In the early seventh century, when Byzantium was defeated and Alexandria, Jerusalem, Antioch and Damascus were conquered by Persian generals, King Khusrow II, renowned for his cruelty and greed, held extravagant banquets. These often consisted of hot and cold meats, rice jelly, stuffed vine leaves, sweet date purée, the meat of young camels, buffaloes and wild donkeys and game dishes prepared with hare and gazelle. Meat was sometimes marinated in yogurt and spices, fruit was often paired with meat, and nuts were ground to thicken sauces or fill pastries. Fruit jams and preserves were popular and dates were stuffed with almonds. The influence of this distinguished Persian

Arab trading ship

cuisine, peppered with Byzantine and Indian traditions, is still evident in many of the dishes throughout the Middle East today.

The spread of Islam, following the death of the Prophet Muhammad in AD 632, changed the face of the Middle East for ever more. With revolutionary fervour, the Bedouin Arabs from the Arabian Peninsula swept into Greater Syria and Persia, conquering one territory after another, converting them to Islam, until they had established a vast Islamic Empire spreading right across Asia and North Africa and into Sicily and Spain. Wherever they went, the Arabs took their own culinary traditions and adopted those of the conquered territories along the way, so that a myriad of dishes and flavours permeated the empire. However, there were a few tiny communities, such as the Christians who entrenched themselves in the mountains of Lebanon, who held on to their ancient cultural beliefs, which have remained unchanged to

Camping in the desert, Wadi Umm al Hayat, Oman

this day. During its first century, the new Islamic Empire was governed from Damascus by the Umayyad dynasty of Caliphs, but it was during the Abassid period, from the late eighth to the twelfth centuries, that cooking really flourished. With Mecca as its religious centre and Baghdad as its capital, the Golden Age of Islam began. Arab ships sailed to China for silk and porcelain, to the East Indies for spices and to Zanzibar and East Africa for ivory and gold. It was a time of intellectual and cultural awakening and a rich period for culinary creativity. During the reign of Harun-al-Rashid (786–809), culinary literature attained the status of an art, in the areas of both pleasure and health. The banquets held at the royal courts of the Caliphs of Baghdad are legendary for their extravagance. Lavish dishes were invented, poems praising the food were recited and diners ate to the sound of music and singing.

Prior to the Islamic Empire, the food of the Arabs, particularly the nomads, was basic. Their daily diet consisted of dates and the milk of camels, sheep and goats, which was curdled or churned into butter and clarified for storing. Meat was a luxury, the usual kind being mutton; occasionally gazelle, hares or ibex were hunted. The nomads supplemented their diet with wild plants, including desert truffles, and the Bedouin consumed grasshoppers, lizards and mice. The settled communities cultivated vegetables and fruit and they made bread from barley or wheat. The dishes were simple, containing few ingredients. Particularly popular were *tharid*, a bread-based meat and vegetable broth, and *hays*, a blend of dates, butter and milk, which were also the Prophet's favourite dishes. Following the conquest, however, Arab cookery was transformed. With the newly acquired lifestyles and culinary techniques of the conquered peoples and the trade routes beyond the empire, a new distinctive cuisine emerged. There came olive oil from Syria, dates from Iraq and coffee from Arabia. Chefs came from Egypt and spices were brought back from India,

Africa and China. But the overwhelming influence came from Persia. The Caliphs of Baghdad adopted the Sassanids' cult of gastronomy, resulting in a food vocabulary filled with Persian words: for example, *turshi* (pickles), *sanbusak* (small, triangular meat pie), *shurba* (soup), *kufta* (minced meatballs) and even the term *mezze*.

In the thirteenth century, a number of Arab culinary books were written, of which only a few have survived. Some were compilations of recipes from the court cuisine, others were concerned with etiquette, diet and health. The *Kitab al-tabikh al-Warraq*, the earliest surviving book, gives detailed accounts of the recipes, ingredients, utensils, table manners and health properties of Abassid cookery. The *Kitab al-tabikh al-Baghdadi*, in which the author refers to food as the noblest of human pleasures and to cooking as an art for which the cook should be intelligent and have a natural flair, is a collection of sophisticated and peasant recipes from the period. And the *Kitab al-Wulsa lla'L-Habib Ibn al-'Adim*, often referred to as the *Wulsa*, was written by an aristocrat who was well acquainted with court cuisine and covers all aspects of food preparation, including distilling and the perfuming of

The camel train from Constantinople to the Black Sea

the body and breath. Some of the recipes and instructions recorded in these manuals could have been written today, so strong are the bonds of culinary tradition.

Thousands of miles further east, in the eleventh century, the first important literary document of the Turks was being composed by Mahmud al-Kashgari. This Turkish-Arabic dictionary recorded aspects of the cuisine and cooking methods of the nomadic Turks, such as the thin flat breads *yufka*, a fondness for yogurt, and the clay oven, *tandır*. As the Turks moved further westwards through Central Asia these fierce warriors and skilled horsemen came into contact with the sophisticated culture and cuisine of the Iranians, but unlike the Caliphs of Bagdhad, who were proud to cook elaborate Persian dishes, they preferred to stick to their ancient culinary tradition of roasted meat on skewers and *mantı*, a kind of pasta dish with yogurt. Around the time that Mahmud al-Kashgari was busy on his dictionary, the Seljuk Turks settled in Konya, from where they ruled Greater Syria for most of the twelfth century. Scholars, poets and mystics from different regions of the Islamic world flocked to Konya as it grew into a brilliant centre of culture and cosmopolitan cuisine. The works of the great mystic and poet Mevlâna Jalal-al Din Rumi provide records of the vegetables, pulses, nuts, pickles, fruits, breads, pastries, milk products and kitchen order of the time, and the tomb of his cook, Atesbazi-Veli, has become a shrine for gastronomic pilgrims.

In 1258 the Abassid Caliphate fell at the hands of the Mongols. The Mongols were then driven out by the Mamluks, a soldier-slave caste of Turks, founded by the military leader Saladin, who had also seized Egypt from the Ayyubid dynasty. The Mamluks were soon in

The Blue Mosque, Istanbul, Turkey

control of the Islamic realm, ruling Egypt, Syria, Palestine and western Arabia for nearly 300 years (1250–1517). Also in 1258 the chief of a pagan tribe of Turks had a son called Osman who converted to Islam and later established the Ottoman (*Osmanli*) Empire, which was to determine the destinies of the Balkans, the Mediterranean region and the Arab world for the next five centuries. By the middle of the fifteenth century, when Mehmet II conquered Constantinople, the Turks had assimilated the culinary traditions of their varied subjects and developed a sophisticated cuisine of their own. Chefs, who were brought from Bolu, specialised in a single culinary method – there was the maker of sweet, syrupy pastries, the *baklavacı*, and the maker of savoury ones, the *börekçi* – which marked the beginning of the celebrated Palace cooking. At the great feasts held in the Topkapı Palace during the reign of Mehmet the Conqueror and Suleyman the Magnificent, the Sultan's table displayed all the indulgent extravagance and glamour of an Abassid banquet. Once more, cooking was regarded as an art and a pleasure, enabling an already sophisticated cuisine to reach new heights

with lavish, sensuously named dishes such as *kız memesi*, young girls' breasts, *kadın göbeği*, ladies' navels, and *kadın buduğu*, ladies' thighs.

In the sixteenth century, the Ottomans came to an agreement with their rivals the Spaniards, so that goods en route from the New World to Spain were transported via the North African coast and Egypt directly to Constantinople. In this way, ingredients such as chilli peppers, maize, aubergines, tomatoes and sunflowers reached the territories of the Ottoman Empire much earlier than parts of Europe. In addition to the introduction of new ingredients and the expansion of the empire, the variety and sophistication of Ottoman cookery were influenced by the fashionable urban life of Constantinople and the unique, dedicated slave system within the palace. Members of the ruling class became slaves to the Sultans, the more able being trained and turned into courtiers and Grand Viziers. The Sultan's wives and members of the household were all slaves, often captured in battle, purchased from pirates or given as gifts. With so many blue-eyed, fair-complexioned followers of the Christian faith, bringing diverse culinary traditions, the Muslim pool was diluted and the cuisine was greatly enhanced. Food was so important to the Ottomans that the insignia of the Janissary force was a pot and spoon and their titles of rank were drawn from the camp kitchen. After four hundred years of complete rule, the Ottoman Empire finally collapsed with the defeat of Turkey in the First World War, but it left a glorious culinary legacy which is still evident on the tables of all its conquered territories, including a large chunk of the Middle East, parts of North Africa, Bulgaria, Hungary, Romania and Serbia and parts of Russia, Greece and Cyprus.

THE MIDDLE EAST TODAY

After the First World War, the French and the British divided up the Ottoman Empire, with France controlling Syria and Lebanon, and Britain administering Palestine, Transjordan, Iraq and Egypt. The French language and cuisine influenced the culinary life of Lebanon in particular and, for the next three decades, Beirut became an international playground and a paradise for food connoisseurs. Stripped of its Arab provinces, the Ottoman Empire was overthrown and the Republic of Turkey was declared under the leadership of Mustafa Kemal, known as Atatürk, in 1923. The cuisine of Turkey is mirrored in its history, which reflects the splendid

sophistication of the Ottoman legacy, seasoned with the diverse culinary traditions of eastern Anatolia – an area that remained relatively untouched during Ottoman rule. The population is predominantly Sunni Muslim, with a minority of Shi'ites, Kurds, Jews and Armenians. At the same time as Turkey was declared a republic, Reza Khan of Persia overthrew the Ghajar dynasty and crowned himself Shah. In 1934, he changed the name of the country from Persia to Iran. The majority of Iranians are Shi'ite Muslims, with a tiny percentage of Sunni Muslims, Jews, Armenians and Assyrians. The cuisine, which is still often referred to as Persian, has changed relatively little since ancient times

Beit Jabri, Damascus, Syria

and is similar to that of Turkey and the neighbouring Arab countries, although it can be distinguished by its unique rice dishes, the preference for a distinct sweet-sour taste and the combinations of meat and fruit.

After the Second World War, when the British withdrew from Palestine, the United Nations divided it into Arab and Jewish states. In 1948, the Jews, who had spread far and wide since Biblical times, flocked to this new state they called Israel, which is still not recognised by many neighbouring Arabs. With them they brought different food customs, to some extent shaped by Jewish dietary laws, and drew from the surrounding cultures. The division of the Jews into Sephardi and Ashkenazi is reflected in their food. The Sephardi Jews, who speak Hebrew, are split into two streams, one that spread westwards to Spain, England and the New World, and one that remained in parts of the Middle East and North Africa; they are sometimes referred to as Oriental Jews. Those who resided in Islamic-occupied Spain and Portugal came under the same culinary influences as their counterparts in the Arab lands. The Ashkenazi Jews, some of whom still speak Yiddish, settled in the Rhine Valley and to the east of it, from Alsace to the Black Sea, so their culinary culture was influenced by the Slavic and Germanic cuisines. The population of the ancient Holy Land is not entirely Jewish, of course, for there are the Palestinians, the Christian Arabs, a small community of nomadic Bedouin, and minority groups such as the Druze, Armenians, Circassians and Samaritans. As a result, the food is an amalgamation of both Jewish branches, with a heavy Arab influence, based on dairy products, wheat, lentils, broad beans, fruit and nuts, raw vegetables, flat breads and lamb.

Dusk over the sandstone façades, Petra, Jordan

The Old City of Jerusalem, which can be traversed in twenty minutes, is the centre of the three most important monotheistic religions. It is where the Way of Sorrow, from Gethsemane where Christ was arrested, to Calvary where he was crucified, is located. It is the site of the third holiest shrine in the Muslim world, the Dome of the Rock mosque, which is built over the rock from which the Prophet Muhammad is said to have ascended to heaven. Below the mosque is the Wailing Wall, believed to be a retaining wall of the Second Jewish Temple, which was destroyed by the Romans in AD 70, and situated between the Dome of the Rock and the Al-Aqsa Mosque is the Temple Mount, the most sacred site for the Jews. The proximity of such sacred sites has been perilous for both resident Muslims and Jews, resulting in a series of Arab-Israeli conflicts, including the Six Day War of 1967, which left Palestinian Arabs refugees. Those who remained in Gaza and the West Bank came under occupation; others fled to neighbouring Arab countries.

Jordan, like other countries in the Fertile Crescent and the Arabian Peninsula, is a new state in an old territory. Its population is largely Sunni Muslim, with more than 60 per cent of it from Palestine. Jordan missed out on oil deposits so it relies heavily on tourism. It is where King Herod's fortress was built and where the Nabataean Bedouins carved a fortress city from rose-red sandstone. Lawrence of Arabia was based at Wadi Rum during the Great Arab Revolt and eight centuries before that the Crusaders built their castles there. As a huge portion of Jordan is barren desert, the food production relies on three micro-climates: the fertile Jordan Valley, where citrus fruits, bananas and vegetables are grown; the high plateau, which yields cereals, pulses, olives and fruit that can be dried; and the desert, where sheep and goats survive. Until recently, the main food culture was that of the villages in the desert and of the nomadic Bedouin, but with such a large Palestinian population and its proximity to Lebanon and Syria, new culinary traditions have been introduced, resulting in a rich and diverse cuisine. It shares with Iraq, Saudi Arabia and Syria the national dish *mansaf*, a whole sheep or camel presented on a bed of rice.

Crac Des Shevaliers, Syria

Both Lebanon and Syria, neighbours on the eastern coast of the Mediterranean, enjoy a favourable temperate climate. Lebanon is tiny with high mountains and a long coastline, at one time famous as a country where one could ski in the morning and swim in the afternoon. Syria, on the other hand, is a vast country with large desert areas and a short coastline. The location of these two countries made the land prey to invasions by the Phoenicians, the Egyptians, the Persians, the Greeks, the Romans (who merged all the states between the Taurus mountains and the Sinai desert into one province called Syria), the Crusaders, the Ottomans and finally the French, each leaving its mark on the culinary culture. The Ottoman influence is the most obvious, as it is throughout the eastern Mediterranean, but the French influence is evident in the refinement of Lebanese food. Both countries share the same ingredients and dishes, with an emphasis on fresh herbs, vegetables, fruit, bulgur, nuts, olives, yogurt, *tahini*, spices, lamb and fish and, with utter conviction, they both claim *hummus*, a garlicky purée of chickpeas and sesame paste, *tabbouleh*, a bulgur salad with onions and parsley, and *kibbeh*, pounded meat and bulgur balls. Given their history, both countries draw from the same pool of dishes but the preparation may differ. The Lebanese use fat and spices sparingly and produce more vegetarian dishes, partly because of the Lenten restrictions of its large Christian community, whereas the Syrians opt for stong flavours with their olive oil and hot Aleppo pepper and they love their sweet dishes and syrupy pastries.

Iraq reflects the same agricultural and culinary divisions as ancient Mesopotamia, with the arid north (Al-Jazirah) and the marshlands in the south (Al Iraq).

Wheat and crops that require winter chill, such as apples, grow in the north while rice and dates grow in the south. Today, Iraq is the world's largest producer of dates. Generally the food of Iraq is a spicier version of the cuisine of Lebanon and Syria. It is also influenced by its neighbour Iran in its dishes combining meat and fruit and in some of its food vocabulary, drawn from medieval texts rather than Arabic. That is apart from the south of Iraq, which relies on its own culinary culture, based on rice, fish and dates, and its own food language, such as *timman* for rice. Relying heavily on grain, Iraqis often combine meat with wheat in dishes such as *kubba*, similar to the *kibbeh* of Lebanon and Syria, *harissa*, a porridge-like soup that is a staple dish for the mountain Kurds, *kashki*, a dish from Mosul that is flavoured and coloured with dried lime, cumin, turmeric and tomato, and *uruq*, also called *ghug*, which consists of meat, cut into small pieces and fried, then mixed with onions and celery leaf in a leavened dough and baked like bread. The Marsh Arabs of the south call the same dish *khubz lahm*, meaning 'meat bread'. The meat from cattle and water buffalo is used more frequently than anywhere else in the Arab world and meat cooked on a skewer is called *tikka*, a term that is adopted in the Gulf, but, is known as *kebab* (*kabab*) elsewhere.

The rivers of Iraq provide freshwater fish, such as carp and catfish, which are cooked in the national dish *samak masquf*, or *simach mazguf* in the south, which involves suspending the gutted fish on stakes around a fire until they are cooked and then sprinkling them with spices, onions, tomatoes and lemon juice. There

Pilgrims and scholars at the shrine of Imam Ali, Najaf, Iraq

are two minority groups in the north-east of Iraq: the non-Arab Muslim Kurds, who speak a language related to Persian, and the Christian Assyrians, who speak a modern dialect of Aramaic. Both cook the heavy meat, grain and vegetable stews suited to their cold winters. The Kurds are known for their syrupy preserves and the Assyrian women are reputed to make the best syrupy pastries and a yogurt soup flavoured with dill, called 'Assyrian soup', throughout Iraq.

Neighbouring Iraq to the south and east are found the member countries of the Gulf Co-operation Council. They include Saudi Arabia, Kuwait, Bahrain, Qatar, the United Arab Emirates and the Sultanate of Oman – a total population of about 25 million. The terrain of this vast area is varied, with extensive desert and a long coastline, the majority of the land receiving occasional rainfall. The food of the whole area is often referred to under the collective banner 'Arabian', or 'Gulf' when excluding Saudi Arabia. Perhaps more than any other region of the Middle East, the food of the United Arab Emirates and Oman has been influenced by distant culinary cultures – Ottoman to the north, Horn of Africa to the west, Iran and India to the east – resulting in an incredibly diverse and vibrant cuisine in the main population centres. Oman has a long history of trade with India and East Africa, resulting in a mixed population of different ethnic groups and, with the proximity of its northern tip to Iran, separated only by the Strait of Hormuz, there is a substantial population of Persian ancestry too. Dubbed the 'playground of the Gulf', the United Arab Emirates, which was formed as recently as 1971, is a loose federation of seven tiny sheikhdoms. Interestingly from a culinary point of view, 85 per cent of the population of almost 2 million is expatriate, from Pakistan, India,

Sri Lanka, the Philippines, North Africa, Europe and America, which has a huge impact on the cuisine. The largest and most populous of the Emirates is Abu Dhabi, the second largest being Dubai. Until almost forty years ago, when commercial exploitation of oil began, both were little more than sand. In Dubai the population was largely nomadic, subsisting on a diet of fish, bread, honey and dates; now there are international restaurants and futuristic shopping malls selling alcohol and pork items, and a ruler who has spent a fortune turning the desert green, so much so that strawberries from Dubai are exported to Europe.

Aside from the external influences, the core food of the Gulf region of Arabia is traditionally Arab, similar to that of Syria and Lebanon. The national dish is *khouzi*, a roasted or baked whole lamb stuffed with chicken, eggs, onions, rice, spices and saffron and served on a bed of rice, garnished with almonds and ghee. Saltwater fish such as *hammour* (grouper) and *zubaidi* (silver pomfret) are popular grilled, and the big Gulf prawns are often cooked with rice and herbs in a dish called *machbous*. Lamb and chicken are roasted on spits in *shawarma* stalls, the Gulf equivalent of the Turkish *döner kebab*. The markets are stacked with all the usual vegetables and herbs, including purslane, rocket, melokhia, fenugreek, coriander and dandelion. Dates are the main fruit, used in sweet dishes and pressed for their molasses, but bananas, mangoes, oranges and watermelons are also common in the Gulf. Coffee is the main drink, sometimes flavoured with cardamom, and tea is drunk black and sweet. Honey is used for sweetening dishes and the combination of Indian spices, the Arab spice mixture, *baharat* and the dried Omani limes, *loomi*, give the food its distinctive character.

Landscape and terraces of the Qadilia Valley, Lebanon

Saudi Arabia, on the other hand, takes itself very seriously. The kingdom is the cradle of Islam and the Arabic language. It is home to the two most sacred Islamic sites – Mecca, the birthplace of the Prophet Muhammad, and Medina, the place of his burial. Mecca, the site to which Muslims bow in prayer five times a day, is also the location of the Ka'bah, the shrine that is said to have been built by Abraham, the father of the Arab race. The unexpected death of the Prophet in the year 632 left a crisis in the Islamic world, as there were no heirs. Followers of his widow, A'isha, eventually became known as Sunni and make up approximately 85 per cent of the Islamic world. The majority of Saudis are Sunni Muslims, as are the Turks, the Jordanians and the Islamic population of the United Arab Emirates. They believe the first four Caliphs were the rightful heirs and don't require the spiritual leader to be a member of the Prophet's family, whereas Shi'a Islam rejects the first three Caliphs and regards Ali, the Prophet's cousin and son-in-law, as the original Caliph. They insist that their imam must be a descendant of Ali and his wife. Most Shi'ite populations are found in Iran, Iraq, Lebanon, Yemen and Azerbaijan, with minorities in Kuwait, the Emirates and Saudi Arabia. The Sunni Muslims of Saudi Arabia are followers of the Wahhabi sect of Islam, the most orthodox of all.

In an area of approximately 1.96 million square kilometres (757,000 square miles), most of which is desert, the bulk of Saudi Arabia's population is centred around Jeddah and Riyadh. The Empty Quarter, the largest sand desert in the world, traversed on foot by the indefatigable explorer Wilfred Thesiger, takes up roughly half the country. After fourteen centuries of receiving Muslim pilgrims from all over the world, on their Hajj to Mecca, and an influx of expatriates involved in oil, Saudi Arabia has quite a diverse population and cuisine. Only the people of Najd in the Saudi heartland remain homogeneous in their pure Bedouin ancestry, which is reflected in their culinary traditions. The Bedouin, who have a strong but basic food culture, were nomadic herdsmen who lived in the deserts of Arabia and North Africa. They depended on their flocks of sheep and goats to provide milk and meat, using their dried hides to make water and food carriers and for churning milk. Their camels provided transport and dung for fuel. Surplus bull calves would be slaughtered for their meat, hide and hair. Dates grew in all the oases and were easy to carry with them and, in the encampments, flat breads would be cooked on a sheet of metal over a fire. With basic needs and animals that could survive in arid conditions, the Bedouin were able to penetrate vast tracts of merciless desert in which others would perish. The Bedouin rules of hospitality, which are still upheld in Bedouin camps and traditional Arab households today, included the provision of accommodation and protection for three days and three nights, and a beast would be slaughtered in the guest's honour to demonstrate the host's wealth. While the beast was being prepared by the women, the men would offer the guest coffee and dates. The slaughtered sheep or camel would be served in the traditional dish, *mansaf*, now the principal hospitality dish of the whole of Arabia and Jordan, and the guest would eat first, followed by the men. The women and children would eat separately, once the men had finished. Today the numbers of nomadic Bedouin are in decline, but their culinary traditions,

such as *mansaf*, have influenced the sedentary populations of the Arab world.

The most arable spot on the Arabian Peninsula is Yemen. It is also the most populous, made up of strong tribal units, all of whom trace their ancestry to Qatan, son of Prophet Hud, who was descended from Noah. Islam is the principal religion but there is a Jewish minority. The northern part of Yemen includes the highest part of the Arabian plateau, where heavy rain falls at the time of the summer monsoon, allowing sorghum, coffee, wheat and maize to grow on the terraced slopes. The oases towns were once on the Spice Road leading to the Mediterranean. In ancient times, frankincense and myrrh grew on the coast of the Gulf of Aden in the southern part of Yemen (formerly the British colony of Aden), which lies on the rim of the Indian Ocean. With its proximity to North Africa and the trade routes with India, there has been a degree of intermarriage between different ethnic groups which is strongly reflected in the culinary culture. Chillies are used more than anywhere else in the Middle East and fenugreek could be seen as the culinary symbol of Yemen. The national dish, *salta*, is a fiery, spicy stew containing pulses and lamb, and the peasants live on a sorghum porridge of

Muslim farmers herding goats, Yemen

ancient origin which is served with spicy clarified butter. Clarified butter is the principal cooking fat and it is often served with honey to dip bread into. Most Yemenis eat with their right hand, using the bread as a scoop.

'The Mother of the World', the birthplace of one of the greatest civilisations, is linked to the body of the Middle East by Sinai, where Moses received the ten commandments on the Mount. Egypt is the most populous country in the Arab world, with most of its people centred in bloated Cairo and the fertile Nile Valley, with Bedouin communities in Sinai. Like Saudi Arabia across the Red Sea, Egypt is a vast country but most of it is desert or marsh. The majority of Egyptians are Muslim, the rest being mainly Coptic Christian, but racially they can be divided into three groups: the Hamito-Semitic race, which has populated the Nile for millennia – this includes the Berbers – the Bedouin Arab nomads and the Nubians. Egypt's recorded history is so ancient, surviving in written documents, wall paintings and tombs, that it reveals a great deal about the food of the early civilisations. Ancient cooking methods, such as lighting a fire inside a concave pottery hearth, outside or on the flat roofs, are still practised today. The Arab and Turkish conquests and the dominant influence of Islam are evident in the *haute cuisine* of Egypt, but the peasant communities still cook the simple dishes of their forebears in Pharaonic times. The national dishes, such as *ful medames*, brown beans with cumin and parsley, and *melokhia*, a soup made with the mucilaginous mallow plant, are of peasant origin. Pigeons are an Egyptian speciality and grilled meat and chicken are standard fare, but the tradition of *mezze*, which is such a fabulous feature of Lebanese, Syrian and Turkish cooking, has almost been lost.

Sailing on the Nile, Egypt

THE PRODUCE

Market stall in Ankara, Turkey

Geographically, the Middle East is extremely varied, with lush, wooded coastlines, high, arid mountains, extensive flat plains, steep, rocky outcrops, marshlands and endless deserts providing different growing conditions for a vast range of plants and crops. Rice grows around the Caspian Sea and in the marshlands of southern Iraq, date palms thrive in the desert areas of Jordan, Iraq and Saudi Arabia, pistachio and olive trees grow where nothing else will, and the lush plains of the Fertile Crescent and Anatolia produce an abundance of fruit and vegetables. On the whole the produce is rich and plentiful, and the people are generous with it.

Fruit and vegetables are sold fresh and dried. The juicy fruits, such as the honey-sweet melons, oozing purple figs, dripping peaches and apricots, black mulberries, grapes and the tart, green plums that are dipped in salt are generally consumed fresh in season. Some of the fresh fruit, such as apples, plums and quinces, are stuffed and cooked, while others, such as figs, dates and apricots, are dried and cooked with meat and vegetables, used in stuffings, or poached in syrup. The white mulberries, originally from China and cultivated in Turkey for the silkworms, are dried and eaten as a snack, rather like raisins. Fresh vegetables, such as the mammoth leeks, giant cabbages, carrots, courgettes, fat bulbous aubergines as well as long, slender ones, knobbly plum tomatoes and scaly globe artichokes, are generally used raw in salads, stewed with meat or pulses, stuffed with rice, or cooked with olive oil and served cold. Some vegetables, such as aubergines, peppers and okra, are dried and hung on strings, like chunky necklaces. Pulses, which were once regarded as a staple of the poor, are enjoyed in many dishes right across the social divide. And wheat is the preferred grain, although rice features highly in the food of Iran and is the staple of southern Iraq.

Beef and the meat of water buffalo, camel and goat are all eaten, but the preferred meat is lamb. Chicken is almost as popular as lamb, and turkey, duck and pigeon are consumed too. Because of Islamic dietary law, pork is rarely eaten, even by the Christians. Islam also prohibits wine, which might be why so many of the meat dishes are given a sweet or sour flavouring for extra interest. Milk is rarely consumed fresh but is made into yogurt, clarified butter, clotted cream and cheese. Surrounded by seas and carved up by some of the world's major rivers, such as the Euphrates and the Nile, there is a wide choice of fresh and saltwater fish.

An Egyptian spread: pigeon stuffed with rice, peas and bread

Herbs, flavourings and spices have been used throughout the Middle East since antiquity, but it was during the early Abassid period that spices began to be extensively employed in the region's cookery. They came from the Arab domains such as southern Arabia, Syria, Persia and central Asia, and from East Africa, India and China. Top-quality spices were expensive and the ability to purchase them was a mark of status. Spices and herbs were essential to the medieval Arab kitchen, valued for their alleged medicinal and aphrodisiac properties. Flavourings such as rose water and orange blossom water have also been used since medieval times. More recently, since the end of the nineteenth century, an unusual flavouring has been extracted from *bois de Panama*, the dried inner bark of the American tree *Quillaja saponaria*. The pale bark has a bitter-sweet taste, with a hint of almond, but it is employed more for its foaming qualities than for its flavour. Boiled and simmered, then strained and whisked, it produces a brilliant white foam which is combined with sugar to make a mousse-like cream, *naatiffee*, which is served with the sweet pastries, *ma'amoul*, favoured by Christians at Easter and by Muslims during *Ramadan*.

The fresh herbs are glorious, sold like large bouquets of flowers and piled high in the markets. They are so popular in the Middle East, they are used liberally and with abandon, often served on their own as a nibble, or to freshen the palate. Dried herbs and spices are often sold in the markets, alongside each other, in large sacks bursting at the seams. The air around them can be quite heady with the pungent aroma of fragrant herbs, warm spices and hot chilli. *Bahar* is the Arabic for spice, *baharat* being the collective word used for the various spice blends. In

Iranian women picnicking on *lavash*, jams and teas

medieval times, one of the spice blends contained distinct echoes of India in its use of betel nut, nutmeg, mace, cardamom, cloves, rosebuds, the fruit of the ash tree and ginger, flavours which still feature in Oman and the Gulf region.

Salt, particularly rock salt, was also an ingredient in medieval Arab cuisine. Several recipes called for scented salt, such as the lemon salt still used in Iran. And salt flavoured with spices, sour pomegranate seeds or toasted sesame seeds was, and still is, popular, like the spice mixture *zaatar*. During the Ottoman era salt formed a lucrative branch of commerce. Great quantities of it were gathered from inland saline lakes, which dry up in the summers and leave an encrustation of high-quality coarse salt. Salt has also been a symbol of hospitality since ancient times – to eat bread and salt with someone is to enter into a covenant of brotherhood. There is a medieval Arab saying, 'Salt is as necessary in food as grammar is in speech.'

Honey, along with the molasses of some pressed fruits, such as mulberries, grapes and dates, is an ancient and vital sweetener. The oldest written reference to the use of honey dates back to Egypt, around 5500 BC, when Lower Egypt was called Bee Land and Upper Egypt was known as Reed Land. Honey is also mentioned on Babylonian tablets for its medicinal uses and it has long been believed to sweeten life and ward off sadness. Today, it is mainly used to sweeten syrupy pastries and is poured over wild duck roasted with almonds and eaten daily with fresh bread or yogurt. One of the joys of honey is its immense range of colours and flavours. Whether it is in comb form or pressed, each one has its own distinct fragrance and taste and, with such an enormous variety of scented blossoms, the villages and markets of the Middle East provide an astounding choice. The most unusual I have ever tasted is the dark *deli bal*, meaning 'crazy honey', which comes from eastern Anatolia, where the bees extract the pollen from the wild opium poppies. Needless to say, it is mildly hallucinatory with an unexpected fiery kick.

MEZZE

The tradition of *mezze* is one of the most enjoyable and relaxing features of Middle Eastern food. The savouring of freshly roasted pistachios, fleshy green olives, juicy melon, delicately flavoured pastries, garlicky aubergine dips, pink-tinged pickled turnips, cubes of white cheese, strips of salted cucumber and thin slices of perfumed quince can be a sensual, mystical experience. It is an ancient tradition, enjoyed by the Greeks, Romans, Persians, medieval Arabs and Ottomans. Traditionally, the *mezze* table was laid out to accompany *araq* (*rakı*) or wine, with the aim of achieving a 'pleasant head' to delight the palate, not to fill the belly. Originally it was a custom enjoyed only by men – traders and travellers, kings, Sultans and noble men – but in the less restricted parts of the Middle East it can be a family affair. The word *mezze* has come to mean a 'pleasant taste', probably derived from the Persian word *maza*, meaning 'taste' or 'relish'.

In Syria and Lebanon the word is *mazza* and in Turkey it is *meze*.

The wonderful thing about *mezze* is that there are no rules. The *mezze* table can be the start of a meal, or completely separate from it. There is no set time or place, just the unspoken understanding that the food should be served in small quantities to be shared and savoured at a leisurely pace and that one should rise from the table feeling contented and comfortable, not stuffed. Generally, though, the partaking of *mezze* tends to be an evening activity, partly because for many it would be unthinkable without *araq*. In some Muslim communities, where the prohibition of alcohol is strictly adhered to, the *mezze* tradition has either been lost or the dishes are accompanied with tea, coffee or sherbet drinks instead. Throughout the Middle East, the Lebanese and the Turks are renowned for their delightful *mezze* spreads.

Ramadan tent at El Hussein mosque in Old Cairo, Egypt

THE QUR'AN AND RAMADAN

Islam is the predominant religion in the Middle East, so it exerts the most influence on the customs, traditions and culinary cultures of the region. The book of Islam is the *Qur'an* (the Koran), which is a collection of revelations or commands from Allah (God) received by the Prophet Muhammad through the Angel Gabriel. As a gift from Allah, food is mentioned throughout the *Qur'an*, especially what is permitted and what is not. Of particular importance are the restrictions on the slaughtering and preparation of meat (p68) and the prohibition of alcohol. However, in the modern world, these laws are observed with varying degrees of laxity. Outside the Christian communities, it is extremely rare for people to eat pork, but the drinking of, or cooking with, alcohol is quite common, although this is a matter of personal preference rather than a national characteristic.

Ramadan is the ninth month of the Muslim calendar, when the Prophet experienced the revelation of the *Qur'an*. Since the Muslim calendar is a lunar one, *Ramadan* falls eleven days earlier in each successive year of the Western calendar. During the month of *Ramadan*, every devout Muslim must abstain from food and drink between sunrise and sunset. Nothing must pass his or her lips. This act of self-discipline and faith is deemed necessary to submit completely to the will of Allah and to engender a sense of compassion for the poor, who are always hungry. When *Ramadan* occurs in the hot summer, the month of fasting can be difficult with the heat and the longer wait to sunset. *Suhur* is the meal taken before sunrise and *iftar* is served to break the fast at sunset. When the new moon is in sight, *Ramadan* comes to an end and the new month begins with *Id al-Fitr* (the Feast of the Breaking of the Fast), a three-day holiday of celebration, sumptuous feasting and exchanging of gifts.

LANGUAGE AND HERITAGE

Arabic is the principal language of the Middle East. The other main languages are Farsi, Hebrew and Turkish. The term 'Arab' really applies to the original nomadic Arabs, distinguished by their language, and the inhabitants of the conquered provinces who adopted Arabic. As the majority of the Arabs live in the Fertile Crescent, renowned for its food produce and culinary delights, I have based a large portion of this book there, under the loose banner 'Arab food',

noting the obvious Turkish and Persian influences and dishes. Also, to keep it simple, the ingredients are listed in Arabic and the recipes in their language of origin, or in the language of the country in which I have tasted them. As there is so much fission and fusion between the countries, a huge number of dishes cross all borders and religious divides. The references to some dishes from Iran as 'Persian' is intentional when they are of ancient origin and are relatively unchanged.

BASIC FOODS

BREAD

(KHUBZ)

Bread is a gift from God. Traditionally it is broken by hand. To cut it with a knife would be to lift up a sword against God's blessing. If a bit of bread falls on the ground, it is picked up and held to the lips and forehead as a gesture of atonement and respect before it is put aside. And it is never thrown away. Instead, stale bread is used in a variety of traditional ways, such as in *fattush* (p181) and the ancient *tharid*.

The first cereal crops are believed to have been grown in Anatolia, Persia and Syria before 7000 BC. So important was the skill of bread-making in ancient times, there are records of full-time bakers amongst the Egyptians, the Phoenicians and the Cappadocians. In Rome, a bakers' guild was set up around 150 BC. In medieval times, bread was primarily made of wheat, although the poor used barley and millet, and it was often flavoured with spices or stuffed with sweet, scented fillings. During the Ottoman period more sophisticated breads emerged and experimentation began with thin flat breads as a pastry dough in savoury and sweet, layered dishes such as *baklava* (p137). Today, there are hundreds of varieties of bread, some savoury, others sweet. Bread is used to break the fast during *Ramadan* and it is broken and blessed in the meal-taking of Orthodox Jews. It is eaten with every meal and some people simply cannot enjoy their food without it.

THE PRODUCTION

First the harvested grains have to be ground into flour, which was traditionally done between two heavy, flat grinding stones. All cereal flours, particularly wheat, consist of starch and protein which react with water to form gluten. As the dough is kneaded, the gluten molecules form strands and absorb water which results in a smooth, elastic dough. For flat bread all that is needed is water but, to produce a risen loaf, some kind of leaven is required. The first leavened loaves are attributed to the ancient Egyptians, who may have accidentally discovered yeast on a batch of dough infected with wild spores. The Israelites left their leaven behind when they fled from Egypt in the Exodus and had to exist on unleavened bread. The Romans introduced ale-barm (brewer's yeast), which had more predictable results. The first breads in tribal encampments would have been cooked on flat stones or metal sheets directly over the fire, much as it is in some villages today. The next developments were to make a freestanding clay cylinder, called a *tinuru*, used for unleavened bread, and a hollow, beehive-shaped

Assorted leavened and unleavened breads

A baker removing loaves from the oven, Yemen

outdoor oven, known as a *tannur*, which produced better risen loaves. This was the precursor to the outdoor clay oven (*tandoor* in Arabic, *tandır* in Turkish), used to bake flat breads throughout the Middle East. Leavened loaves are often baked in a hot, communal oven, called a *furn* (Arabic) or *firin* (Turkish), which can also be used for unleavened breads by sticking the flat dough to the inside hot walls or on the outside. The most traditional of all the flat breads is as wide as an arm-length and as thin as fine cloth. It takes years of practice and great skill to shift a small ball of dough from hand to hand, and then arm to arm, carefully stretching it and keeping it taut and circular, until it resembles a thin sheet of paper.

APPEARANCE AND TASTE

There are hundreds of different kinds of leavened and unleavened breads, from the round rings scattered with seeds, such as *semit*, to the paper-thin sheets, called *fila* in Arabic and *yufka* in Turkish, which come in different grades for savoury and sweet pastries. All have their own unique taste from the flour or the oven used,

from the baker or the hand that made them. One thing is sure, they all taste and smell delicious. There is the ubiquitous pitta bread, known in Arabic as *khubz* or *eish shami*, which is a round or oval flat bread made with refined wheat flour, with a hollow pocket demanding to be filled. The Egyptian *eish baladi* is a whole-wheat version, often flavoured or sprinkled with the spice mixture, *dukkah* (p163). There are many other flat breads, each with its own characteristic, such as the wholemeal *nan-e lavash* and *nan-e tâftoon* of Iran, and the thick *pide* of Turkey. There is village bread, sometimes made from barley or corn, Armenian bread padded like a quilt, Jewish bread made with egg doughs, olive bread, sweet breads and savoury, spicy or herb breads.

BUYING AND STORING

In the Middle East, bread-making is such a part of daily life that people often bake their own or send their dough along to the communal oven. Almost every village has a baker, who bakes batches of fresh bread once or twice a day. If you don't bake your own, you will have to look for Middle Eastern-style loaves

and flat breads, such as pitta and *fila*, which are now readily available in supermarkets and specialist shops, or look for the real thing in Middle Eastern shops. As bread goes stale quickly and fresh bread is so easily attainable in the Middle East, storing is not a problem. Fresh bread is eaten immediately and stale bread has many uses. If *fila* is sealed in an airtight bag, it will keep for a few weeks in the refrigerator or for two to three months in the freezer.

CULINARY USES

Leavened and unleavened bread is eaten with food at every meal. It is a scoop, a mop, a palate cleanser and an essential part of the overall enjoyment. Warm fresh bread is usually eaten for breakfast with cheese, olives, dates and honey. A choice of buns, dried breads and the savoury bracelets called *kahk* (p163) are eaten as a snack. Toasted or stale bread is used in village vegetable soups and the Syrian peasant dish *fattush* (p181), a lovely, crunchy, herb-laden salad made with broken flat bread. Stale bread is also soaked in a syrup made from poached fresh fruit topped with the strained fruit and served with clotted cream. Hollow breads are often filled with grilled meat balls or *falafel*

(p113) with parsley, onions, tomatoes and a squeeze of lemon or yogurt. Some flat-bread doughs are filled with eggs or minced meat (p188)– such as *lahma bi ajeen* – or with a sweet *tahini* paste before being baked. A particular characteristic of Middle Eastern food is to use the flat bread as a base for other ingredients: the Turkish dish *Iskender kebabı* consists of grilled meat, a tomato sauce and yogurt, layered over thick *pide*. Similarly, there are the Arab *fatta* dishes (*fatut* in Yemen) which involve breaking toasted or stale bread and soaking it in a broth or stock with vegetables or meat before topping it with yogurt. This dish, which was known as *tharid* in Arabia, was the favourite dish of the Prophet Muhammad, who praised his favourite wife in this way: 'A'isha surpasses other women as *tharid* surpasses other dishes.' In ancient times this dish was made plain with bread sopped in broth or stew but some modern versions alternate layers of stew and flat bread. The thin sheets of flat bread, known as *fila* are used for a variety of savoury and sweet pastries. In Turkey, the *yufka* is used to make a series of different-shaped, filled pastries, called *börek*, and the thin sheets of dough are layered with nuts and soaked in syrup to make some sweet pastries. In Egypt, *om Ali* (p133), a popular syrupy dessert, is made with nuts, cinnamon and crumpled sheets of *fila*.

Bread airing after the heat of the oven in a bakery in Giza, Cairo

Bedouin women making fila bread, Syria

Fatta dishes are wholesome family meals that are popular throughout the Arab world. The word *fatta* describes the crumbling or breaking of the bread into pieces and the dish probably originated as a method of using up stale bread. All *fatta* dishes have a bed of toasted bread soaked in stock or cooking broth, followed by a layer of minced meat, chicken, chickpeas, or vegetables, topped with a layer of thick, creamy yogurt, over which toasted pine nuts or Middle Eastern red pepper is sprinkled. Pitta breads, lightly toasted or crisped up in a hot oven, are the best breads to use for *fatta*.

FATTET HUMMUS
(CHICKPEAS WITH TOASTED BREAD AND YOGURT)

Serves 4
Preparation time 5 minutes (+ at least 6 hours' soaking)
Cooking time roughly 1 hour 20 minutes

110g (4oz) chickpeas, soaked for at least 6 hours, or overnight
2–3 dried bay leaves
1 tablespoon olive oil and a little butter
1 onion, chopped
½ teaspoon cumin seeds
A scant teaspoon ground coriander
Juice of ½ lemon
500ml (18fl oz) thick, creamy, set yogurt
2–3 cloves garlic, crushed
2–3 large pitta breads
A small handful pine nuts
Salt and freshly ground black pepper

Simmer the chickpeas with the bay leaves in plenty of water for at least 1 hour, until they are very tender. Drain them and reserve some of the cooking liquid. Remove any loose skins from the chickpeas and heat up the reserved cooking liquid with a little salt.

Heat up the oil and butter in a frying pan and stir in the onion and cumin seeds. Once the onions begin to brown, stir in the coriander and the chickpeas. Toss them about until they are well mixed, then add the lemon juice and season to taste with salt and black pepper.

In a bowl, beat the yogurt with the garlic and season to taste. Then open out the pitta breads and pop them in a hot oven for a few minutes, until they are crisp and brown. Meanwhile, heat up a small heavy-based pan, toss in the pine nuts and roast them until they look nicely browned and oily.

Break up the toasted breads with your hands and lay them in a serving dish.

Spoon some of the heated cooking liquid over them, making sure they are well soaked, then spoon the chickpeas on top, followed by the yogurt and a sprinkling of roasted pine nuts. Serve immediately.

Generally known as *khubz* in Arabic and *eish shami* in Egypt, these flat breads with a hollow pocket just begging to be filled are known outside the Middle East as pitta bread. The same bread made with wholemeal flour is called *baladi*, and olives or spices can be added to the dough. In Turkey, a similar, thicker bread, *pide*, is often filled or used as the base for many kebab dishes. In Iraq, the same bread dough is mixed with minced meat to make the special *khubz abbas*, while the plain *khubz* was traditionally distributed to the poor with melted butter and sugar on top.

Selling assorted sweet and plain bread on the street, Turkey

KHUBZ
(PITTA BREAD)

Serves 6–8
Preparation time approximately 3½ hours
Cooking time 6–10 minutes

10g (½oz) fresh yeast, or 5g (¼oz) dried yeast (a scant teaspoon)
½ teaspoon sugar
Roughly 300ml (½ pint) lukewarm water
450g (1lb) plain flour
½ teaspoon salt
Sunflower oil

Dissolve the yeast with the sugar in a little of the water and leave in a warm place for 15 minutes, until it bubbles and froths.

Sift the flour with the salt into a large bowl. Make a well in the centre and pour in the yeast and most of the water. Using your hands, draw in the flour and knead the dough, adding more water if necessary, until it forms a pliable ball. Place it on a floured surface and knead for about 15 minutes, until it is smooth and elastic. Pour a drop or two of oil into the bottom of the bowl, roll the dough in it, cover the bowl with a damp cloth and leave the dough to rise in a warm place for at least 2 hours, until it has doubled in size.

Punch the dough down and knead it briefly. Divide the dough into lumps – the size of a pomegranate for large pitta breads, the size of an apricot for small ones – and flatten them with the palm of your hand, or a rolling pin, on a floured surface, until they are roughly ½cm (¼in) thick. Lay a clean cloth on a flat surface and dust it with flour. Place the flat doughs on top, with a gap for expansion between them, and sprinkle with flour. Dust another clean cloth with flour, lay it over them, and leave them for about 1 hour, until they have expanded.

Preheat the oven to 220°C/ 450°F/gas mark 8 (or even hotter, if you can). Lightly grease two baking sheets and place them in the hot oven for 10 minutes, just before baking. Quickly pop the flat doughs onto the hot baking sheets, sprinkle a little cold water over them to prevent them from browning, and bake for about 8 minutes. As soon as they are ready, slip them off the baking sheets onto a wire rack and leave to cool – if your oven is hot enough, the bread should be soft and white with a hollow pouch. They firm up on cooling so, if you want them to remain soft, put them into a plastic bag until you are ready to use them.

COFFEE

(KAHWA) *Coffea arabica*

Ground coffee

The coffee plant is thought to have originated in Ethiopia, where it grows wild. The discovery of the plant in Arabia is interwoven with myths of dancing goats and sleepy monks. The berries would have been eaten first and the fermented pulp then made into a kind of wine. The earliest record of coffee as a drink was in the writing of Rhazes, an Arabian physician in the tenth century, but the practice of roasting the beans didn't begin until the thirteenth century. According to legend, coffee became popular amongst the Sufis of Yemen, as they believed that it helped them perform their religious ceremonies, bringing on mystical raptures and prolonging the hours of prayer. By the end of the thirteenth century in Yemen, the drink was known as *qahwah*, probably because of its stimulant qualities as the word was originally a poetic name for wine. The dervishes and Muslim pilgrims contributed to the spread of coffee throughout the Middle East and, by the end of the fifteenth century, cultivation had begun in Yemen, with plants transported from Ethiopia. The Ottoman Turks refined the art of coffee-making and spread it throughout their empire in the sixteenth century, giving the name of Turkish coffee to a drink that was originally of Arab origin.

SOCIAL ROLE

Coffee is the main drink in the Arab world, particularly in Saudi Arabia, Yemen, Jordan, Syria and Lebanon. It is part of the social life. The Bedouin are reputed to drink so much of it, they would almost collapse without it, although tea is drunk just as often. In the rural parts of Turkey and Iran, coffee is reserved mainly for ceremonial occasions, tea being the common drink. In Iran it is served at funerals and in Turkey it plays a traditional role in the selection of a bride: a young girl must serve coffee to her prospective mother-in-law so that she can inspect her beauty and grace.

Throughout the Middle East, the serving and drinking of coffee are entrenched in tradition and ceremony. As a mark of hospitality, it is the first thing a host prepares for visitors and it is rude to refuse. In the serving of coffee, strict rules of etiquette must be observed – a person of high rank, or the father of the household, must be served first, followed by the older guests or relatives, and men are always served before women. Amongst the Europeanised communities of the large cities, such as Amman, Beirut and Istanbul, these rules have been waived and women are generally served first.

In the Arab countries, coffee is the principal social drink for men. They spend hours drinking in the coffee houses, talking, joking and playing backgammon, sometimes soaking up the coffee with a sweet, syrupy pastry, or a piece of *lokum* (Turkish Delight). At one time, Islam seemed to be under threat as attendance at the mosque slackened while the coffee houses filled. In the Arab communities, business in the marketplace, in the office, or in the home is always conducted with a small cup of coffee, whereas tea would usually be served in those situations in Turkey and Iran, unless it was immediately after a meal.

A Bedouin man brewing coffee over an open fire in Wadi Umm al Hayat, Om

PREPARATION AND PRESENTATION

In the Middle East, two types of coffee are made: Arabic coffee, which is drunk solely in Arab communities, particularly in Saudi Arabia, Yemen and by the Bedouin; and Turkish coffee, which is fashionable in the cities, especially in the ones influenced by the Ottoman Empire, and in Turkey. Arabic coffee is made in two pots (*dallahs*) – brewed in the first and poured into the second – always without sugar. Turkish coffee is brewed in small, long handled, tin-lined brass pots (called *kanaka*, *rakwi* or *ibrik* in Arabic and *cezve* in Turkish).

The coffee beans are always freshly roasted and then pounded or ground to a very fine powder which is added to the water in the pot. As the coffee is sweetened during the preparation, guests are always asked whether they would like theirs sweet (*helou* or *hilweh* in Arabic, *şekerli* in Turkish), medium (*mazbout* or *wassat* in Arabic, *orta* in Turkish), or plain (*murra* in Arabic, *sade* in Turkish), hence the need for several coffee pots in each household. However, at happy, festive occasions, the coffee is often made sweet for everyone, whereas at sombre occasions such as funerals, it is a solemn drink, black and unsweetened. Milk is never added to coffee, although there is a drink in Lebanon and Syria called 'white coffee' which, in fact, has nothing to do with coffee but is made with orange blossom water. In the Arab countries such as Yemen, Saudi Arabia and Jordan, a cardamom pod is often added to the coffee pot for flavouring. Cardamom is also added to coffee in Iran, but it rarely features in the coffee of Turkey, and ground ginger is often added to the coffee in Yemen.

The coffee cups are small and cylindrical and, in some societies or social circles, they are delicate with no handles, so as to slot into ornate metal holders, matching the patterned or inscribed serving tray, usually made of brass or silver. When the coffee has been drunk, it is customary to turn the cup upside down on the saucer to let the sediment dribble down the sides of the cup. Once the cup has cooled, it is lifted up and the pattern of coffee-grain rivulets formed on the inside is read to determine the individual's fortune. The saucer is then held up and read too.

BUYING AND STORING

To make authentic Arabic or Turkish coffee, any *arabica* bean can be used. Mocha from Yemen is popular but beans from Brazil and Kenya are used too. The beans must be ground to a very fine powder, otherwise the coffee will be too gritty and you won't get the creamed, foamy effect. Tins and packets of Turkish coffee are available in Middle Eastern stores and some specialist shops.

Arabic coffee pot and cup

Kahve, Turkish coffee

The Turks have been promoting their coffee for a long time. The first British coffee house was opened in Oxford by a Turkish Jew in 1650. A little later, in 1688–9, the Turkish Ambassador to France encouraged the Parisian élite who attended his lavish parties to drink Turkish coffee. Dressed in decorative oriental costumes, his black slaves served hot, fragrant Mocha coffee in tiny porcelain cups on gold or silver saucers.

KAHVE
(TURKISH COFFEE)

Serves 2
Preparation time –
Cooking time 2–3 minutes (with practice)

All you need is a *cezve* that holds 2 coffee cups of cold water, to which you add 2 coffee spoons of finely, ground coffee and the required sugar on top. Using a teaspoon, carefully stir the sugar and coffee into the surface of the water, making sure the spoon doesn't go anywhere near the bottom of the *cezve*. This little stir gives the froth a kick-start.

Place the *cezve* over a medium flame and heat the water up, gradually stirring the outer surface edges into the middle to create an island of froth.

Pour about a third of the coffee into each cup to warm it up, return the *cezve* to the heat, and continue to gather the froth in the middle. Just as it is about to bubble up, take the *cezve* off the heat and pour the hot coffee into the warmed cups (some people spoon a little of the froth into the cup before pouring in the coffee).

Serve the coffee immediately, while it is hot and frothy, but, before you drink it, leave it to stand for a minute to let the coffee grains sink to the bottom of the cup.

TEA
(CHAI)

Linden tea

Hibiscus tea

Although coffee, surrounded by tradition and ritual, is the king of drinks in the Middle East, tea occupies an important place in Iran and Turkey, where it is the drink of the masses. In Iran, coffee is mainly reserved for funerals and, in rural Turkey, it is only drunk on ceremonial occasions, so tea is the everyday beverage.

It wasn't always the case, though. Tea, thought to have first arrived in Iran with the early Persian caravans, didn't make an impact until comparatively recently. Instead, coffee was the most popular drink. Brought from Arabia in the ninth century, it was blessed by Islam and drunk at religious ceremonies, making coffee houses the focal point of communities throughout the Middle East. But in Iran, between the seventeenth and twentieth centuries, the coffee houses were suspected of fostering political and religious dissent, as well as encouraging acts of vice, much the same as the evils attributed to the drinking of alcohol. In the 1920s, coffee was finally banned in Iran and new types of tea, imported from China,

A group of men taking refuge from the heat with tea and water pipes, Yemen

took its place and filtered through to Turkey. Now where there are packed coffee houses in the rest of the Middle East, there are busy tea houses and tea gardens dotted around the towns and villages of Iran and Turkey. In both these countries, it is often the first drink to be offered to a guest in a home, or when conducting business in an office or the bazaar. It is also the first drink of the day and the last, with many in between. It seems to be served endlessly throughout the day until your bladder is ready to burst.

Tea is also a popular beverage in Syria, Lebanon and Jordan, where, according to legend, it was originally introduced by the Circassians. The Bedouin, who have a reputation for drinking gallons of coffee, are equally keen on tea. No Bedouin camp or compound can be visited without the customary partaking of tea. In these regions, the tea is prepared and drunk much the same way as in Iran and Turkey, although it is often flavoured with spices like cinnamon and aniseed, or with fresh spearmint leaves. Aromatic infusions, or herbal teas, drunk for pleasure or medicinal purposes, are also popular throughout the Middle East. Rose petals are recommended for colds and mallow or lime flowers for coughs. Dried pomegranate flowers are believed to relieve intestinal complaints, mint and aniseed to aid digestion and infusions of dried thyme are reputed to cure a number of ailments, as well as acting as an aphrodisiac.

A boy delivering tea in Istanbul, Turkey

BUYING AND STORING

In Turkey tea is grown in the damp hills at the eastern end of the Black Sea and in Iran it grows in the Caspian littoral and very little is exported. Some Middle Eastern stores may stock it, otherwise you will have to use a loose-leafed tea of your choice, preferably organic. I tend to use the fragrant Darjeeling or a mixture, in equal proportions, of Assam and Earl Grey. All loose-leafed teas should be kept in an airtight container in a cool place, otherwise they lose their aroma and flavour quite quickly.

PREPARATION AND PRESENTATION

Traditionally tea is prepared in a samovar, originally imported from Russia. Often an elaborate brass vessel, the early samovars consisted of a compartment at the bottom for burning coals to heat up the water in the 'kettle' section, on top of which sat a small teapot in which the tea brewed all day and was continually topped up with fresh water and tea. Some households and tea houses still use the old samovars, but many people have converted to a lighter, more practical version, made out of tin or enamel. Although less impressive to behold, the principle is the same: placed on the stove, the larger pot acts as the kettle while the tea brews in the smaller pot placed on top. In theory, by constantly replenishing the tea leaves and water, tea is available throughout the day.

Tea is served in glasses. In Turkey, these glasses are shaped like tulips, a legacy of the 'Tulip Period' during the reign of Ahmet III (1703–30). The glasses usually rest on glass or silver saucers and are presented on a tray. Sugar lumps are offered with the tea, but rather than stir them in as you would expect, it is customary to place them on the tongue and sip the tea through them.

Two-pot tea system

Sage tea

CHAI
(A POT OF TEA)

To make a light, fragrant, amber-coloured tea, select tea leaves of your choice and use one teaspoon per pot. Add a sprinkling of sugar (and of herb or spice, if you like) and a splash of water to moisten the leaves. Fill the larger kettle pot with water, place it over the stove or flame, and put the teapot on top.

When the water has boiled in the kettle pot, fill up the teapot and pour some water into the tea glasses to heat them up. Top up the water in the kettle pot and place it back over the heat with the teapot on top.

Wait for the water in the kettle pot to boil again, allowing the tea to brew gently, then tip the water out of the glasses and pour in the tea, about two-thirds of the way up. Top each glass up with the boiled water and serve with sugar lumps.

Add some more tea leaves to the pot, top it up with water, top the kettle up, and start all over again.

Tea served in a tulip-shaped glass

YOGURT

(LABAN)

Yogurt has been a basic food in the Middle East since the earliest nomadic and pastoral tribes and, as with cheese, the discovery of it probably came about by accident when a batch of fermenting milk was invaded by bacteria. Ancient methods of curdling milk to make yogurt are still used in the Middle East. In eastern Anatolia, some nomads use crushed ants' eggs as a yogurt culture, mountain shepherds use a specific herb, and in the Mediterranean regions, villagers often use a fig branch, as the sap produces a chemical reaction that turns the lactose in milk into lactic acid. Referred to as 'Persian milk' in medieval manuals, yogurt is known as *laban* in Arab countries, *laban zabadi* in Egypt, *mâst* in Iran and, in Turkey, *yoğurt*, from which the English word derives. The very same word was used by the ancestors of the Turks, who roamed Central Asia and valued yogurt so highly they offered it to the gods, the sun and the moon. The Turks add yogurt to practically everything and get through a million tons a year.

APPEARANCE AND TASTE

The sour taste associated with yogurt comes from the lactic acid, produced by bacteria during fermentation. Sometimes, the bacteria are joined by yeasts, which make it taste fizzy and slightly alcoholic, a feature of many rural yogurts in the Middle East. It is made from the milk of cows, sheep, goats, water buffalo and, occasionally, camels – all of which lend a distinctive texture and flavour. All yogurt should be creamy and tangy, not watery and tasteless. Cow's milk yogurt, which is the mildest and thinnest, curdles easily, so it needs to be stabilised (p42) if used in cooking. Sheep's milk yogurt, which is thick and creamy, and the strong-tasting goat's milk yogurt are both good for cooking as they tend not to curdle. The yogurt made from water buffalo's and camel's milk is extremely rich and thick, but slightly sweeter than the others, and can be used in cooking too. When yogurt is strained through a suspended piece of muslin, it loses its whey and reduces in quantity, intensifying the flavour and creaminess. If it is mixed with a little salt and left to drain for a long time, 1–2 days, it gets thicker and firmer until it is the consistency of dense cream cheese. Often referred to as 'yogurt cheese', this is known as *labna* in Arabic.

A tub of strained yogurt

BUYING AND STORING

Yogurt is always in constant supply in the Middle East. In rural areas, it is still made in the home, stored in tin-lined copper urns, but practically everywhere else freshly made yogurt is sold by street sellers, in the markets and in local shops. Making it yourself is very easy but nowadays we're spoilt for choice in most big supermarkets, wholefood shops and Middle Eastern and Asian stores. Look for live, organic yogurt, with nothing added. Strain it yourself through a piece of muslin cloth or buy one of the Greek brands of ready-strained yogurt. All yogurt needs to be kept covered in the refrigerator and used by the sell-by date. If you make it yourself, it should last for two weeks.

MEDICINAL USES

The lactose found in milk is converted to lactic acid during the fermentation process, making yogurt much more digestible than milk and more suitable for people who suffer from lactose intolerance – a common condition in the Middle East. Containing significant amounts of calcium, yogurt has long been regarded as a nutritional, health-giving and healing substance. It is rich in minerals and vitamins, it soothes skin conditions such as rashes and sunburn, it contains antibiotic properties, it aids the digestion and it contributes to longevity.

A traditional tin-lined copper yogurt urn from Trabzon, Turkey

CULINARY USES

Yogurt
In the Middle East, yogurt has multiple uses. It is like a staple food. It is eaten for breakfast with honey, it is eaten as a snack, often sprinkled with powdered sugar, it is diluted to make the refreshing drink *ayran*, it accompanies most meals and is an integral part of many dishes. The one thing it is rarely served with is fish. It is often served with meat dishes, such as kebabs, or it is spooned over them, as in the Turkish speciality *yoğurtlu* (p51) *paça*, which consists of poached sheep's feet on a bed of toasted flat bread, topped with yogurt and melted butter, and is served at the Islamic festival *Kurban Bayramı*. In Iran, this everyday yogurt is used to marinate meat and it is mixed with egg yolk and saffron to form the crunchy bottom of the famous Persian rice dishes. In Turkey, it is mixed with crushed garlic and used as a sauce for grilled and fried vegetables, for egg dishes, such as *çılbır*, and for *mantı*, an ancient dish of pasta parcels filled with minced meat, chickpeas or nuts. A similar pasta dish, *shish barak*, which is a speciality of Syria and Lebanon,

Fresh yogurt, strained through cloth, Iran

is prepared with a hot yogurt sauce. Also in Lebanon there is *immos*, meaning 'his mother's milk', which is a rather morbid dish that calls for the meat of a young lamb to be cooked in yogurt made from its mother's milk. Owing to their dietary laws, this dish is prohibited among Jews. In Iran, Lebanon, Syria and Turkey, a number of dishes involve cooking meat in yogurt, or adding yogurt to soups and stews to impart a creamy, lemony flavour. Yogurt is also used in a number of refreshing salads with cucumbers, lamb's lettuce, beetroot, peppers, courgettes and aubergines. Strained yogurt is ideal for the sumptuous, creamy *mezze* dishes made with cooked vegetables that have been chopped or pulped, like spinach and smoked aubergine, known as *ezme* in Turkey and *boorâni* in Iran. And the thick, creamy strained yogurt, *laban* (*süzme* in Turkish), is often served on its own or mixed with white cheese and flavoured with garlic or herbs, like mint and dill, as a dip for bread.

In the Middle East, some recipes call for yogurt to be used as the cooking liquid. It is often made in batches and stored in the refrigerator to be used in a variety of dishes during the week. Yogurt made from sheep's

and goat's milk tends not to curdle, but cow's milk yogurt does, so it needs to be stabilised by using egg white or cornflour. To stabilise a litre of yogurt, beat it in a pan until it is liquid, then stir in one egg white or a tablespoon of cornflour (first made into a paste with a little water or milk) and a scant teaspoon of salt. Slowly bring the liquid to the boil, stirring all the time in one direction, and then leave it to simmer over a very low heat for about ten minutes, until it looks thick and creamy. Use it immediately in a dish or leave it to cool and store in the refrigerator.

Yogurt cheese
Labna is often eaten as a *mezze* dish on its own, drizzled with oil and sprinkled with fresh herbs or Middle Eastern red pepper, and it is used in thick *mezze* dips and in some desserts. It is also served as a healthy, sweet snack with a dribble of honey and a dusting of cinnamon. *Labna* is also used to make *labna bi zayt*, which are balls of yogurt cheese marinated in olive oil and served as a *mezze* or snack with bread and herbs.

An ancient product using *labna* is a dried curd, particularly popular in Jordan and among the Bedouin. Balls of yogurt cheese are dried in the sun until they become hard, then they are crumbled and rubbed with the fingers, or grated, until they resemble fine breadcrumbs, before being dissolved in water to make a nourishing drink for journeys. Sometimes, the freshly strained *labna* is mixed with flour and left in the sun to dry into hard cakes (the Bedouin do this on top of their tents). These are called *jameed* in Jordan, where they are used to make a sauce that is poured over the country's national dish, *mansaf*, and in a lentil and rice dish, *reshuf* (*rajuf*). Similarly, in Turkey, the yogurt cheese is left to ferment and dry in the sun and is then rubbed into pellets to be used to thicken soups and stews. Or it is mixed with cracked wheat and pulped vegetables, fermented, dried and crumbled and called *tarhana*. The soup made with it is called by the same name. These crumbled pellets are also used to make a kind of peasant porridge, or they are mixed with crumbled cheese and eaten for breakfast. Occasionally, *tarhana* is chewed as a snack. The Arabs make a fermented product with yogurt and bulgur, called *kishk* (p125), which derives from the Persian tradition known as *kashk*, meaning crushed wheat or barley. In modern Iran, *kashk* tends to refer to dried whey or buttermilk, which is employed in the popular creamy, sour-tasting aubergine dish *kashk-e bâdenjân*.

Known as *doogh* in Iran, *laban* in parts of the Arab world and *ayran* in Turkey and Lebanon, this refreshing drink was enjoyed by Persian kings and the ancient ancestors of the Turks, who also called it *ayran*. It is a popular drink in the Middle East, usually flavoured with fresh mint, although basil is used in Iraq, and it is served chilled, or with ice. It is prepared in homes, cafés, kebab houses and by street vendors to quench the thirst in hot weather. Traditionally it is drunk as an accompaniment to meat dishes, especially lamb kebabs.

AYRAN
(YOGURT DRINK WITH MINT)

Serves 3–4
Preparation time 2 minutes
Cooking time –

600ml (1 pint) chilled thick, creamy yogurt
600ml (1 pint) cold water
A pinch of salt
A few fresh mint leaves, coarsely chopped, or 2 pinches dried mint

Beat the yogurt in a bowl and gradually add in the water, until it is well blended. Alternatively, whiz them together in an electric mixer.

Season it to your taste – a little salt just lifts it – then pour it into tall glasses, with ice if you like, and sprinkle the mint over the top.

Yogurt soups are popular throughout the Middle East. In Turkey and Iran, cold yogurt soups, made with cucumber and mint, are refreshing in the hot summer months. In Egypt, the traditional yogurt soup, *labaneya*, is made with spinach or beet and served hot. The Iranians also make a hot yogurt soup, *eshkeneh Shirazi*, which is flavoured with walnuts and fresh fenugreek; the Armenians add noodles to the traditional yogurt soup, *tutmaj*. The following recipe is for the Turkish yogurt soup, made hearty with the addition of chickpeas and rice and usually flavoured with dried mint or safflower. If you prepare the chickpeas in advance, it doesn't take long to make.

YOĞURT ÇORBASI
(YOGURT SOUP)

Serves 4
Preparation time 5 minutes (+ at least 6 hours' soaking of chickpeas)
Cooking time 35 minutes (+ 50 minutes' simmering)

Roughly 25g (1oz) chickpeas, soaked for at least 6 hours
1 onion, finely chopped
1 tablespoon clarified butter or ordinary butter
1–2 tablespoons flour
1.2 litres (2 pints) well-flavoured lamb or beef stock
50g (2oz) long-grain rice, rinsed
425ml (¾pint) thick, creamy yogurt
Salt and ground black pepper
Dried mint for serving

Simmer the chickpeas in plenty of water for about 50 minutes, until they are tender.

In a deep saucepan, soften the onion in the butter. Quickly stir in the flour, off the heat, and pour in the stock. Bring the liquid to the boil, stir in the rice and the cooked chickpeas, cover the pan and leave the soup to simmer for about 20 minutes, until the rice is cooked. Then season.

Beat the yogurt in a bowl and add it gradually to the soup, stirring all the time, making sure you only heat it through and don't boil it, as it would curdle. Serve immediately with dried mint sprinkled over the top.

Ayran

kaşar peynir

CHEESE

(GEBNA)

Cheese stored in sheep's stomach

Cheese dates back to the earliest pastoral societies. Once there were herds, there was milk and the act of cheese-making may have come about by accident from the fermented products. The ancient Egyptians are known to have made cheese; traces of it were found in a tomb dating back to 3000 BC. It was a staple food of the ancient Greeks and Romans, and Abraham gave milk from his cattle to the poor when he first migrated to the land of Canaan. However, milk is rarely consumed fresh in the Middle East. According to Islamic custom, it should have ceased flowing before it is consumed, so it is used for milk puddings and made into cheese, yogurt, butter and clotted cream. Medieval Arab sources reveal that a variety of cheeses was produced throughout the Islamic Empire and that Jerusalem was famous for its milk and cheese. More sophisticated blocks of white cheeses were made during the time of the Ottomans, when the milk of sheep and goats and, in some parts, buffalo, was treated with rennet. Today, the cheese is made following the traditional ways using the milk of the same animals. In the rural villages and Bedouin camps, cheese is made in goatskins to make it easy to carry.

Blocks of white cheese kept fresh in brine at a market, Turkey

APPEARANCE AND TASTE

A whey cheese, similar to ricotta, with a creamy texture and a mild flavour is popular in most parts of the Middle East, often eaten with honey or sugar. A firm, crumbly white cheese, in the style of feta, made from sheep's or goat's milk, is salted and preserved in brine. This is the most common, everyday cheese with a slightly salty, lemony taste, delicious with olives. *Hallum* is a salty, semi-hard cheese made from sheep's milk. It is matured in whey and often sprinkled with nigella seeds. Lebanon and Cyprus are known for their *hallum* (*haloumi* in Cyprus). Of the many village cheeses, some are buried underground in clay pots and left for months to mature, and there is a special cheese made in the spring from the milk of nursing ewes. There is also a hard, yellowish cheese with a tangy flavour, encased in a rind. It too is made from sheep's milk and is called *kashkawan* in Arabic (*kaşar* in Turkish). And there is a curious stringy, white cheese, *jibna majdula* or *dil peyniri*, that looks a bit like a plastic block of compressed thin layers – these peel off in strips.

BUYING AND STORING

There is a large selection of cheeses to choose from in the Middle East, the only difference sometimes being the village they come from. However, outside the region, only a handful are available. The crumbly white cheese, sometimes called 'Turkish feta' is sold in Middle Eastern stores; this can easily be replaced by Greek feta in the recipes. *Kaşar* is sold in some Middle Eastern stores and can be substituted with a dry, tangy Cheddar or Pecorino, and *haloumi* from Cyprus is available in Middle Eastern stores and most supermarkets. All cheeses need to be stored in the refrigerator.

CULINARY USES

Fresh white cheese is often eaten as a snack with a hunk of bread or for breakfast with olives, dates and honey. A classic Turkish breakfast will include freshly baked bread, thin slices of white cheese, a choice of the local black and green olives, honey or rose petal jam, slices of ripe tomatoes and cucumber and fresh figs. White cheese is also a popular *mezze*, either with a little olive oil drizzled over it, sprinkled with dried oregano and flaked Middle Eastern red pepper (p152), or served with cubes of juicy, honey-sweet melon. It is used as a filling for savoury pastries, such as the ubiquitous *börek*, and it is mixed with vegetables in patties and in

the Turkish dish of minced turkey balls, *gelik köftesi*. The soft ricotta-style whey cheese and a denser, creamier cheese are often eaten with honey for breakfast, or used in sweet pastries and semolina desserts. The soft and crumbly white cheeses are often mixed with herbs or strained yogurt to make a dip for bread, such as the Iranian *poloor* (p176). These cheeses and dips are sometimes sprinkled with *zaatar* (p196) or nigella seeds and they are occasionally combined with ground walnuts and red pepper paste in the delicious *mezze*, *muhammara* (p136). The same white cheeses are used in Turkey to make *peynir tatlısı*, small sponge puddings bathed in syrup, and in Syria and Lebanon they are used in a cheese-flavoured version of the

A *mezze* spread including *hummus*, yogurt dips and slices of white cheese, Lebanon

semolina pudding, *ma'mounia*. The hard sheep's cheese *kaşar* is eaten on its own with bread, or is used as a filling in savoury pastries and in dishes that require melted cheese. Baked cheese-filled aubergines are a popular Jewish dish and *haloumi* and *kashkawan* are sometimes dredged in flour and deep-fried as an appetiser, served with

Beyaz peynir stored in water to reduce the salt content

Bedouin shepherd with kid in Petra, Jordan

BEĞENDİ

(SMOKED AUBERGINE PURÉE IN A CHEESE SAUCE)

Serves 4
Preparation time 15 minutes
Cooking time 10 minutes

2 big aubergines
Roughly 25g (1oz) butter
1–2 tablespoons flour
600ml (1 pint) milk
175g (6oz) kaşar or other cheese, grated
Salt and ground black pepper

Place the whole aubergines directly over a gas flame, on a barbecue, or in the embers of a fire. Leave them to smoke, turning them from time to time, until they feel soft when pressed. Split them open with a knife to spoon out the flesh, or hold them under running cold water to remove the skin. Chop the flesh into a pulp.

Melt the butter in a saucepan and, off the heat, stir in the flour to make a roux. Place the pan back over the heat and pour in the milk, stirring all the time, until the sauce begins to thicken.

Gradually stir in the grated cheese, then beat in the pulped aubergine. Make sure it is mixed together well, season to taste. Serve with bread to mop it up.

Konafa (called *künefe* or *kadayif* in Turkish) is a speciality of Antakya, in the southern-most region of Turkey where the atmosphere is Arab in character, and it is one of the most popular desserts in Jordan, particularly amongst the Palestinian community. It is also popular in Lebanon, where some people eat it for breakfast, sandwiched inside sesame bread. Made with the famous pastry that looks like shredded wheat, sometimes called *kadaif*, it is not practical to make from scratch at home – the batter needs to be tossed through a sieve onto a metal sheet over a fire, then as soon as it sets it has to be scraped off quickly before it cooks. The good news is that ready-prepared packages of the shredded pastry can be bought in the same specialist shops that make *börek* and *yufka* or *fila* and, outside the Middle East, they are sold in Middle Eastern and Greek shops. Although the shredded pastry can be filled with chopped nuts, it is the cheese filling that makes *konafa* so unusual and delectable. Each region uses its own white cheese, including the stringy *dil peyniri*, for which mozzarella is the best substitute.

lemon. They are also fried with peppers, *çökelekli,* or with eggs, *beid bi gebna maqlia.* The stringy white cheese is a popular snack with adults and children alike – it is such a delight to peel off the layers and eat them with pickles. And it has one major culinary role as a filling in the delectable syrupy desert *konafa,* which is made with thin strands of pastry that look like shredded wheat.

There is a Turkish dish called *Hünkâr beğendi,* meaning 'Sultan's Delight': it obviously pleased one of the great Ottoman rulers. Traditionally, the dish is made with meatballs cooked in a tomato sauce, or a meat and tomato stew, served on a puréed bed of smoked aubergine in a cheese sauce – the *beğendi.* The following recipe is for the purée, which is delicious on its own, or served with meatballs or roasted meats. In Turkey, the cheese used is *kaşar,* the hard, tangy sheep's cheese, but one could substitute a strong-tasting hard cheese such as mature Cheddar or Parmesan.

Sheep lined up for sale, Syria

KONAFA

(SYRUPY SHREDDED PASTRY WITH A CHEESE FILLING)

Serves 6
Preparation time 20–25 minutes
Cooking time 1¼ hours

225g (8oz) sugar
150ml (5fl oz) water
Juice of ½ lemon
225g (8oz) ready-prepared shredded pastry
110g (4oz) clarified butter (ghee), melted
350g (12oz) mozzarella, sliced (you can use other cheeses, such as ricotta)

Preheat the oven to 160°C/325°F/gas mark 3.

Prepare the syrup: put the sugar and water into a pan and bring it to the boil, stirring all the time. Add the lemon juice, then reduce the heat and leave to simmer, until the syrup thickens a little and coats the back of a spoon. Leave to cool, then place the syrup in the refrigerator.

Put the shredded pastry into a bowl and separate the strands as much as possible. Pour the melted clarified butter over them and, using your fingers, rub it into the strands to make sure they are well coated. Put half the pastry into an oven-proof dish or individual dishes and lay the slices of mozzarella over the top. Cover the cheese with the rest of the pastry, tucking it down the sides of the dish to seal in the cheese, and flatten the top with the palm of your hand. Pop the dish, or dishes, into the oven and bake for about 1 hour, then zap up the oven to 220°C/425°F/gas mark 7 for about 15 minutes, until the *konafa* turns golden brown. Take the *konafa* out of the oven and pour the cold syrup over it. Serve straight away as *konafa* is best eaten warm.

Konafa

COOKING FATS

Olive oil

SHEEP'S TAIL FAT
(ALYA)

The flavoursome, rendered fat from the tail of Awassi sheep, a long-fleeced Asian breed with enormous, podgy, bulbous tails, has been used in the cooking of the Middle East since the time of the early nomadic and pastoral tribes. These sheep don't need lush pastures and can survive in hot, arid temperatures as, similar to the hump of a camel, the fat stored in their tails provides them with all the sustenance they need. Marco Polo was one of the first Europeans to write about his encounter with the sheep, which he described as being as big as a donkey with a thick fat tail, weighing 30 pounds (13.5kg) or more. He also noted that they were delicious to eat. The fat was put to good use in the many medieval Arab recipes which began with instructions to melt or fry the tail.

Nowadays, this heavy, strong-tasting fat is really used only in rural areas, such as the mountainous regions of eastern Turkey and northern Iraq. Sheep's tail fat is known as *alya* or *aliya* in Arabic, *kuyrukyağı* in Turkish, and *roghan-e donbeh* in Farsi.

CLARIFIED AND ORDINARY BUTTER
(SAMNA)

Butter replaced sheep's-tail fat. It was made from the milk of sheep, goats or buffalo, which gave it a strong, distinctive, almost rancid smell and taste. Among the Bedouin and peasant communities, it fell to the women to churn it, in goatskins suspended on sticks. The nomads carried the butter in the goatskins to supply the towns. The kitchens of Aleppo and al-Karak (now in Jordan) were famous for their lavish use of butter. In order to preserve it, the butter was melted over boiling water and then strained through dampened muslin to clarify it – a process that still takes place in most rural communities. Clarified butter or ghee (*samna* in Arabic) is rich and strong with a slight nutty taste, and only a small amount is required for a dish. It is easy to make at home by melting butter in a pan until it froths, then straining it through a piece of muslin to remove the impurities. Pour the clarified butter into a jar or container, leave it to cool and solidify, then cover it and store in a cool place.

Clarified butter

OLIVE OIL AND OTHERS
(ZEIT ZAYTUN)

Olive oil is the principal cooking oil of Turkey, Syria, Lebanon and Jordan, where it has been produced for thousands of years. The ancient Romans spread its cultivation throughout their empire, as a fuel for oil-burning lamps as well as for cooking. The ancient Hebrews used it for anointing and in temple offerings. In the Middle Ages, Syrian olive oil was regarded highly in the Islamic world. Traditionally, many Christians in the Middle East cook only with olive oil during their religious fasts. The Jews use it to deep-fry morsels at *Hanukah*, in commemoration of the miraculous oil that features in the story of Judas Maccabaeus' victory. Olive oil didn't make an impact on Turkey until the late seventeenth century, when it was employed in the famous Ottoman Palace dishes, which involved gently poaching vegetables, balanced with 'warming' or 'cooling' herbs and then leaving them to cool in the oil before serving. Prior to that in Turkey, olive oil had been used only as a lighting fuel in the mosques.

The olives used to make olive oil need to be gathered when they are quite ripe and undamaged. The flesh then has to be crushed without breaking the stones and pressed to extract the oil. The fluid that is extracted is left to settle so that it separates naturally into oil and a bitter watery substance (this is removed from olives for eating by soaking them in a lye solution). Olive oil is extremely healthy, containing no cholesterol, and it has long been used for its medicinal properties, to nourish dry skin, to soothe sprains and earaches, and as a laxative. In fact, an ancient Roman prescription for longevity involved drinking wine and cooking with olive oil. Early and medieval Arab recipes used a variety of other oils, including pistachio, walnut, sesame, safflower, cotton seed, sunflower and corn, some of which are still used today.

BUYING AND STORING

Unless you know a breeder of Awassi sheep or go to a Middle Eastern shop supplied with its own butcher, I would imagine sheep's-tail fat is impossible to find in the West. Clarified butter, however, is readily available in Indian and Middle Eastern stores and some supermarkets, often sold in tins as ghee from India. It keeps for a long time in a cool place and doesn't have to be stored in the refrigerator. The choice of olive oils in the shops is growing all the time but it is rare to find one from a Middle Eastern country. This is partly because the olive-growing regions don't produce enough and, until recently, it wasn't sufficiently refined for export. This is changing now and Turkey, in particular, is beginning to export a satisfying, comparable product, but, alas, in the name of progress all the depth and character of the crude, pungent, virgin oils made in the villages have virtually disappeared. Sunflower, sesame, walnut and corn oils are all available in supermarkets. All oils need to be kept in a cool dark place.

Olive oil factory

Frying sweet pastries in the Bayt Al Faqih market, Yemen

CULINARY USES

In Turkey, the whole sheep's tail is boiled and consumed with bread during the feast of *Kurban Bayramı*, which marks the near-sacrifice of Isma'il (p69). In the rural parts of the Middle East, the flabby tails of the Awassi sheep are burnt to release the fat to use in meat and grain dishes. Its distinct flavour is unique to a number of peasant dishes.

Clarified butter is popular throughout the Middle East in savoury dishes that are cooked and eaten hot, particularly meat stews and soups, and in grain dishes. It also gives a distinct characteristic to some sweet pastries and sweetmeats which keep moist for months without tasting rancid. In urban areas though, ordinary butter, made from the milk of cows or sheep, is often used.

The mellow, fruity flavour of olive oil is favoured for vegetable dishes, fish and in dishes that are served cold, such as the numerous, delectable *mezze* dishes. It plays a principal role in the special Ottoman-inspired olive oil dishes (*zeytinyağlı*), coating vegetables such as artichokes, broad beans, celeriac, leeks, stuffed peppers and stuffed aubergines. It is also used as a preserving oil for olives, prepared vegetables such as roasted pimento peppers, and for the balls of yogurt cheese.

In areas where olive oil is expensive or difficult to obtain, a cheaper oil such as sunflower or safflower might be used for most dishes. Otherwise, the completely tasteless and lighter sunflower oil is reserved for frying and deep-frying. Sesame and walnut oils tend to be used only in cold dishes involving sesame seeds or walnuts, such as the Circassian chicken, *Çerkez tavuğu* (p62).

This is a Turkish speciality, a legacy of the Ottomans. It is called İmam bayıldı, meaning 'the Imam fainted', as it is believed that the quantity of olive oil used in this tender and delicious dish caused him to keel over. Whether he fainted from shock or pleasure, no one knows.

İMAM BAYILDI
(STUFFED AUBERGINES IN OLIVE OIL)

Serves 4–6
Preparation time 20–25 minutes
Cooking time 1 hour

1 large onion, finely sliced
3 large tomatoes, skinned and chopped
4 cloves garlic, finely chopped
A bunch of fresh parsley and dill, chopped
1 teaspoon salt
150ml (5fl oz) olive oil
2–3 long aubergines, partially peeled in zebra-stripes and soaked in salted water for 5 minutes
50ml (2fl oz) water
1 tablespoon sugar
1 lemon, cut into wedges, to serve

In a bowl, mix the onion, tomatoes, garlic and herbs with the salt and a little of the olive oil. In a frying pan, heat up enough oil to just cover the base. Pat the aubergines dry and pop them into the pan to soften them quickly on all sides.

Place the aubergines on a board and, carefully, slit them open from top to bottom, making sure you create a deep pocket to fill. Pack the onion and tomato filling into the pockets and place the aubergines, side by side, in a deep pan.

Mix together the remaining olive oil and water and pour it over the filled aubergines. Sprinkle with sugar and cover with the lid.

İmam bayıldı

Buying and selling sheep, Kuwait

Cook the aubergines gently for about 1 hour, basting them from time to time, until they are soft and tender and only the olive oil is left in the bottom of the pan. Leave them to cool and serve cold with a little of the oil spooned over them and lemon wedges to squeeze.

At the Islamic festival *Eid-el-Kurban* (*Kurban Bayramı* in Turkish), a day that marks the near-sacrifice of Isma'il (p69), a sheep is slaughtered and almost every part of it is cooked in the fat from the tail. In Turkey, the following is made with the feet.

YOĞURTLU PAÇA
(SHEEP'S TROTTERS IN YOGHURT)

Serves 4
Preparation time 15 minutes
Cooking time approximately 4¼ hours

6–8 sheep's trotters, scrubbed clean in salted water

For the stock:
Juice of 1 lemon
1 onion, quartered
3–4 cloves garlic, smashed
2 dried bay leaves
1 teaspoon coriander seeds
A few peppercorns
Salt

4 pitta breads or 6–8 slices day-old bread, with the crusts removed
2–3 tablespoons sheep's-tail fat
300ml (10fl oz) creamy yogurt
2 cloves garlic, crushed
1 tablespoon clarified butter
1 teaspoon Middle Eastern red pepper (p152)

Preheat the oven to 180°C/350°F/gas mark 4.

Blanch the trotters in boiling water for about 5 minutes, then drain. Put them into a large pan with the stock ingredients and cover with water. Bring to the boil, then simmer gently for 3–4 hours. Drain the trotters, reserving the stock, and take the meat off the bone. Reduce the stock and season it to taste.

Heat the sheep's-tail fat in a wide pan, fry the bread until crisp, then lay the pieces in a shallow, oven-proof dish. Arrange the meat on top, moisten with a little of the stock, cover with foil and place the dish in the oven for about 10–15 minutes.

Meanwhile, beat the yogurt with the garlic and season it to taste. Melt the butter in a pan and stir in the red pepper. Take the meat out of the oven, spoon the yogurt onto it and pour the butter over the top. Serve immediately.

green olives

OLIVES

(ZAYTUN) *Olea europaea*

Known as the 'sultan of the table', olives appear at almost every meal. A handful of olives and a lump of white goat's cheese have sustained peasants and nomads since ancient times. Wild olives originated in the eastern Mediterranean, where the small, bitter fruit was gathered by Neolithic peoples. The tree was first cultivated in Syria or Palestine, long before 3000 BC, and gradually spread westwards to Crete and Greece and upwards and eastwards into Anatolia and parts of Central Asia. The ancient Greeks claimed the first olive tree was given by the goddess Athena to mankind. Along with the Romans, they held the fruit in high esteem, the olive branch being a symbol of peace. It was regarded as a sacrilegious act to destroy an enemy's olive tree. Olive motifs feature on some ancient Egyptian artefacts and the polished stones of the fruit are used throughout the Islamic world as prayer beads, flicked between thumb and finger. Today, Syria, Lebanon, Jordan and Turkey are all producers of olives and olive oil.

Ripe black olives

Olive trees outside Nazareth

HOW THEY GROW

Wild olive trees (*Oleaster*) still grow in their regions of origin but the bitter fruit contains more stone than flesh. The cultivated olive tree produces larger, fleshier fruit which are delicious on the table and ideal for pressing to extract the oil. Olive trees are evergreen with silvery-green leaves and deep roots. They are slow to mature, but can live for a long time in poor, stony soil, up hillsides and on uneven ground. There is an old Arab saying that the olive tree remains a strong and useful wife, in spite of neglect and hardship. Some trees live for hundreds of years and still produce a crop of fruit. The tree flowers in spring- time and the fruit is harvested, by shaking the tree and gathering up the fallen fruit, in late autumn and on into winter.

APPEARANCE AND TASTE

In spite of their bitter and almost soapy taste, the green wild olive fruits are prized by some people as a table olive. All other olives are fleshy, round or oval, and come in a variety of colours: shades of green, sometimes tinged with red or pink, red wine, violet, deep purplish-black like some aubergines, muddy brown, and jet black. The only difference between them all is in the ripeness, the black ones being fully ripe and the oiliest. The

A huge variety of olives on sale at market, Turkey

green ones, picked immature, must first be soaked in a lye solution to remove the glucoside, which makes the fruit very bitter, before they are preserved in brine. The sweeter black olives, which have been left to ripen on the tree, can be picked and put into brine straight away. Generally olives are cured whole, but to speed up the process, some olive growers make small incisions in the flesh, or crack them by striking them gently with a mallet. Not all olives are cured in brine; some are repeatedly rinsed in water, others are soaked or rubbed in oil, and the ripe black olives are often sprinkled and turned in salt, which crinkles the skin and softens the flesh, turning it brown.

Black olives left to ripen on the tree

BUYING AND STORING

Most supermarkets, delicatessens, Italian, Greek and Middle Eastern shops have a wide selection of olives. If you can, buy them in brine, rinse them well and marinate and flavour them yourself. They keep well in olive oil in a sealed jar in a cool, dry place, away from the light.

CULINARY USES

All table olives are enjoyed as they are. No *mezze* table is complete without a bowl of the shiny green ones, bathed in oil and flavoured with coriander seeds, or the crinkled black ones tossed in oil and fresh mint. The most common marinade is a combination of olive oil and lemon juice, to which a variety of spices or herbs can be added, the favourite being dried marjoram, oregano or thyme, fresh mint, flaked Middle Eastern red pepper,

coriander seeds and crushed garlic. Olives are also popular for breakfast, eaten with white cheese and bread.

Green olives are crushed with garlic and coriander seeds to make a tasty paste for bread known as *çakiste* in northern Cyprus and southern Turkey. In Egypt and other parts of North Africa, green olives are sometimes cooked with chicken, duck or pigeon. In the Mediterranean regions, black olives are added to bread doughs, cold fish dishes and bean salads, such as the Turkish *fasulya piyaze*. Black olives are also used for garnishing many dishes and in some coastal regions they are added to a delicious potato dish with tomatoes or cooked with squid in a wine and tomato stew, Greek and Italian style.

The Egyptians are fond of pigeon, stuffed, baked, grilled, roasted or stewed. Along with quails and chickens, some

families even raise them in their gardens for the pot. Qasr Al Nil, the road which leads to the pyramids, is lined with restaurants serving charcoal-grilled pigeon, refreshed with lemon juice and chopped herbs. The pigeons in Egypt are different from the ones in the West, but this spicy recipe, with its tart bursts of lemon juice and olives, works well with wood pigeon too. If you have already made up the Arab spice mixture *baharat* (p162), you can use 1–2 teaspoons of that instead of the spices listed.

HAMAM BIL ZAYTUN
(SPICY PIGEON WITH OLIVES)

Serves 2
Preparation time 10 minutes
Cooking time approximately 1¼ hours

2 teaspoons tomato paste
½ teaspoon paprika
½ teaspoon ground cinnamon

½ teaspoon ground ginger
¼ teaspoon ground cloves
A little grated nutmeg
A sprinkling of sugar
1–2 tablespoons clarified butter (ghee)
2 pigeons, cleaned and split in half lengthways
2–3 dried bay leaves
Juice of ½ lemon
Roughly 16 green olives
Salt and freshly ground black pepper

Mix together the tomato paste, spices and a sprinkling of sugar.

Heat the clarified butter in a heavy-based pan and add the pigeons and bay leaves. Brown the pigeons and then stir in the spicy paste, the lemon juice and roughly 250ml (8½fl oz) water. Cover the pan and simmer gently for about 1 hour, until the pigeons are tender.

Add the olives and simmer with the lid off for a further 15 minutes. Season and serve with bread to mop up the sauce.

Çakiste

This olive paste is a popular *meze* dip in southern Turkey and northern Cyprus, where it is often pepped up with hot red pepper. It is always made with tart green olives, although crushed black olives make a delicious paste too, and is served along with other *meze* dishes (p28) such as cubes of white cheese, bathed in olive oil, cubes of honey-sweet melon and pickles.

ÇAKİSTE
(GREEN OLIVE AND CORIANDER DIP)

Serves 4 as part of meze spread
Preparation time 15–20 minutes
Cooking time –

Roughly 225g (8oz) green olives
2–3 cloves garlic
1 teaspoon coriander seeds
A squeeze of lemon juice
Salt
A sprinkling of Middle Eastern red pepper (p152) or chopped red chilli

Cut the olive flesh off the stones.

Using a mortar and pestle, crush the garlic and coriander seeds to a smooth paste. Add the olive flesh and pound it to a coarse paste. Stir in a little lemon juice and season with salt, if necessary.

Tip the paste into a bowl, sprinkle the red pepper or chilli over the top and serve with toasted flat bread.

Olives spiced with chillies and thyme make a delicious *mezze* dish in Syria, Lebanon, Turkey and Jordan. They are often served with cubes of firm, salted white cheese which is either drizzled with olive oil or fried. *Hallum* is particularly good for this.

ZAYTUN MSABBAH
(OLIVES SPICED WITH CHILLIES AND THYME)

Serves 4–6 as mezze
Preparation time 2–3 hours
Cooking time –

225g (8oz) fresh green olives, soaked in water for 1–2 days
1 fresh, hot chilli, chopped or 1 teaspoon Middle Eastern red pepper (p152)
1 teaspoon dried thyme
Roughly 120ml (4fl oz) olive oil
Juice of ½ lemon

Drain the olives and cut 3 or 4 slits in each one. Put them into a bowl, pour in the olive oil and mix well. Add the chilli and thyme and leave to marinate for a few hours.

When ready to eat, squeeze a little lemon juice over them, sprinkle with a little salt if you like, and serve with cubes of white cheese and bread to mop up the chilli oil.

Pickled aubergine parcels

PICKLES
(MEKHALEL)

Fruit and vegetables are an important part of the Middle Eastern diet. In order to enjoy the abundant supply of freshly harvested fruit and vegetables throughout the year, some of them have to be preserved. In season they are tasty and cheap, so every traditional household reserves a quantity for drying, poaching in syrup, pressing into molasses, or for pickling in vinegar – delectable delights that will nourish the soul and brighten up the cold winter.

The medieval Arabs adopted their food preservation methods from the Greeks, the Romans and the Persians. The most common method of all was pickling, which was applied to fruit, vegetables, nuts, chicken, eggs, small fish, birds and even lamb and goat. Today, the method has not changed but, with the year-round availability of imported produce and refrigeration, some of the ingredients have. Tongue and brains are still pickled and fish is still popular (in fact the Turks of the Black Sea don't believe a fish is worth eating if it can't be pickled) but, on the whole, most pickles consist of fruit and vegetables. They are so popular, there are shops and street-vendors dedicated to them. The arrays of jars containing colourful pickles, stacked in shop windows or in the bustling bazaars, have a dazzling and enticing effect on passers-by, who can't resist stopping for a quick pickle snack. And, in the hot weather, the pickling juice is often drunk to quench the thirst.

APPEARANCE AND TASTE

The majority of Middle Eastern pickles are made with a combination of vinegar and salt; a few are made with brine. The vinegar is commonly made from dates, grapes or apples, although other fruit can be used. Nuts, garlic and a wide variety of spices, seeds and herbs, such as nigella, tarragon, angelica seeds, spearmint and cinnamon, are added for flavouring, but nothing else. And Middle Eastern pickles are always sour, never sweet. The fruit and vegetables are often picked immature and raw, so that they retain a delightful crunch throughout the pickling process, or they are lightly poached. Green walnuts are pickled, as are the unripe almonds still in their furry green skins. Immature apricots and watermelons are popular, and baby aubergines are often stuffed and wrapped in celery or vine leaves. Grapes, beans, peas, garlic, cauliflower, peppers, chillies, carrots, lemons, chickpeas, pears, melons, tomatoes, cucumbers, artichoke hearts, turnips and cabbage are all pickled. Fruits, nuts and vegetables are pickled individually or mixed together in a variety of personal combinations. The ratio of vinegar to salt varies too, according to personal taste. And some people like to throw in a few slices of beetroot to give a pink hue, or use red cabbage for its purple tint.

Pickled vegetables, including chillies, cabbages and stuffed aubergines stacked in a shop window, Istanbul, Turkey

Pickled olives, gerkins, stuffes pepper, beetroot and cabbage

TORSHI LEFT
(PICKLED WHITE TURNIPS)

Makes 2 big jars
Preparation time 20 minutes
Cooking time –

1kg (2¼lb) small white turnips,
  peeled and cut into quarters
1 beetroot (or 2 if you want a
  strong pink), peeled and sliced
A few celery leaves
Roughly 75g (3oz) salt
850ml (1½ pints) water
300ml (½ pint) white wine vinegar

Pack the turnips into sterilised jars, interspersing them with the beetroot slices and celery leaves.

Stir the salt in the water until it has dissolved, then mix in the vinegar. Pour the pickling juice over the turnips and seal the jars tightly. Leave the pickles to sit for 2 weeks before tucking into them.

The vegetables, herbs and their quantities can be altered according to taste – just make sure they are all well washed and patted dry before using.

Pickled vegetable stall, Turkey

BUYING AND STORING

In the Middle East, if you don't make your own pickles, then you go to the pickle shop. It's quite simple. Elsewhere, you will have to look for them in Middle Eastern and Asian stores. The vinegar-based pickles are designed to keep for a year but, if they are unopened and stored in a cool place, away from direct light, they keep for a couple of years.

CULINARY USES

Pickles are often served as *mezze*, or as an accompaniment to some main courses, particularly grilled meat dishes. In Turkey, they are eaten with slices of *pastırma* (p198) and *sucuk* (p166) as a snack, and they are often served with the popular late-night stomach filler, or early-morning hang over cure, *işkembe çorbası* (p208), tripe soup. In other parts of the Middle East, pickles are often

tucked into pitta bread with *hummus* or *falafel* (p113), and they are always served with bowls of *ful medames* (p116), the Egyptian brown beans. Invariably, pickles are eaten as a snack with cheese and with bread to mop up all the vinegary juice.

The following recipe is for pickled turnips, a great favourite in Egypt, Syria and Lebanon. The small white turnips are traditionally coloured pale or bright pink by adding slices of raw beetroot to the jar.

TORSHI-YE LEETEH
(PICKLED VEGETABLE RELISH)

Makes roughly 1.8kg (4lb) relish
Preparation time approximately
 1 hour
Cooking time –

*110g (4oz) carrots, peeled and
 chopped*
*110g (4oz) white cabbage,
 chopped*
1 onion, peeled and chopped
2 celery sticks, chopped
1 leek, chopped
1 courgette, chopped
1 green pepper, chopped roughly
6 cloves garlic, peeled
1 aubergine, cut into cubes
*Roughly 600ml (1 pint) white
 wine or cider vinegar*
*A large bunch parsley and
 coriander, chopped*
*A small bunch mint and dill,
 chopped*
Roughly 2 tablespoons salt
½ tablespoon nigella seeds
½ tablespoon coriander seeds
A few peppercorns

Put all the chopped vegetables
except the aubergine into a
bowl with the garlic. Put the
aubergine cubes into a shallow
pan. Pour in enough of the
vinegar to just cover and bring it
to the boil for just under a
minute. Tip the aubergines and
vinegar into the bowl of
vegetables and mix thoroughly
with the herbs, spices and salt.

Push the vegetable mixture
through the large hole of a
mincer, then spoon it into
sterilised jars, leaving a gap
(roughly the depth of a
thumbnail) at the top. Pour the
remaining vinegar into the gaps,
then seal the jars. Leave the
relish to sit for about 2 weeks
before opening.

Pickled hot or sweet peppers
are popular throughout the
Middle East, often served with
cheese as a *mezze* dish. They
are also popular with kebabs,
meatballs and *falafel* (p113). The
following recipe is for the long,
slender, perfumed green
peppers which can sometimes
be a bit sharp.

Torshi felfel

TORSHI FELFEL
(PICKLED GREEN PEPPERS)

Makes 2 big jars
Preparation time 5 minutes
Cooking time –

450g (1lb) long, green peppers
600ml (1 pint) water
300ml (½ pint) white wine vinegar
1 tablespoon salt

Pack the peppers into a jar. Mix
the water and vinegar with the
salt and pour it over the
peppers. Seal the jar tightly and
store in a cool place for 2
weeks before opening.

MEAT & FISH

Goose and chicken seller, Egypt

CHICKEN

(DJAAJ) *Gallus domesticus*

The wild ancestors of the chicken are thought to have been native to the Indian subcontinent, but they have been domesticated in the Middle East since the ancient Romans bred them for meat. Poultry was so highly regarded in the medieval Arab kitchen that numerous recipes for chicken were recorded in the *Wulsa*. Some of these included rhubarb and mulberries, quince and pomegranates, walnuts and almonds, rose water and musk, echoes of which exist in many of the recipes of today. During the Ottoman period, the markets were full of feathered creatures, such as chickens, turkeys, geese and ducks, and there was an abundance of game birds including some exotic species, too. Game birds such as partridge

and pheasant still feature on the tables of the Middle East, particularly in the hunting areas. Pigeons are eaten in Egypt and duck is favoured in Iran and Iraq, but none of these are used as frequently as chicken, which is almost as popular as lamb. If a festive occasion doesn't call for the slaughtering of a sheep, chicken will often be served instead. Among Jewish communities, chicken is the traditional food eaten before *Yom Kippur*, the Day of Atonement, which is a day of fasting and prayer. On the eve of the fast, a light chicken soup is served and, to break the fast, a number of chicken dishes are prepared, such as stuffed roast chicken, elaborate chicken stews, and thick chicken and vegetable soup.

Egg and potato stall at the Bayt Al Faqih market, Yemen

BUYING AND STORING

Chickens and other poultry are often bought live in the markets in the Middle East. They cluck, cackle and squawk in caged crates, while the buyers poke and prod them as they haggle over the price. The purchased bird is either killed and plucked on the spot, or carried home alive and squawking, held upside down by its feet, to meet its fate in the kitchen. In the rural areas, hens are free-range, fed on a diet of corn, and the meat is beautifully lean and tasty. With the emphasis on mass production in the West, the only way to acquire a tasty bird is to raise it yourself, or to buy the more expensive, certified organic, free-range chickens. However, with the rising population in the Middle East, there has been an increased demand for poultry and egg production in the last few decades, resulting in hens reared industrially on imported feed. Fresh chickens should be eaten within three or four days, but they can be stored in a freezer for about three months.

CULINARY USES

Often small chickens and other small birds are split down the back bone, flattened out, marinated in spices and grilled over charcoal. The tender, tasty meat is then eaten with fruit-based sauces, such as sour cherry or pomegranate, or stuffed into pitta bread with onions, parsley, lemon and yogurt. This is a particularly popular way of eating chicken outdoors and the smell emanating from the chicken grilling in the streets, or in the open country air, is quite irresistible. Chicken kebabs are also popular, in small rural kebab houses and gardens, as well as in sophisticated urban meat restaurants. For festive occasions, large chickens are often boiled first to obtain a stock for soup, and the meat is then served with rice. Large chickens are also cooked with vegetables, such as okra, spinach, and aubergines, or added to rice, with saffron, nuts, vegetables or fruit, to make a substantial meal.

The Iranians, who specialise in dishes using fruit, make a delicious stew with chicken and

Free-range hens, Northern Iran

oranges, *khoresht-e naranj*, and they are responsible for the famous *fesenjân*, which can be made with chicken, duck or fish, combined with walnuts in a pomegranate sauce. The Iranians also make a splendid baked rice and chicken dish, called *tahcheen-o morg*, which is served inverted so that the crusty bottom is on top. In Egypt, chicken is served with rice and the special *melokhia* soup, which is spooned over like a sauce. Also in Egypt, chicken is cooked with a calf's foot, eggs and wheat grains in a medieval dish called *ferique*. In Jordan and Lebanon, the Palestinian dish *musakhan* (p189) is popular. It consists of sautéed chicken, richly flavoured with sumac (p188) and spices, and served inside pitta bread with lashings of thick yogurt. And in Turkey, *Çerkez tavuğu*, a dish of Circassian origin, is favoured as a *meze* dish in restaurants or as a meal in the home.

Throughout the Middle East, all birds, large and small, are stuffed. Quails and pigeons are often stuffed with bulgur, while chickens, ducks, and turkeys are usually stuffed with rice, which might be flavoured with saffron, herbs and spices, and contain meat, fruit, or nuts. The most impressive of all stuffed chicken dishes must be the Iranian *koofteh tabrizi*, which is a huge dumpling made from rice, yellow split peas and minced lamb, inside which a whole, boned chicken, stuffed with apricots and walnuts, is concealed. Chicken livers and kidneys are often popped into stock or stuffings and, in Turkey, they are used in an extremely tasty rice dish, *iç pilavı* (p161). The most unusual of all the dishes using chicken has got to be the chicken breast pudding, *tavuk göğsu*, a fabulous creation of the Ottoman Palace kitchens.

Chicks dyed bright colours for sale at festivals, Abu Dhabi

Although pigeon, quail, duck and pheasant are eaten in other parts of the Middle East, the Turks rarely sway from chicken and Çerkez tavuğu is one dish that they have put their stamp on. Having said that, the dish is originally Circassian and the heavy use of walnuts is echoed in a number of classic Persian dishes. Moreover, a true Çerkez tavuğu is said to be flavoured with fresh coriander, a herb that features little in Turkish cookery. But although the dish has moved away from its origins, it is still delicious, served with the characteristic Turkish topping of melted butter and red pepper.

ÇERKEZ TAVUĞU
(CIRCASSIAN CHICKEN)

Serves 6
Preparation time approximately 35 minutes
Cooking time 1 hour

1 whole medium-sized, free-range chicken

For the stock:
2 onions, quartered
4 cloves
4–6 allspice berries
4 black peppercorns
3 bay leaves
1 teaspoon coriander seeds
Salt

3 slices day-old white bread, with crusts removed
150ml (5fl oz) milk
175g (6oz) walnuts
3–4 cloves garlic, crushed
Salt and freshly ground black pepper
Roughly 25g (1oz) butter
1 scant teaspoon Middle Eastern red pepper (p152)

Remove any excess fat from the chicken and place it in a large pan with all the stock ingredients. Pour in enough water to just cover the chicken

and bring it to the boil. Lower the heat and leave the chicken to simmer for about an hour.

Remove the chicken from the pan and leave to cool a little before taking the meat off the bone. Discard the skin, tear the meat into thin strips and put it into a bowl. Meanwhile boil up the stock for about 15 minutes to reduce it. Season it with salt and strain it.

Soak the bread in the milk. Grind the walnuts and garlic to a paste and beat in with the soaked bread (or blend them together in a mixer). Add the mixture to the chicken and bind together with spoonfuls of the seasoned stock. Keep adding stock until the mixture is light and creamy.

Season to taste, then spoon the mixture onto a serving dish. Melt the butter, stir in the flaked red pepper and spoon it over the top.

'Eat sweet, talk sweet', say the Turks, who are fond of their milk puddings and syrupy pastries. And, of all the puddings they will insist you try, tavuk göğsu is the one in which they take most pride. Probably originally a dish of the Romans, adopted by the Turks who migrated to Anatolia, once the hub of the Eastern Roman Empire, tavuk göğsu reached its pinnacle of sophistication during the height of the Ottoman Empire. Regarded as an Ottoman pudding, it is one of the most delectable creations of the Topkapı Palace kitchens.

TAVUK GÖĞSU KAZANDİBİ
(CHICKEN BREAST PUDDING)

Serves 6
Preparation time 15 minutes
Cooking time approximately 45 minutes

1 chicken breast
5 tablespoons rice flour
850ml (1½ pints) milk
300ml (10fl oz) single cream
¼ teaspoon salt
175g (6oz) sugar

Place the chicken breast in a pan with a little water. Bring it to the boil, reduce the heat and simmer until the meat is cooked. Drain and tear the breast into very fine threads.

Mix the rice flour to a loose paste with a little of the milk. Put the rest of the milk into a saucepan with the cream, salt and sugar, and bring to the boil.

Add a few spoonfuls of the hot liquid to the rice-flour paste, mix well, pour it into the pan, and beat vigorously. Reduce the heat and keep stirring until the mixture begins to thicken. Beat in the fine threads of chicken and continue to cook the mixture until it is very thick.

Tip the thick mixture into a heavy-based frying pan and place it over the heat for 5–10 minutes to burn the bottom of the pudding. Move the pan around over the heat so that the bottom is burnt evenly and don't stir.

Leave the pudding to cool and firm up in the pan, then cut it into rectangles. Using a spatula, lift out of the pan and place them on a plate or flat surface. Roll each rectangle into a log and place on a serving dish.

Serve chilled or at room temperature, sprinkled with a little cinnamon, if you like.

**Left: Cooking chicken on an outdoor grill in the Bekaa Valley, Lebanon
Right: Tavuk göğsu kazandibi**

FISH AND SHELLFISH

(SAMAK)

With the Black Sea, the Aegean, the Mediterranean, the Red Sea, and the Arabian Sea, the Middle East is not short of fresh seafood. Only Iraq and Jordan are without extensive coastlines. The varieties of fish include sole (*samak Moussa*), named after Moses (it is said to be so thin because it was cut in half when he separated the Red Sea), red mullet (*Sultan Ibrahim*), the favoured fish of the Romans, grey mullet, sea bass, grouper, red snapper, sea bream, anchovies, swordfish, flounder, mackerel and tuna, along with shrimps, prawns, squid and mussels. Of the freshwater varieties found in the lakes and rivers of the Middle East, the most common are trout, different species of carp, and barbel. In former times, the fish was often salted and dried so it could be transported inland or taken on long journeys but nowadays only a few fish, such as mackerel and anchovies, are preserved this way as a matter of preference. One of Iran's crowning glories is the sturgeon of the inland Caspian Sea, from which the finest caviar is produced.

A common feature in the recipes of the Middle East, in both the early cookery manuals and those of the present day, is that the fish to be used is not specified. Generally, people cook the fish of their region, or the fish they like. When grilling and frying, almost any fish will do, but there are dishes where the size, oiliness, or flavour of a certain fish means it works better than others. Another feature of fish cookery in the Middle East is that yogurt and milk are almost never used. I say almost never, as al-Baghdadi had a recipe for fish cooked with milk in his medieval culinary manual, and I have eaten grilled fish with a yogurt sauce in the home of an Armenian family. But the belief that the combination of fish and milk could be harmful is fairly widespread.

The shape of a fish is also significant in the Middle East. Carved in early tombs and in metal, it has traditionally been a symbol of Christianity but, among many communities, it is also believed to ward off the evil eye. At New Year, the Iranians eat fish to cleanse their bodies of evil and the Jews display a fish head in the centre of the table to indicate that they will always be at the 'head'.

Selling fish at Karaköy on the Bosphorous, Istanbul, Turkey

Fresh anchovies displayed in market, Lebanon

CULINARY USES

All fresh fish is delicious grilled over charcoal; known as *samak meshwi*, the fish is whole or in chunks that have been marinated. Red mullet is particularly delicious grilled, so very often, that is the only way it is cooked. Lemons and limes are served to refresh the fish, and sumac (p188) is often sprinkled over it while it is cooking. Ingredients used in the marinade could include allspice, coriander, fenugreek, cumin, chillies, garlic and onion juice, and the preferred fresh herbs to serve with fish are parsley, coriander and dill. Generally grilled or fried fish is popular served with a garlicky *tarator* sauce, usually made with crushed walnuts, pine nuts, and almonds, or a *tahini* sauce.

Another popular way of eating fish is with rice, as in the Arab dish *sayyadiah*, which is often coloured and flavoured with saffron, and garnished with fresh herbs or nuts. On the Black Sea coast, where the anchovy is king, the rice dish, *hamsili pilav*, is famous and served at every opportunity. Fillets of fish are combined with bulgur to make light *kibbeh* in Syria and Lebanon. Similarly in Turkey, they are combined with spices and

bread crumbs to make *köfte*.

The Turks also specialise in fish, particularly mackerel, cooked in olive oil and served cold. In all regions, fish is baked with vegetables, such as tomatoes, celeriac, carrots, and onions, and it is baked in sauces made with *tahini* or crushed nuts. In the northern provinces of Iran, whole fish are stuffed with apricots, prunes and walnuts, bound with sour pomegranate syrup and then baked. In the southern provinces, the stuffing for a whole, baked fish is fruity and spicy with tamarind, turmeric, chilli, and fenugreek. Medieval Arab culinary manuals call for fish to be baked with a walnut stuffing, a combination put to best effect in the resplendent stuffed mackerel dish, *uskumru dolması*, a legacy of the lavish feasts of the Ottomans.

Fish also features in a variety of soups and stews. Most of the hearty fish soups of the Mediterranean region, which are more akin to a stew than a soup, have been inherited from the Phoenicians, Greeks and Romans. They are often packed with vegetables and flavourings as well as the day's catch and are mopped up with lots of fresh bread. In Iran, there is a fish *fesenjân*, cooked with walnuts and pomegranate paste, just like the duck equivalent. Also in Iran, there is a delicious fish stew, *ghaliyeh mâhi*, with tamarind,

BUYING AND STORING

The fish markets of the Middle East are busy and noisy, with stalls of the gleaming live or gutted catch. In ports and seaside resorts, fish are often sold from the boats, sometimes cooked there and then as a snack. And along the rivers, small makeshift stalls are set up for the day's catch. One thing is

sure: the fish is always fresh. At the end of a day, the stalls are empty and washed down with water in preparation for the next day. There really is only one golden rule with fish – buy it fresh and eat it that day. It is not meant to be stored, unless you freeze it immediately, salt and dry it, or marinade it in vinegar.

Drawn from the very same waters and on a par with the better-known Russian caviar, Iranian caviar is now available in specialist stores and some supermarkets.

Drying sardines on the beach, United Arab Emirates

turmeric, fenugreek, chilli and garlic – the distinctive Indian flavours of the Persian Gulf. A similar stew, *ghaliyeh maygoo*, is made with prawns.

Shrimps, prawns and octopus are often grilled or pan-fried and served as salads. Prawns also feature in some stews, particularly in the Arabian Gulf. In most of the coastal regions, scallops, mussels, and prawns are sautéed with rice. In Turkey, squid and mussels are popular coated in a beer-batter and deep-fried, then served with a *tarator* sauce – a dish that is served in high-class restaurants and as snacking fodder in the streets. Squid are also stuffed with bulgur or rice and baked, and mussels are stuffed with an aromatic rice in the Turkish delicacy *midye dolması* (p183).

In the Middle East, fish is often grilled over charcoal for the lovely smoky aroma it lends to the flesh. In rural communities, the fish is rubbed with onion juice or clarified butter and spices, before being impaled on a stick, which is passed through the mouth and set above the glowing coals. This recipe, popular in Arabia and among the Marsh Arabs in southern Iraq, is particularly delicious as the fish is rubbed with puréed dates. In these regions, a freshwater fish, such as carp or barbel, would be used, but a firm-fleshed fish, such as trout or red mullet, works well. If possible, cook the fish over a barbecue: it tastes so much better.

SAMAK MASHWI
(GRILLED FISH WITH DATES)

Serves 4
Preparation time approximately
  1 hour
Cooking time 10 minutes

225g (8oz) dried, pitted dates
2 onions, grated
2 cloves garlic, crushed
Salt
1 teaspoon turmeric
1 teaspoon baharat spice mixture
  (p162)
1 good-sized trout or 4 medium-
  sized red mullet, with scales on
  but gutted and cleaned

Soak the dates in water until they are soft – if the dried dates are moist this won't take long – then rub them through a sieve or purée in a food processor.

Mix together the onions, garlic, salt and spices, rub the mixture around the inside of the fish and close the cavity with a skewer or stick, piercing the skin. Push a long stick or skewer through the mouth and stand it in a tall jug, or in the ground, so that the fish is supported freely, upside down.

Rub the date purée all over the fish and leave for about 15 minutes.

When the charcoal is glowing, hold the fish above it and cook each side for about 5 minutes (less if using red mullet).

Serve immediately, removing the skin before you eat the delicious, fruity-flavoured flesh.

The morning's catch at a fish market, Lebanon

Sayyadiah

This popular Arab dish, found all over the Middle East, varies from region to region. Some bake it in a mould and turn it out with the whole fish on top; some fry a whole fish and add it to the rice; and others add fish fillets to the rice. The following is an Egyptian version which works well with most firm-fleshed fish, such as sea bass, sea bream, turbot, haddock or halibut.

SAYYADIAH
(FISH WITH RICE)

Serves 4–6
Preparation time 15 minutes (+ 1 hour for making the stock)
Cooking time 45 minutes

900g (2lb) fish fillets (keep the bones and head for stock), cut diagonally into 2 or 3 pieces
450g (1lb) long-grain rice, well rinsed
2 onions, sliced or chopped
2–3 tablespoons clarified butter or olive oil
1 teaspoon cumin seeds
Salt and pepper
A handful pine nuts, lightly roasted

For the stock:
1 onion, quartered
1 carrot, roughly chopped
1 celery stick and leaves, roughly chopped
A few peppercorns
A few saffron fronds
Salt and black pepper

Preheat the oven to 150°C/300°F/gas mark 2.

Put the fish head and bones into a pot with the stock ingredients, cover with water and bring to the boil. Reduce the heat and simmer for about 1 hour. Drain the stock and season it.

Pour about 600ml (1 pint) of the stock into a pan and bring it to the boil. Throw in the rice and boil vigorously for a minute, then reduce the heat and simmer until almost all the liquid has been absorbed. Turn off the heat, cover the pan with a clean tea towel, followed by the lid, and leave the rice to steam for about 15 minutes.

Meanwhile, fry the onions and cumin in the butter or oil. Once the onions begin to colour, add the fish, tossing it gently in the pan. Season with salt and pepper and turn off the heat.

Tip the rice into a baking dish and carefully toss in the fish and onions. Pour a little of the extra stock over the top to keep it moist, or melt a tablespoon of clarified butter and pour that over it instead.

Sprinkle with the pine nuts and place the dish in the oven for about 20 minutes and serve immediately.

LAMB
(QOUZI)

Historically, the only food products to rival the date and the olive in the diet of the Middle East are those from livestock and, throughout the region, the preferred meat has traditionally been mutton or lamb. The most highly prized meat comes from the fat-tailed sheep, which are thought to have originated in the Middle East around 3000 BC. Like the hump of a camel, the tail stores the fat, which acts as an emergency supply in arid climates and periods of drought. Ever since the early nomads herded their sheep for sale into the villages and towns, the meat has been added to the daily diet of bread, bulgur, rice or beans. Regarded as a high-status food, enjoyed with regularity by the wealthy but a rarity for most, it had to be used sparingly and imaginatively, cut into small pieces or minced, to make a little go far. One custom that dates back to the early pastoral nomads was to fry pieces of mutton in the melted fat from the carcases and tail, which were then packed into earthenware jars, sealed with clay, and stored in a cool place, or underground. This method of preserving meat, called *qawarma* in Arabic and *kavurma* in Turkish, still practised in some rural communities today, enabled the nomads and villagers to impart a meaty flavour to their winter soups and stews.

Medieval recipes just state 'meat' without specifying what kind because, apart from the occasional kid, camel, rabbit or gazelle, and the occasional wild boar among the Christian communities, only lamb and

General sheep market, Kuwait

mutton were consumed. Beef was seldom eaten as the cows and oxen were valued for their milk and labour in the fields. Nowadays, lean beef or veal is often substituted for lamb in stews and meatballs, particularly in Iraq; water buffalo is popular in Egypt; and goat is often roasted whole for rural festivities. Nevertheless, lamb and mutton still reign supreme at ritual slaughters, which occur at births, funerals and weddings, the blessing of a new house, the well-wishing or thanksgiving at the start or end of a long journey, the honouring of an important guest, and religious festivals and ceremonies.

The sacrifice of Isaac (Isma'il in the *Qur'an*)

The Jews recall Abraham's near-sacrifice of Isaac at *Rosh Hashanah* (the New Year) with the tradition of baking a sheep's head in the oven, signifying the ram that Abraham saw and sacrificed to God instead. In many modern households, it's now quite common to substitute brains or tongue for the sheep's head. In the *Qur'an*, Ibrahim (Abraham) offers Isaac's brother, Isma'il, for scarifce. Throughout the Islamic world, Muslims mark this near-sacrifice at the festival called *eid-el-Kurban* in Arabic, or *Kurban Bayramı* in Turkish, held on the tenth day of the last month of the Muhammadan year. The sheep are paraded for sale through the streets and villages and every family that can afford to buys one and takes it home to sacrifice, first turning its head towards Mecca and then uttering the words 'In the name of Allah' as its throat is slit. Some families rub the carcases with onion juice, herbs and spices before roasting it whole over an open fire, while others carve up the carcases to distribute meat to the poor, reserving a little for themselves. A local butcher may be invited to do the carving to ensure that every bit of the animal is used. The tenderloin is cut into small pieces and threaded onto skewers, often alternated with pieces of sheep's tail fat. Other cuts of meat will be cooked in soups and stews, or simply fried in fat from the carcases. The podgy tail is boiled and eaten with bread, the intestines are used for soup, or they are stuffed with other offal and spices, and the liver and kidneys are mixed with rice and spices and used as stuffing, or they are grilled or fried. The sheep's head, complete with eyes, is used to flavour soup; the brains may be boiled separately and eaten cold as a delicacy, and the feet are either used in soup or boiled and served with yogurt on bread.

Whole carcases hanging in a butcher's shop, Egypt

Dietary laws

For Muslims and Jews, there are certain restrictions regarding meat. The *Qur'an* forbids an animal to be slaughtered in any other manner than by cutting its throat; it forbids the consumption of an animal's blood; it forbids the consumption of an animal slaughtered for any other god; and it forbids any form of pork. Traditionally, all Jews adhered to the dietary laws of *kashrut*, which were revealed to Moses on Mount Sinai. Detailed and strict, they formed the basis of what was *kasher* (permitted or kosher) and what was *terefah* (forbidden). Today, many of the archaic laws, such as Jews being forbidden to eat in the home of a non-Jew, have been dropped in most communities, but some of the laws regarding the slaughtering and cooking of animals remain. Basically, only those that 'chew the cud' and have cloven hooves are permitted. They must be slaughtered by cutting the throat and draining the blood. The consumption of blood is forbidden, so all traces of it must be removed to render the meat kosher. First, the meat has to be soaked in cold water for half an hour. It is then sprinkled with salt and left to sit for an hour to draw out the bloody juices, before being washed three times in cold water. And meat and milk must be kept completely separate.

BUYING AND STORING

There are a variety of sheep breeds in the Middle East, but, as has been said, the most popular is the fat-tailed. As all the fat is stored in the tail, the meat is very lean and tasty and, in traditional and rural dishes, the tail fat is used as a cooking fat. Although fat-tailed sheep are bred outside the Middle East, the meat may be difficult to find. There is no substitute for the tail fat, but organic breeds of sheep can yield lean, tasty meat. You are best advised to contact organic breeders or ask your butcher. Fresh lamb keeps in the refrigerator for a week, but it can be frozen for at least three months.

CULINARY USES

In the Middle East, every part of the sheep has a culinary use. The head, eyes, brains, tongue, lungs, intestines, trotters, tail and even the testicles are all considered delicacies and, as a mark of respect or hospitality, it is these parts that are often offered to guests — every Westerner's nightmare! The whole animal or cuts of meat are generally roasted over open fires, grilled on skewers, stewed with vegetables and fruit, stuffed and roasted, or baked. The minced meat is layered with vegetables and baked, as in *mousakka*, pounded with herbs and spices into meatballs, *kofta* (*köfte* in Turkish), or pounded with bulgur to make *kibbeh* (p126), which in turn are sometimes filled with minced lamb and spices. Minced meat is also combined with rice and spices and used as a filling for vegetables, poultry and fruit.

Slicing meat for a *döner kebab*, Turkey

Kebabs

The ubiquitous lamb kebab, meaning chunks of lamb grilled on a skewer, served with rice, has become almost synonymous with parts of the Middle East. Tourists visiting Turkey and Iran often think it is the national dish. Kebabs, however, cover a wide range of grilled or roasted meat, from the primitive method of grilling cuts of meat over a fire, called *meshwi* in Arabic, to the long sheaths of minced meat grilled on swords in open ovens and deposited on the table with a flourish. The portable, outdoor grill (*mangal* in Turkish, *manqal* in Farsi) provides one of the simplest and most effective means of grilling kebabs. They can be set up on balconies, on verandas, in the street, and in the countryside. The enticing aroma of meat cooking in the open air is mouth-watering. Almost all kebabs have one thing in common — the skewer. Made of metal, which conducts heat, skewers of different widths are used for livers, kidneys, chicken, chunks of lamb and beef, and minced meat. Minced meat kebabs, such as the fiery *Adana kebabı*, require a great deal of pounding and kneading so that the mixture holds together.

The *şiş kebab* from Turkey is perhaps the best known of all kebabs. It is reputed to have been created during the Ottoman Empire by the Turkish soldiers who, forced to camp out for months on end, threaded chunks of meat onto their swords and grilled them over the open fires. The same kebab is called *lahma mashwi* in Arabic. Another common type of kebab is the *shawarma* of the Arab world, *döner* to the Turks, which involves threading slices of marinated lamb onto a vertical spit (sometimes alternated with sheep's-tail fat, onions and peppers) to form a huge cone shape which is trimmed and grilled by slowly rotating the spit in front of a tiered charcoal fire. The meat is skilfully cut off the sides as it cooks, landing in a pan placed underneath. The hot, cooked meat is then eaten inside, or on top of, pitta bread, with sliced onions, tomatoes, parsley, pickles, *tahini* or yogurt.

Another interesting kebab in Turkey is *çöp şiş*, literally meaning 'rubbish kebab', as it is made with tiny scraps of meat. Marinated in onion juice and flavoured with cumin, the meat is grilled on thin skewers then pushed onto a thin, pliable flat bread, topped with onions, flat-leaf parsley, and a squeeze of lemon. The flat bread is then folded or rolled up and eaten just like that.

Kebab skewers

Roasted and stuffed meat

A traditional Bedouin dish, *mansaf*, meaning 'large tray', is a communal feast served to honour guests or to celebrate special occasions. The huge tin-lined copper or silver tray is covered with flat bread, topped with a mound of rice, on top of which sits chunks of boiled lamb, or a whole roasted lamb. Over all this is poured a sauce, *jameed*, made with the juices of the cooked meat and dried sheep's-milk yogurt. It has become the national dish of Jordan, served at weddings and state banquets, which can call for such astounding proportions of *mansaf* that one is reputed to have included a whole baby camel that had been stuffed with several sheep, inside which were turkeys that had been stuffed with chickens — just like a Russian doll.

Stuffing cavities, such as hollowed-out vegetables and fruit, is a popular activity in the Middle East and it is put to its most flamboyant in the stuffing of whole lambs or kids, which are then roasted over a fire and served with a huge dish of rice. At one time, this way of serving meat was practised by the wealthy and the imperial courts, but now it is a special dish prepared for communal festivities. Examples of this way of roasting are found in the *çebiç* of Turkey, the *barreh tu por* of Iran, and the *qouzi* or *kharouf mahshi* of Saudi Arabia. The shoulder of lamb is also often stuffed with a mixture containing nuts and dried fruit, such as apricots. The Persian-inspired Arab dish *dala' mahshi* is probably the most delicious example of this — the breast of lamb is stuffed with rice, minced beef, pine nuts and raisins, and served with stewed apricots, apples, quince or black cherries.

Street-seller grilling *kokoreç* – stuffed intestines

Meatballs and dumplings

Meatballs are popular all over the Middle East. Whatever the dish, all meatballs have to be kneaded and pounded well to make them light and hold together. They can be made with grains, pulses or vegetables, such as aubergines or courgettes. In Iran, the ordinary minced meat balls are called *cottlet*, whereas the *koofteh* are more like dumplings, blended with rice or pulses and cooked in stock – an elaborate example being the mammoth *koofteh Tabrizi*, which consists of a whole, boned chicken, stuffed with walnuts and dried apricots, encased in a dumpling mixture of minced beef or lamb pounded with rice and yellow split peas, and cooked in a tomato-based stock. In Turkey, the *köfte* are generally made with meat and onions, sometimes flavoured with spices and herbs, and grilled or fried. Only a few Turkish meatballs are pounded with bulgur or rice, such as the Ottoman favourite *kadın buduğu*, meaning 'ladies' thighs'. Sometimes meat is the filling, as in *içli köfte*, meaning mother-in-law's *köfte*, and the stuffed potato balls of both Iran and Turkey. Also in Turkey there is a fabulous dish of meatballs or minced meat served on a bed of smoked aubergine and yogurt purée called *ali nazik*, and

another dish inherited from the Ottomans called *Hünkâr beğendi*, which consists of meatballs served with a hot smoked aubergine and cheese purée. Similarly the *kibbeh* (p126) of Syria and Lebanon, called *kubba* in Jordan and Iraq, are made with meat which is usually pounded with bulgur and grated onions until the mixture resembles a paste. Done by hand, this generally takes a long time, so the making of *kibbeh* is often a communal activity for special occasions, such as the Christian feast day *'Id al-Salib*, which marks the day Queen Helena, the mother of the Roman emperor Constantine, was said to have found the Crucifixion cross on a basil-covered hill in Jerusalem. *Kibbeh* are extremely popular raw or cooked. Mixed with spices and eaten raw with lettuce leaves, they are known as *kibbeh naye* in Arabic, a dish that is similar to the spicy *çiğ köfte* of Turkey. Some stuffed *kibbeh* are cooked in a tomato or yogurt sauce, as in the Arab dish *shish barak*, while others are moulded and simply fried or baked. Small *kibbeh* are sometimes added to stews and soups. All *kibbeh* require practice and skill and come under much scrutiny. Only some women are considered to have the knack.

Soups and stews

Jewish meat cookery is characterised by long, slow cooking in soups and stews, for kosher meat, which has not hung for very long and has been salted and washed, is generally tough. The Egyptian speciality *dfeena* is a popular stew for the Jews on the Sabbath. It can be left to simmer from the Friday and consists of cubed meat, often beef, cooked with a calf's foot, eggs in their shells, and chickpeas or haricot beans. Lamb or mutton is used in a number of soups, often to celebrate a happy event, such as *düğün çorbası*, the cinnamon-flavoured wedding soup of Turkey. Lamb or mutton is also combined with vegetables and pulses to make a substantial meal, such as the Iranian *âbgoosht*, which is served in two courses – the soup is strained and the broth is served as an appetiser while the meat and pulses are served separately with bread.

This way of cooking meat, in light vegetables stews, is common daily fare in households throughout the Middle East. It is called *yakhnie* in Syria and Lebanon, and *yahni* in Turkey. Cooking meat with fruit is another popular method found in the Middle East, inspired by the old Persian fruit

and meat stews, *khoresht*, designed to be served as a sauce for rice. Meat from head and legs is used to make *fatta* (p34), a layered dish of bread soaked in a broth, usually flavoured with lamb. The bones and cheaper cuts of meat are also used to impart flavour to the porridge-style dish known as *harissa* in the Arab world, *keşkek* in Turkey, and *haleem* in Iran. The early cookery manuals called for meat to be cooked in milk or yogurt, a method that is still popular in parts of the Middle East and is best illustrated in the Lebanese dish *immos*, literally meaning 'his mother's milk', as the young lamb or goat must be cooked in its own mother's milk – a dish that goes against Jewish dietary restrictions.

Offal

Throughout the Middle East offal is popular. There are street-sellers with their cooked specialities and shops and restaurants devoted just to tripe, or brains, or one of the many spicy, stuffed stomachs. Among Jewish communities, kosher meat was always expensive, reserved for the Sabbath and special occasions, so the cheaper offals, such as the brains, liver, intestines, and feet became popular. Generally, liver is lightly fried in olive oil or clarified butter and flavoured with red pepper, thyme or mint. Brains are

Freshly cleaned offal and intestines hanging for sale

usually poached and served hot or cold, and the feet are often used to flavour soups. In Turkey, the feet are gently cooked and served on a bed of pitta with lots of garlic-flavoured yogurt in the Anatolian dish *yoğurtlu paça* (p51).

Intestines are often used as a preservative casing for the many spicy meat and offal sausages, and they are stuffed with minced mutton and ingredients such as rice, chickpeas, onions and spices in the popular specialities *kokoreç*, which is grilled, and *krush mahshiyya*, which is boiled. Tripe is particularly popular in soup, often served with pickles, as a pick-me-up late at night. It is also used like pasta in parts of Syria and Lebanon, where they cut the stomach into small squares, spoon a little spicy meat mixture onto each one, then fold them over and sew the edges together so that they can be boiled. Kidneys, sweetbreads, and rams' testicles are usually grilled and served with melted clarified butter, while in eastern Anatolia there is a preference for the much larger bulls' testicles.

Bedouin woman spinning wool, Jordan

Whole lambs or kids are stuffed and roasted for festive and ceremonial occasions throughout the Middle East. It is a feast for the rich and the poor, although many of the poor can only afford to eat meat at *Eid-el-Kurban*. The following dish is a Saudi Arabian speciality. Traditionally, the whole kid or baby lamb is stuffed, roasted over charcoal in a pit and served on a huge tray, surrounded by mounds of rice, sliced raw onion, hard-boiled eggs and lots of fresh parsley.

At home, you can use a whole spring baby lamb, which a butcher can help you to prepare, and cook it over a barbecue or, as I have done in this recipe, in a conventional oven. If you prefer, you could use a breast of lamb and reduce the quantities in the recipe.

KHAROUF MAHSHI
(ROASTED STUFFED LAMB)

Serves roughly 16 people
Preparation time approximately 40 minutes (if the butcher has prepared the lamb for you)
Cooking time almost 2 hours

Bedouin herding a flock of sheep through the desert

An 8kg (18lb) baby lamb, cleaned, with entrails and head (some leave it on) removed
Juice of 3 onions, which have been grated and pressed
2–3 tablespoons ground coriander
1 tablespoon ground ginger
Salt and black pepper

For the stuffing
Roughly 1kg (2¼lb) long-grain rice, well rinsed
2 pinches saffron fronds
2 onions, chopped
2 tablespoons clarified butter (ghee)
110g (4oz) almonds, coarsely chopped
110g (4oz) pistachios, coarsely chopped
110g (4oz) walnuts, coarsely chopped
175g (6oz) raisins
1 teaspoon ground coriander
1 teaspoon ground cumin
A scant teaspoon ground fenugreek
Salt and freshly ground black pepper
Big bunch of flat-leaf parsley, coarsely chopped

Preheat the oven to 220°C/ 425°F/gas mark 7.

Rinse the lamb inside and out, and wipe it dry. In a bowl, mix together the onion juice, coriander, ginger and salt and pepper, and rub all over the lamb, inside and out, and put it aside.

Put the rice into a pan and cover with just enough water. Bring it to the boil, stir in the saffron, and cook for about 10 minutes, until the rice is tender. In a wide pan, fry the onions in the clarified butter until they begin to colour, then stir in the nuts, raisins, and spices. Tip in the rice, mix well, and season with salt and pepper.

Stuff the lamb with the rice, packing it in tightly, and sew up the opening with a strong thread. Place the stuffed lamb on a large baking tray and pop it into the preheated oven. After 20 minutes, reduce the oven to 160°C/325°F/gas mark 3 and roast it for about 1½ hours (or more if you like your meat well done), basting it in its own juices. Serve the lamb on a large dish, or tray, with lots of fresh flat-leaf parsley and extra rice prepared in the same way as the stuffing.

Of all the kebabs in the Middle East, these are my favourite. Traditionally made with scraps of meat, hence the name 'rubbish kebab', they can also be made with a lean, tender cut of meat. The key to these kebabs is to cut the meat into very small pieces, so that they take minutes to cook and can be wrapped up in the flat breads which are made at the same time. For this recipe, which is designed for the barbecue, it is easier to have two cooks at the end, one to turn the meat on the skewers, the other to flip over the flat breads.

ÇÖP ŞİŞ
(ANATOLIAN LAMB KEBABS)

Serves 6
Preparation time roughly 3–4 hours
Cooking time 5 minutes

A 900g (2lb) shoulder of lamb, cut into small bite-size pieces with most of the fat removed

For the marinade:
2 big onions, peeled
Roughly 1 tablespoon salt
2 cloves garlic, crushed
2–3 teaspoons cumin seeds, crushed

For the flat breads:
225g (8oz) strong white flour
50g (2oz) wholemeal flour
1 teaspoon salt
175–225ml (6–8fl oz) lukewarm water

To serve:
2 red onions, finely sliced
A big bunch of flat-leaf parsley, roughly chopped
3–4 lemons, halved or quartered, ready to squeeze

Grate the onions into a bowl (or in a food processor) and sprinkle a generous quantity of salt over the top. Cover and leave to weep for about 10 minutes. Push the salted onion pulp through a sieve into another bowl, making sure you squeeze out all the juice. The liquid collected in the bowl is your onion juice for the marinade.

Stir in the garlic and cumin seeds and, using your hands, toss in the pieces of lamb until well coated. Cover the bowl and leave to marinate for at least 2–3 hours.

Meanwhile, sift the flours and salt into a bowl. Make a well in the centre, add the water gradually, drawing the flour in from the sides, and knead into a firm dough. On a floured board, divide the dough into 24 pieces and roll each piece into a ball. Leave the balls to rest on the floured surface, covered with a damp cloth, for at least 30 minutes.

While your charcoal grill is heating up, roll out each ball of dough into wide, thin circles. Keep them dusted with flour so they don't stick to one another and keep them covered with a damp cloth at all times to prevent them from drying out.

Thread the meat onto skewers and place over the hot charcoal. While the meat is cooking, quickly flip the flat breads, one by one, onto a hot griddle or flat pan. Each side takes just seconds as they brown and buckle a little.

Push the cooked meat off each skewer onto the flat breads, throw on some onions and parsley, squeeze lemon juice over and wrap it up into a parcel that you can hold and eat.

Çöp şiş

FRUIT

Dried barberries

BARBERRY

(ZERESHK) *Berberis vulgaris*

In medieval times, barberries were fashionable in England and Europe, often preserved in jams and jellies. In North America, the early settlers regarded them as 'the poor man's redcurrant' and preserved them in syrup and vinegar. These tart, bright little berries are still popular in Iran.

HOW IT GROWS

Many species of the berberis shrub grow wild in temperate regions of Europe and Asia but it is the B. vulgaris with its edible, sour berries, that grows in Iran.

APPEARANCE AND TASTE

The berries hang in clusters and look like bright red jewels, the size of a small redcurrant. They are really too tart to eat fresh, so they are dried in the sun and used in cooking for a burst of colour and their refreshing, sour flavour.

BUYING AND STORING

Dried barberries are available in Iranian shops and Middle Eastern stores. They keep well in an airtight container, or in the freezer, and will need to be picked over for stalks and washed before using. Like currants, they spring back into shape when soaked in water or sautéed in oil.

A barberry dish such as *Khoresht-e zereshk* is often served at traditional weddings in Iran

CULINARY USES

Dried barberries add a sour punch to a number of Iranian and Persian-inspired dishes. They are sprinkled over stews and pilafs, added to stuffings and the Iranian herb omlette, *kookoo-ye sabzi*, but they are best known for their role as a brilliant jewel in the stunning Persian rice dish, *morasa' polow*, and in the wedding dish *khoresht-e zereshk*.

In Iran, most wedding dishes are sweet, designed to ensure happiness for the newlyweds. However, this tart dish is also traditionally served at weddings, to remind the newlyweds that there is sadness in life too.

KHORESHT-E ZERESHK
(BARBERRY AND NUT STEW)

Serves 4–6
Preparation time 25 minutes
Cooking time approximately 1 hour

2 tablespoons olive oil
2 onions
450g (1lb) lean lamb, trimmed and cut into cubes
225g (8oz) blanched almonds, chopped or cut into slivers
225g (8oz) pistachios, chopped or cut into slivers
2 pinches saffron fronds
2 tablespoons sugar
110g (4oz) dried barberries
Salt and freshly ground black pepper

Heat the oil in a heavy-based pan and fry the onions until golden brown. Stir in the meat and brown it, then pour in enough water to cover, put on the lid, and simmer for about 40 minutes. Stir in the nuts and simmer, with the lid off, for a further 15 minutes.

Meanwhile, using a pestle and mortar, grind the saffron fronds with a teaspoon of sugar and pour in a little boiling water to extract the colour.

Heat up a splash of extra oil and toss the barberries in it, to plump them up. Sprinkle them with the remaining sugar and add to the stew with the saffron. Season the stew to taste and spoon it over plain rice.

Morasa' polow

This sumptuous rice dish is as beautiful to behold as it is to eat. It is a light saffron rice dotted with little barberries, which look like rubies amongst other dried fruits and nuts resembling precious stones and jewels. The fruits and nuts vary a little in the Gulf, Iraq and Turkey; the dish is of Persian origin.

MORASA' POLOW
(JEWELLED RICE)

Serves 6
Preparation time 5 minutes (+ 20 minutes' soaking)
Cooking time 30 minutes

450g (1lb) basmati long-grain white rice
75g (3oz) dried barberries
50g (2oz) dried sour cherries or cranberries
1–2 tablespoons bitter orange peel, cut into slivers
2–3 tablespoons olive oil with a little butter
2 pinches saffron fronds
75g (3oz) raisins or golden sultanas
75g (3oz) dried apricots, cut into slivers
110g (4oz) blanched almonds, cut into slivers
110g (4oz) pistachios, chopped or cut into slivers

Rinse the rice well and leave it to soak in water for 20 minutes.

Place the barberries, sour cherries, and bitter orange peel in individual bowls, pour a little boiling water over them and leave to soak for 10 minutes. Drain the rice, barberries and sour cherries but reserve the bitter orange soaking water.

Boil the rice in plenty of salted water for about 10 minutes, until it is al dente, then drain.

In a large, heavy-based pan, heat the oil and butter. Stir in the saffron, then tip the rice in with all the other ingredients and a sprinkling of salt. Carefully, mix it all together, adding a little extra oil to coat it.

Cover the pan with a clean tea towel, followed by the lid, and steam the rice over a very low heat for 15–20 minutes, until it is tender. Serve hot or at room temperature.

LIME

(LOOMĪ) *Citrus aurantifolia*

There are various kinds of lime but the *citrus aurantifolia*, which originated in Malaysia, is often referred to as 'the true lime'. It is thought to have travelled to the Middle East with the Arab traders in medieval times. Amongst the leading producers of this lime is Egypt, where it is known as *limun baladi*; it is also grown in Iran. The *Citrus limettoides*, a sweet and juicy lime, often referred to as the Palestine lime, is also popular in the Middle East and is known as *limun helou*, or *limun succari* in Egypt. What is interesting about limes in the Middle East is that they are often left in the sun to dry before use. In their dried form, they are known as *noumi basra* in Iraq, as *limoo amani* (Omani limes) in Iran and, in Oman itself, they are simply *loomi*.

Fresh limes

CULINARY USES

Neither fresh nor dried limes are used much in the food of Turkey, Lebanon and Syria – they feature more in the food of Egypt, the Gulf, Iraq and Iran. Fresh limes are used much like lemons to lend a citrus flavour to a sauce, or to accompany fish in the lime-growing regions. Whole dried limes, on the other hand, are in demand for the musty, tangy flavour they lend to stews such as *gheimeh*, an Iranian vegetable stew. In the Arabian Gulf, they are often cooked with fish, particularly in *samak quwarmah*, a popular way of cooking fish with spices. The limes are also ground to a fine green powder to add to stews or stuffings, such as the Iraqi speciality *koubba helwa*, a dumpling filled with lime-flavoured meat and cooked in a tomato sauce. Ground dried lime is also sprinkled over soups and stews for a splash of tartness. And a refreshing tea, *chai hamidh*, is made by breaking open the dried limes and pouring boiling water over them.

HOW IT GROWS

Most limes grow mainly in tropical climates, but some grow in milder climates. In the Middle East, they grow in the Arabian desert and in Egypt and Iran.

Dried limes

APPEARANCE AND TASTE

We tend to think of them as a green fruit, because they are picked before they are ripe. If they were left on the tree, they would turn orange, then yellow, and look rather like lemons. The *limun baladi* is quite tart to taste but the *limun succari* is sweet and juicy. The Omani limes are pale or dark in colour, depending on how long they have been dried. They are selected according to the colour of the soup or stew that is being prepared but, in Iran, the paler, more delicate-tasting limes are preferred. They sound hollow when tapped and give a distinct musty, tangy, sour flavour to a dish.

BUYING AND STORING

Fresh limes are available everywhere nowadays but the dried fruit are available only in Middle Eastern stores. Powdered dried lime is also available in packets in Middle Eastern stores. Both the dried limes and powder should keep for about a year.

Lime powder

The following recipe from the Arabian Gulf, where the flavours are often influenced by Indian cuisine, is an example of many such dishes involving fish, seafood or chicken. The use of fresh ginger and dried limes is typical of this region.

SAMAK QUWARMAH
(SPICY FISH WITH GINGER AND LIME)

Serves 6
Preparation time 5–10 minutes
Cooking time approximately 40 minutes

A chestnut-sized piece of fresh ginger, peeled and chopped
2–3 cloves garlic
2 tablespoons clarified butter (ghee)
700g (1½lb) fish steaks (e.g. tuna, grouper, sea bass, trout)
2 onions, chopped
½ teaspoon hot chilli pepper
1 teaspoon ground turmeric
1 teaspoon baharat (p162)
A piece of cinnamon bark
4–5 tomatoes, skinned and chopped
1 teaspoon sugar
2 dried limes
Salt

Samak quwarmah

Using a pestle and mortar, grind the ginger with the garlic to form a paste.

Heat the clarified butter in a heavy-based pan and sear the fish steaks on both sides. Remove from the pan and stir in the onion.

Just as the onion begins to colour, stir in the ginger and garlic paste, the spices, and the cinnamon bark.

Add the chopped tomatoes, sugar and dried limes (pierced twice with a skewer). Pour in a little water, roughly 150ml (¼ pint), and simmer gently for about 15 minutes.

Season the sauce with salt and place the fish steaks in it. Cover the pan and simmer for a further 15 minutes, until the fish steaks are cooked.

Remove the cinnamon bark and dried limes and serve with rice.

This unusual dish is an Iraqi speciality. Although, in essence, it is really a filled *kibbeh*, it has one distinct characteristic – the sharp, musty flavour of the dried limes.

KOUBBA HELWA
(IRAQI DUMPLINGS)

Serves 4–6
Preparation time 40–50 minutes
Cooking time approximately 40 minutes

225g (8oz) semolina
Salt and freshly ground black pepper
225g (8oz) minced beef
1 onion, grated
1 dried lime, pounded in a mortar to a powder
A little plain flour for dusting

For the sauce:
1 tablespoon clarified butter (ghee)
1 onion, chopped
2 cloves garlic, chopped
1 courgette, thinly sliced
1½ tablespoons tomato paste
1 teaspoon sugar
A small bunch fresh parsley and coriander, chopped
A squeeze of lemon juice

Put the semolina into a bowl with a little salt and pour in enough water to make a thick paste. Knead it with your hands to make it doughy.

In another bowl, mix together the minced meat, onion and ground dried lime. Season it with salt and pepper and knead with your hands to form a smooth paste.

Once you've washed and dried your hands, dust them with flour, and take a chestnut-sized lump of the semolina paste. Roll it into a ball, flatten it in your hand and place a heaped teaspoon of the meat filling in the centre. Fold the semolina shell over the filling, pinching it together, and pat it back into a ball.

Repeat with the rest of the mixture, rolling each finished ball in a little flour, so they don't stick together.

Heat the clarified butter in a wide, heavy-based pan and stir in the onion. When it begins to colour, add the garlic and courgette and cook for a minute or two. Stir in the tomato paste, sugar, herbs, and a squeeze of lemon juice.

Pour in enough water to just cover the dumplings and bring to the boil. Season with salt and pepper, then reduce the heat and gently drop in the dumplings.

Cover and cook gently for 25–30 minutes, until the semolina is soft and the dumplings begin to float. Scoop out the dumplings and keep them warm while you boil the sauce vigorously to reduce it. Serve the dumplings hot with the sauce and rice.

LEMON

(LAMOUN) *Citrus medica*

The lemon tree is thought to have originated in India and found its way to the Mediterranean at the end of the first century AD, when the Romans discovered they could reach India from the southern end of the Red Sea. Arab traders spread the lemon tree westwards along the Mediterranean to North Africa and eastwards to China.

While the lemon was still rare and expensive in Europe in the Middle Ages, the Arabs of the eastern Mediterranean were exploring its culinary uses, making lemon syrup and preserves, recipes that are still in use today. Before the arrival of lemons in the Middle East, the juice of sour pomegranates or sour grapes was used as a souring agent but nowadays it is lemons that grace practically every meal. In Iran, a classical Persian meal will always include lemon or a combination of lemon and saffron.

Fresh lemons

Buying fruit and vegetables in the market

HOW IT GROWS

Lemon trees grow in the coastal regions of the Mediterranean and in Iran. The fruit is usually harvested in September.

APPEARANCE AND TASTE

The lemons of the Middle East are small and round or oval, yellow in colour, sometimes with a tinge of green. They have thin skins and are very juicy, with a sharp, tart taste, as you would expect.

BUYING AND STORING

Lemons are readily available all year round, but the best lemons are bought in season. Harvested in September, when they are juicy and fruity, they keep for weeks in a cool, dry place.

Ripened lemons ready for harvest

CULINARY USES

Fresh lemons serve as an accompaniment to fish, seafood or lamb. The juice enhances numerous savoury dishes and makes a refreshing, clean-tasting dressing for salads and steamed vegetables. It also brings out the flavour of other fresh fruits, such as olives and melon. Lemon juice is a crucial ingredient in some strong-flavoured sauces, such as *tarator*, a garlicky nut sauce served with fish and seafood in Lebanon, Syria, and Turkey, and *tahini* dressing for raw root salads in the same regions. It is combined with egg to make a slightly tart sauce for poached and steamed vegetables, and for

Lemon juice seller, Turkey

the Turkish dish of meatballs in lemon sauce, *terbiyeli köfte*. The popular Arab *mezze* dish of smoked aubergine purée with *tahini* and lemon, *baba ghanoush*, requires a lot more lemon juice than one thinks. The juice, pith and seeds are a source of pectin for jam-making and the zest, which contains all the oil and intensity of flavour, is ideal for puddings and baking. Fresh lemons are pressed for their juice to flavour thick syrups to pour over sweet pastries and are used as the basis of a cooling sherbet drink. They are also dried, pickled, or preserved in salt or sugar.

Strongly flavoured with lemon and garlic, this tangy chicken broth is favoured by the Egyptians. Traditionally, it is served either as a sauce for plain rice or, during a meal of several courses, first as a soup and then as a sauce for the rice. This recipe is for the basic broth, which is really like a well-flavoured stock, to which other vegetables could be added.

HAMUD
(EGYPTIAN CHICKEN AND LEMON BROTH)

Serves 6–8
Preparation time 1 hour for stock
Cooking time 50 minutes

A chicken carcass, giblets and
  bones, cooked or uncooked
Celery leaves
1 tablespoon clarified butter
4 celery stalks, sliced
4 cloves garlic, sliced
Juice of 2 lemons
110g (4oz) long-grain rice, washed
Salt and freshly ground black
  pepper

Put the carcass, giblets and bones into a pan with the celery leaves and cover with water. Bring to the boil, simmer for 1 hour, then strain the stock. Pick the bits of chicken off the bones and add to the stock. Keep aside roughly 1.8 litres (3 pints).

Melt the clarified butter in a deep pan and stir in the celery. Cook for a minute or two and add the garlic. Just before the celery and garlic begin to colour, pour in the stock and bring it to the boil.

Pour in most of the lemon juice, reduce the heat and simmer for about 30 minutes.

Toss in the rice, bring the soup to the boil once more, then simmer for a further 20 minutes, until the rice is cooked but not mushy. Pour in the rest of the lemon juice and season to taste.

This creamy, tangy aubergine and *tahini* dip is an old favourite, almost as popular as the ubiquitous *hummus*. Also known as *moutabal*, the strong flavours are sharpened by what seems to be a lot of lemon juice, but it can stand it. The quantities vary according to personal taste, as some people like their *baba ghanoush* lemony, while others like the strong taste of the *tahini*. Usually, it is served as a *mezze* dish with lots of bread to scoop it up.

BABA GHANOUSH
(SMOKED AUBERGINE DIP WITH TAHINI AND LEMON)

Serves 4–6
Preparation time 25 minutes
Cooking time –

2 aubergines
2–3 cloves garlic
Salt
Roughly 4 tablespoons tahini
Juice of 2 lemons
A small bunch of flat-leaf parsley,
   chopped
A few black olives

Place the aubergines directly onto the gas flame, over charcoal, or under the grill, and cook them until they are soft and oozing. Hold them by the stem under running cold water, peel off the skin, and squeeze out the juices. Using a fork, mash the flesh in a bowl, then crush the garlic with a little salt and beat it into the aubergine, until it is smooth and creamy. Add the *tahini* and lemon juice alternately, beating all the time, then season to taste.

Spoon the purée into a serving bowl, garnish with chopped parsley and black olives, and serve with flat bread.

Literally translated as 'well behaved' *köfte*, these meatballs are also known as *ekşili* (sour) *köfte*. Served with, or cooked in, a tart egg and lemon sauce, they are a speciality of Turkey.

TERBİYELİ KÖFTE
(MEATBALLS IN AN EGG AND LEMON SAUCE)

Serves 4-6
Preparation time 25minutes
Cooking time 45 minutes

450g (1lb) minced lamb or beef
1 onion, grated
1 tablespoon long-grain rice,
   washed and drained
A small bunch of fresh dill and
   parsley, finely chopped
Salt and freshly ground black
   pepper
Flour
2 egg yolks
Juice of 2 lemons

Put the minced meat, onion, rice, herbs and seasoning in a bowl. Knead well and pound to form a paste. Take walnut-sized portions in your fingers and shape them into balls. Roll in a little flour and put aside.

Bring roughly 900ml (1½ pints) water to the boil. Drop the *köfte* into the water, cover the pan and bring the water to the boil again. Reduce the heat and simmer for about 35 minutes, until the rice has cooked in the *köfte*.

Meanwhile, beat the egg yolks in a bowl, until light. Beat in the lemon juice and a little of the hot cooking liquid from the pan. Make sure it is well blended and seasoned, then sit the bowl over a pan of water and gently heat the egg and lemon mixture through, taking care not to curdle it, until it is thick and hot.

Drain the *köfte* from the cooking liquid and pop them into the egg and lemon sauce. Serve hot with plain rice.

Baba ghanoush

ORANGE

(NARANJ) *Citrus sinensis*

The sour orange (*C. aurantium*) travelled westwards from China and India with the Arab traders, who probably introduced it to Sicily and Spain, but the sweet orange (*C. sinensis*) didn't appear in the Mediterranean region until the fifteenth century. The Arabic word for orange is *naranj*, which is said to come from an old Sanskrit term, *narunga*, meaning 'fruit like elephants'. The Persian word for bitter orange is the same as the Arabic, but the word for sweet orange is *portoghâl*, like the Turkish word, *portakal*, which reflects its origins in Portugal, where a superior sweet orange was cultivated shortly after the Portuguese explorer, Vasco da Gama, returned from his voyage around the Cape of Good Hope in 1498. The main oranges in the Middle East are Jaffa, which originated in Palestine in the mid-nineteenth century and is now grown in Cyprus and Turkey; the navel orange, which is thought to be the orange brought to Portugal from China, and now grown extensively in Turkey; and the bitter orange, grown in Iran for its peel.

Fresh oranges

Dried orange peel

HOW IT GROW

Generally oranges thrive in subtropical climates. The Jaffa orange originated as a bud mutation on a Beladi tree near Jaffa. The navel orange, which matures early, is seedless and has to be propagated by cuttings. And the bitter orange has grown in the Caspian region for 2,000 years.

APPEARANCE AND TASTE

Jaffa oranges are almost seedless with a fine, sweet flavour. Navel oranges are aptly named as each fruit contains a 'baby' or mini orange in its apex. They are large with quite thick skins, so they are easy to peel and they are sweet, juicy and seedless. The bitter oranges of Iran are similar to Seville oranges.

MANUFACTURING

In Adana, in southern Turkey, a sweet fragrant wine is made from the juice of pressed oranges, but it is not exported. And, in Turkey and Iran, the blossoms of the bitter orange tree are distilled to make a fragrant essence which, in its diluted form, is sold as orange blossom water.

BUYING AND STORING

Both Jaffa and navel oranges are available in most supermarkets. If Jaffa oranges are picked when they have fully ripened, they keep well and remain juicy. The bitter oranges from Iran may be available in Iranian and other Middle Eastern stores but Seville oranges, which are available in the marmalade season, are a fine substitute. Packets of dried bitter orange peel can be bought in Middle Eastern stores; it keeps well in an airtight container but if you are only going to use it very occasionally, the finely sliced peel of a fresh orange will work just as well. Orange blossom water is available in bottles in almost every Middle Eastern, Oriental, or wholefood store.

CULINARY USES

In Iran, two wonderful syrupy conserves are made for spooning over creamy rice puddings: *morabbâ-ye khalâl-e nâranj* is made with wide strips of bitter orange peel rolled into the shape of rosebuds and poached in syrup with cardamom seeds – it is a joy to look at and deliciously aromatic; *morabbâ-ye bâhar nâranj* is made

Piles of oranges at the market

Assorted candied orange segments, often used for decorative purposes

with the blossoms of the bitter orange, soaked in limewater and poached gently in a rose-flavoured syrup – it is delicate in both appearance and flavour.

Throughout the orange-growing regions of the Middle East, oranges are preserved in syrup – they are peeled and poached whole or in thick slices in a sugar syrup, sometimes flavoured with orange blossom water and orange zest. They are also boiled and pulped to make the light, moist orange and almond cakes for the Jewish Passover. Other light cakes, flavoured with orange zest, are popular too, such as the Turkish semolina cake, *Revani*, which is soaked in a lemon syrup. Fresh oranges or their juice often added to raw root vegetable salads, which echo the flavours of North Africa but are often served with spicy food in southern Turkey and Syria. In both Iran and Turkey, oranges are married with chicken and cinnamon in popular stews. The juice of fresh oranges is used to make a simple custard-based ice cream, or a refreshing sorbet, often flavoured with orange blossom water as well.

Like rose water, orange blossom water is splashed into many fruit compotes, creamy

puddings and confections for its perfumed flavour, and it is often added to sugar syrups to pour over the traditional sweet pastries. Mix it with lemon juice to make a fragrant salad dressing. A drop is sometimes added to Turkish coffee, and a teaspoon of orange blossom water stirred into a coffee cup of boiling water, with or without sugar, makes a healthy, soothing tisane called 'white coffee' in Lebanon. Dried bitter orange peel from Iran can also be used to make a digestive tisane, but it is mostly used in stews and aromatic rice such as *morasa' polow* (p77).

So many dishes in the Middle East are claimed by Arabs and Turks, Jews and Kurds, but I have only ever had the following dish in an Armenian household. Like the Persians, the Armenians have long enjoyed the combination of fruit and meat.

ERİK KURUSU DOLMASI

(STUFFED PRUNES WITH ORANGES)

Serves 4–6
Preparation time 25–30 minutes
Cooking time 30 minutes

225g (8oz) minced lamb or beef
1 small onion, grated
2–3 tablespoons pine nuts
1 teaspoon dried mint
1 teaspoon ground cinnamon
Salt and freshly ground black pepper
2–3 fresh oranges, sliced
450g (1lb) moist, pitted prunes
150ml (¼ pint) fresh orange juice
1 tablespoon olive oil
1 tablespoon sugar
A small bunch fresh mint and coriander, finely chopped

Preheat the oven to 180°C/ 350°F/ gas mark 4.

Put the minced meat in a bowl

with the onion and knead it with your hands. Add the pine nuts, dried mint, cinnamon and seasoning and knead until it resembles a paste.

Line a baking dish with half the orange slices. Then, using your finger, enlarge the opening of each prune, stuff some of the meat mixture in and arrange them on top of the oranges.

Mix together the orange juice, olive oil and sugar and pour over the stuffed prunes. Cover them with a lid or some foil and pop them in the oven for about 30 minutes, until the prunes are tender and slightly caramelised.

Lift the prunes onto a serving dish, leaving the orange slices behind. Sprinkle the prunes with mint and coriander and then garnish with the orange slices.

This exquisite-looking preserve is a Persian speciality, often spooned over creamy rice or milk puddings. It is made with the native bitter oranges, for which the Seville variety can be substituted. A little time is required for preparation, but it is well worth the effort.

Orange-seller, Syria

MORABBÂ-YE KHALÂL-E NÂRANJ
(ORANGE-PEEL PRESERVE)

Makes 3–4 jars
Preparation time approximately
13 hours
Cooking time 25 minutes

8 bitter oranges, well washed and
dried
350g (12oz) sugar
1 tablespoon whole cardamom
pods

Peel each orange in a thin, wide, continuous strip. Cut each strip into four equal bits and roll them into the shape of a tight rosebud. Pack the rosebuds into a deep bowl or container so that they don't unravel and cover with cold water. Leave them to soak for approximately 12 hours.

Squeeze the peeled oranges and keep the juice aside.

Drain the orange rosebuds and put them in a heavy-based pan. Cover with water and bring to the boil. Reduce the heat and simmer gently for an hour. Drain and refresh them under running cold water.

Put the sugar into a heavy-based pan with roughly 1.5 litres (2 pints) water and bring to the boil, stirring all the time. Boil gently for about 5 minutes, then stir in the cardamom pods, orange-peel rosebuds, and orange juice. Reduce the heat and simmer gently until the rosebuds are transparent and tender and the syrup is thick. Remove from the heat and pack the orange-peel rosebuds into sterilised jars. Pour in the syrup, through a strainer to catch the cardamom pods, and seal the jars immediately.

Salads of oranges and onions, often with herbs and olives, are popular in the orange-growing regions of Turkey, Syria and Lebanon. This recipe is from Syria, where lemons are also added to the salad.

SALATA NARANJ
(ORANGE AND ONION SALAD)

Serves 4

Preparation time 15–20 minutes

3 sweet, juicy oranges, peeled, with
pith and pips removed and
sliced
1 juicy lemon, peeled, with pith
and pips removed, sliced
1 red or white onion, finely sliced
Roughly 12 black olives
½ teaspoon cumin seeds, crushed
A small bunch fresh mint leaves,
chopped, or a teaspoon fresh or
dried thyme, or oregano
Salt
2 tablespoons olive oil

Arrange the orange and lemon slices on a dish. Place the onion slices and black olives on top.

Sprinkle with the cumin seeds, herbs and salt, and drizzle the oil over it all. You can toss it lightly and serve at once, or leave it for a while for the flavour to mingle.

Salata naranj

MELON

(SHAMAMA) *Cucumis melo*

Fresh melon

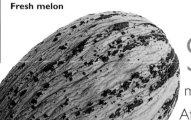

Some people say that the best melons come from Afghanistan and Iran. This may be true, as wild ancestors of the modern melon were thought to have grown naturally in the area stretching from Egypt to Iran and north-west India, but it wasn't until after the fall of the Roman Empire that the melon was first cultivated. Watermelon, *Citrullus lanatus*, on the other hand, is not from the same genus as the melon and has a longer history of cultivation. It was grown and eaten in Egypt before 2000 BC. Although quite distinct from one another, I have joined melon and watermelon here as they are often sold side by side and consumed in much the same way, as a *mezze* or dessert fruit. The seeds of both are also eaten, roasted and salted as a snack, or blanched.

Fresh watermelon

HOW IT GROWS

Melons are one of the world's agricultural wonders. Like weeds, they sprawl over the soil and grow at great speed. If allowed to, they would take over. Harvested in the hot summer months, they are much appreciated to quench the thirst. And those harvested in the winter provide a burst of honey-sweet, fruity delight. As mentioned earlier, the best are reputed to be grown in Iran, but all the regions of the Middle East grow a range of delicious specimens.

APPEARANCE AND TASTE

Nothing beats a ripe, golden-fleshed melon with a taste of pure honey. Most of the melons in the Middle East are like a cross between a cantaloupe and a honeydew, often with a green skin and orange or yellow flesh, or they are of the netted variety. All have juicy flesh that is so sweet it's like nectar. Winter melons, such as the Turkish Casaba melon, are more oval-shaped, like a rugby ball, and they have a green, or green and yellow, rough skin with a pale yellow flesh. In Iran, some of the melons are white-fleshed and taste like candyfloss. Watermelons are generally large and round, like footballs, and a deep green, sometimes striped with light green or tinged with yellow. They are incredibly refreshing and dribble with juice as you tuck into the mild, pink flesh.

A netted melon ready to harvest

BUYING AND STORING

The best way to tell if a melon is ripe or not is by pressing the end opposite the stem to see if it yields or not. With some melons, such as galia and other cantaloupe varieties, you can tell if it's sweet or not by smelling the same end. Watermelons should have a rich, hollow sound when tapped. Both keep for weeks in a cool, dry place.

Melon sellers, Istanbul, Turkey

CULINARY USES

Ripe melons and watermelons are generally eaten fresh as *mezze* or dessert. A popular Turkish *meze* consists of cubes of sweet melon with cubes of white, feta-style cheese. Sweet melons are also served stuffed with other summer fruits and scented with rose water, or crushed and made into a chilled dessert or drink. The pale flesh of unripe watermelons, or the white flesh near the rind of a ripening fruit is often pickled or used for making a syrupy jam. Even the watermelon rind is preserved in a cardamom – flavoured syrup in Iran.

In the heat of summer in Iran, the following recipe is often served as a chilled dessert or, diluted with ice, as a refreshing drink. Sprinkle crushed, scented rose petals over the dessert for an air of sophistication.

PÂLOODEH GARMAK
(ICED MELON WITH ROSE WATER)

Serves 2–4
Preparation time 10–15 minutes
Cooking time –

1 sweet, ripe melon (e.g. galia, honeydew or cantaloupe)
2 tablespoons rose water
1–2 teaspoons sugar
2 pinches of rose petals

Halve the melon, scoop out the seeds and cut out the flesh. On a plate to catch the juice, chop the flesh and crush it lightly with the back of a fork. Tip it and the juice into a bowl, then stir in the rose water and sugar. Put it into the refrigerator to chill and serve ice-cold with crushed rose petals sprinkled over the top.

Fruit often forms part of the *mezze* table in the summer and autumn months, and melon is very popular. Sweet and juicy, it complements white cheese beautifully, and it acts as a refreshing palate cleanser between dishes or courses. As a variation on the theme, modern recipes like this one crop up in the more cosmopolitan cities of the Middle East. It is not traditional, but very characteristic. The firm, crumbly regional cheeses can be replaced by feta and, although the ingredients for the salad can be prepared ahead of time, they should only be mixed together just before eating as the melon tends to weep.

KAVUN SALATASI
(MELON SALAD)

Serves 3–4
Preparation time 10–15 minutes
Cooking time –

1 ripe, juicy melon
200g (7oz) white cheese (feta)
A small bunch fresh purple basil and mint, chopped
2–3 tablespoons olive oil
A squeeze of lemon juice
2–3 tablespoons black olives

Halve the melon, scoop out the seeds, and cut out the flesh. Chop it into bite-size cubes and cut the cheese into similar-sized cubes.

Watermelon jam

Put the melon and the cheese into a bowl with the herbs.

Dress with the oil and a squeeze of lemon and garnish with the black olives.

Kavun salatası

QUINCE

(SAFARJAL) *Cydonia oblonga*

Fresh quince

In the Song of Solomon, the 'apples' mentioned are likely to be quinces, as this ancient, scented fruit was cultivated in the Levant before the apple. It is also believed that the 'golden apple' given by Paris to Aphrodite, which led to the fall of Troy, was a quince. The name *Cydonia* comes from Kydonia in Crete, where a superior variety of quince was cultivated. The Romans called the quince *melimelum*, derived from the Greek for 'honey apple', because the sour fruit was always preserved in honey. Other fruit and vegetables had been preserved in honey or vinegar by this time, but the quince was the first to be cooked before being preserved, which led to the discovery of pectin. Quince preserves with honey – the first jam – appeared in the medieval Arab world and are still enjoyed today throughout the Middle East.

Quince jam

HOW IT GROWS

The quince, which is related to the apple and the pear, originally came from the Caucuasus, where the wild, twisted trees still grow. It is cultivated throughout the Levant, Turkey and Iran.

APPEARANCE AND TASTE

The quince is usually matt yellow or golden in colour and looks like a large, bulging pear. The flesh is firm and simultaneously sour and scented, with lots of pips. The raw fruit has a distinctive texture that can make your tongue feel as if it is sticking to the roof of your mouth but, when cooked with sugar, it turns a pretty shade of pink and emits a lovely, floral fragrance that wafts enticingly through the house.

BUYING AND STORING

The fresh fruit keeps quite well in a cool place. They are available in Middle Eastern stores and some well-stocked fruit shops from October to February. Most quince preserves keep for months and are intended to last the year.

CULINARY USES

In Turkey, the fresh fruit is cut into thin slices, with a little lemon juice squeezed over them so they don't discolour, to eat as *meze* or as a refreshing nibble with a drink. Throughout the Middle East, quinces are preserved in a sugar syrup, flavoured with the juice of lemons or limes, or they are cubed or shredded and made into a syrupy jam, sometimes flavoured with cloves or cardamom seeds. They are poached with sugar to make a fragrant, pink dessert, served with clotted cream, and cooked quinces are puréed to make a fruity paste that is eaten as a sweetmeat, decorated with blanched almonds. The Armenians combine quince with other vegetables in soups and stews and they often sauté them with sugar and cinnamon to serve as an accompaniment to poultry or lamb. In Iran and Turkey, quinces are often cooked with meat or poultry in stews, or they are cooked whole and filled with a minced meat stuffing.

When the Arabs spread Islam throughout the Middle East, they also spread restrictions on all consumption of wine and spirits. The transition was slow but, for those who had enjoyed wine for so long, something had to be found to replace it. And so the sherbet, *sharab* ('drink' in Arabic), came about. Based on a fruit syrup, diluted with water and served chilled with ice, sherbets are varied and refreshing.

One of the earliest, and most unusual, sherbets was made from a mint and vinegar syrup, just one step away from the forbidden wine, but the more common syrups are made from lemons, sour cherries, pomegranates, mulberries and rose water. This delightful syrup is from Iran.

SHARBAT-E BEH-LIMOO
(QUINCE AND LIME SYRUP)

Makes roughly 850ml (1½ pints)
Preparation time 10 minutes
Cooking time approximately 40
  minutes

500g (18oz) sugar
225ml (8fl oz) water
1 large quince, peeled, cored, and
  chopped into small cubes (keep
  in cold water with a splash of
  lime juice as it goes brown very
  quickly)
110ml (4fl oz) fresh lime juice

Put the sugar and water into a pan and bring it to the boil, stirring all the time. Drain the quince and add it to the pan.

Bring the liquid back to the boil, then reduce the heat and simmer for about 15 minutes. Strain the syrup through a muslin cloth, pressing the quince with the back of a wooden spoon to extract the flavour.

Return the strained syrup to the pan, stir in the lime juice, and boil it gently until the syrup is thick. Leave it to cool in the pan, then pour into a sterilised bottle.

To serve, drop some ice cubes into a tall glass and put it in the freezer to frost. Pour one or two tablespoons of the syrup over the ice and dilute with it cold water.

This is a classic autumn dessert, enjoyed particularly in Turkey. It is quite magical as the pale yellow fruit transforms into a pretty shade of pink, and the natural pectin in the fruit and seeds turns the syrup into a jelly. If for no other reason, it is worth making this dessert for the heavenly perfume it emits in your kitchen.

AYVA TATLISI
(QUINCE DESSERT)

Serves 6
Preparation time 15 minutes
Cooking time approximately
  1 hour

225g (8oz) sugar
425ml (¾ pint) water
Juice of ½ lemon
6–8 cloves
1kg (2¼ lb) fresh quinces, peeled,
  halved from head to stalk, and
  cored – retain the seeds (keep
  them in water with a splash of
  lemon juice until you're ready to
  use them)

Put the sugar and water into a heavy-based pan and bring it to the boil, stirring all the time. Add the lemon juice, cloves, and quince seeds.

Slip in the quince halves, then reduce the heat and poach gently for about 50 minutes, until the fruit is tender and has turned pink.

Pick out the quince seeds and leave the quinces to cool in the syrup, which will become jelly-like.

Serve chilled or at room temperature with clotted cream.

Ayva tatlısı

Fresh figs

Fig

(TEEN) *Ficus carica*

Muhammad is reputed to have said that if any fruit came from Paradise, it was the fig. In the West, figs are something of a luxury and are often disappointing as they haven't matured on the tree, but in their natural habitat they are juicy and sweet and grow in abundance. The cultivation of figs first began somewhere between 4000 and 2700 BC in Egypt or Arabia. By 800 BC, figs were growing in mainland Greece and acquired the species name *carica* as the Greeks thought they had originally come from Caria in Asia Minor. Figs are often referred to in the Bible.

Dried figs

HOW IT GROWS

The fig tree is descended from a wild tree, the caprifig, which spread from Western Asia to the Mediterranean region in prehistoric times. Its evolution involved one of nature's little wonders. If a fig tree was to bear formed, edible fruit, the flower had to be visited by a tiny fig wasp. Amazingly, Aristotle was aware of this fact in the fourth century BC. This is still true of the caprifig and Smyrna figs, but in the long period since the Roman Empire new types of fig have appeared that don't require a wasp. With the caprifig though, the wasp inhabits the immature syconium, the vase-shaped outer shell, which contains both male and female flowers that are unable to fertilise one another. Once she is impregnated, the female wasp crawls around inside the syconium, getting covered in pollen from the male flowers, and finds a way out through a little hole opposite the stem. She then flies to another syconium, crawls through the hole and lays her eggs down the style of a female flower, managing to pollenate the other female flowers as she passes them, so that they form seeds.

Botanically, the fig fruit is regarded as a series of fruits but as you eat it it looks more like a pocket full of seeds.

APPEARANCE AND TASTE

Smyrna figs still grow in their natural habitat in Turkey and closely resemble their ancient ancestors from Asia Minor all those years ago. Bigger than the ones we are used to and amber in colour, they have a nutty flavour. In Turkey, Greece, North Africa, and California, where they now grow, they are eaten fresh, but for export they are dried. Also common in Turkey are Bardajic figs which, are reddish-brown with a pinkish flesh, and Franciscan figs which, with their purple-black skin and red, sweet flesh, are the ones most of us are familiar with. Dried figs taste quite different from the fresh ones and in parts of the Middle East the fruit is picked when very small and dried, so that you can just pop them in your mouth like chewy, honey-flavoured sweets.

BUYING AND STORING

When buying fresh, ripe figs make sure they are soft to the touch so that the juice will ooze out of them. If they are firm, they will usually be tasteless and a bit dry. Really ripe figs need to be eaten straight away. Dried figs, on the other hand, keep for quite a long time if stored in an airtight container in a dry, cool place. The semi-dried figs are still moist and can just be popped into the mouth.

Crates of fresh figs, Egypt

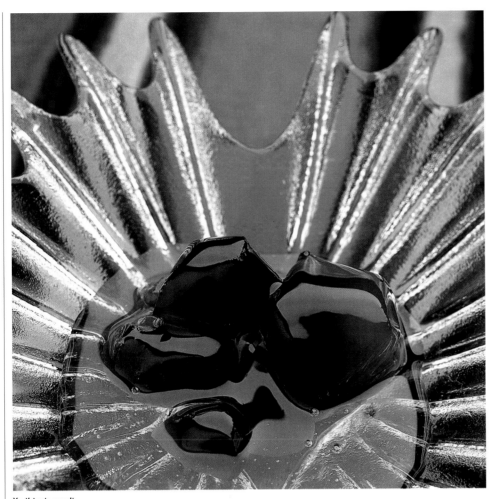

Yeşil incir reçeli

CULINARY USES

Fresh, ripe figs are generally eaten as they are with the juice dribbling down one's chin. Dried figs are added to fruit compotes, are used in stuffings and stews, poached into jam, and are occasionally used to make *rakı*, Turkey's national alcoholic drink. Dried figs are also stuffed and baked with honey and milk or cream. Immature figs are picked when they are small and green and are poached with sugar to make a delectable, honey-tasting, syrupy jam, which is more akin to a conserve.

Both fresh and dried figs are delicious baked with honey. Dried figs are also popular baked in a scented syrup, as in this homely winter dish which is moist and sticky with a hint of roses.

İNCİR TATLISI
(STUFFED FIGS BAKED IN ROSE SYRUP)

Serves 4
Preparation time 15–20 minutes (+ soaking overnight)
Cooking time 20–25 minutes

225g (8oz) dried figs, soaked overnight, or boiled for 5 minutes, until soft and plump
75g (3oz) blanched almonds, chopped
75g (3oz) walnuts, chopped
225g (8oz) sugar
125ml (5fl oz) water
2 tablespoons rose water

Preheat the oven to 180°C/ 350°F/gas mark 4.

Drain the figs and cut off the stalks. Push a teaspoon of chopped nuts inside each fig, and place them all upright in a shallow oven-proof dish. In a pan, bring the sugar and water to the boil, stirring all the time. Reduce the heat, stir in the rose water and simmer for 10–15 minutes, until the syrup coats the back of a spoon. Pour the syrup over the figs and place them in the oven for about 20 minutes, until they are tender and sticky. Serve hot or cold with clotted cream.

Some of the Middle Eastern jams are exquisite. There is the scent of antiquity in the delicate rose petal jam, a striking novelty to the magnificent aubergine jam, and a delectable honeycomb flavour to this glorious conserve of tender, baby green figs floating in syrup. To stabilise the colour, shape and texture, the freshly picked, immature fruits are soaked in lime-water (slaked lime powder diluted with water) before being poached in syrup. This, of course, may not be possible in your home, in which case the figs in the resulting jam will lose shape and become soft. The jam will still taste delicious, though.

YEŞİL İNCİR REÇELİ
(GREEN FIG JAM)

Makes roughly 1.2 litres (2 pints) of jam
Preparation time 5–10 minutes
Cooking time roughly 30 minutes

450g (1lb) small, immature green figs, washed and patted dry
450g (1lb) sugar
300ml (½ pint) water
Juice of ½ lemon

If the figs are perfect with unblemished skins, there is no need to peel them; if not, remove the skins and trim the stalks.

Put the sugar and water into a heavy-based pan and bring to the boil, stirring all the time. Stir in the lemon juice and figs and boil rapidly for about 5 minutes.

Reduce the heat and simmer for about 20 minutes, until the syrup thickens and the figs are beautifully tender.

Leave the figs to cool in the syrup, then spoon them into scalded jars. Leave them to stand for a few days before eating them.

DATE

(TAMR) *Phoenix dactylifera*

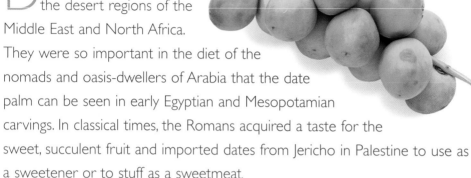

Fresh dates on a stick

Dates are a staple food in the desert regions of the Middle East and North Africa. They were so important in the diet of the nomads and oasis-dwellers of Arabia that the date palm can be seen in early Egyptian and Mesopotamian carvings. In classical times, the Romans acquired a taste for the sweet, succulent fruit and imported dates from Jericho in Palestine to use as a sweetener or to stuff as a sweetmeat.

Finding dates in the desert must have been like stumbling across gold. Delicious fresh or dried, they could be carried by travellers and nomadic herdsmen, such as the disappearing Bedouin. They have a high sugar content and are fairly nutritional, so some desert Arabs thrive for long periods of time on a diet of dates and fermented milk. The Arabs say that the Bedouin can't get to sleep under the palms with the fruit hanging over their heads, such is their love of dates and all things sweet.

As the date is integral to the lives of both the nomadic and settled Arabs, it is one of the most extensively cultivated crops in the Middle East. Such is the appreciation of the date in Iraq and the Gulf, there are reputed to be over 350 varieties in Basra alone. Generally, the dates fall into three main types: soft, juicy dates, which are grown for eating fresh, although some of the crop is dried and compressed into blocks; hard, dry, fibrous dates – also known as 'bread' or 'camel' dates, which used to be the staple date of Arab nomads and which are dried further for their intense, sweet flavour or ground to a powder; and semi-dry dates, which are less sweet but moist and popular in Iran. Believed to increase prosperity and enhance life, dates play such an important role in the culinary cultures of the Middle East that the biggest producers, worldwide, are Egypt, Iraq, Iran, and Saudi Arabia. Even the degree of ripeness is internationally classified in Arabic.

HOW IT GROWS

Dates are the fruit of a palm tree that grows in irrigated environments as well as in extreme desert conditions, for its deep rooting system can reach water other crops can't. Like all palms, they flower and fruit at the top and, if left, they can grow to 30m (107ft) in height. Obviously, this makes them difficult to harvest, so commercial growers tend to cut the trees at about 15m (54ft) Harvested in late summer, the fruits grow in large bunches that may contain as many as a thousand dates. A single tree can produce anything from 50–150kg (110 –330lb) of fruit.

APPEARANCE AND TASTE

Generally speaking, a fresh date fruit is roughly 5cm (2in) long and yellow in colour. However, its colour, taste, quality and uses vary according to the variety being grown. In Iraq, there is the *Asharasi* date, which is dry with a nutty taste; the soft, richly flavoured *Khadrawi* from the south; the *Khustawi*, which is so sweet and delicious it is generally eaten as a dessert date; and the *Zahidi*, which is Iraq's main commercial date, sold in different stages of maturity from soft to dry. In Arabia there are the *Bahri* and the *Khalas*, both of which are

Dried dates

rich in flavour, fresh and dried; and the *Hilali*, which has a lovely flavour but eaten only fresh as it doesn't dry well. Egypt has the large maroon-coloured *Khidri* date, which is chewy with a mild flavour and the Gulf region has the small, sweet *Mactoum*, which originally came from Iraq. In Oman and the UAE, there is the reddish-brown *Fardh*, which is a staple date, and the *Naghal* which ripens early and eaten fresh.

BUYING AND STORING

Some fresh dates have better keeping qualities than others. For example, the *Fardh* and *Khustawi* keep well. Dried dates, on the other hand, keep for a long time, if stored in a cool, dry place. Most often, dried dates are packed in bags or boxes and dry out on keeping, but look for the moist, dark dates of Iran (available in Iranian and Middle Eastern stores), which are packed semi-dried in boxes or tins: they keep well in the fridge.

MANUFACTURING

In the Middle East, the principal manufactured products from date palms are sugar and molasses. As the *Zahidi* palm is prolific, producing fruit with a high sugar content, it is used as an industrial source of sugar. And a thick, sticky molasses (*pekmez* in Turkey, *dibs* in the Arab world) is extracted from the pressed fruit of a variety of date palms. It is sold in jars and used as a sweetener, or it is spooned onto bread like honey. Date syrup mixed with *tahini* makes a nourishing spread or dip.

Dibs (pekmez):
date syrup

Carrying freshly picked dates and melons, Bahla, Oman

CULINARY USES

Fresh and dried dates have been combined with poultry and lamb since ancient times in the Arab world. The medieval recipe *rutabiya* consists of meatballs stuffed with almonds, flavoured with spices, and garnished with dates. Throughout the Middle East, dried dates are often stuffed with blanched almonds, rose-scented almond paste or crushed pistachios and served as a sweetmeat. Pounded with cinnamon and a little rose water or orange blossom water, dried dates are often used as a filling for *ma' amoul* (p143), the special melt-in-the-mouth biscuits baked by Christians at Easter and Muslims at *Ramadam*. Soft dates are used in Iraq to make little date-filled pies called *babee bi tamr*. In Iran, a delicious fudge-like sweet, *ranginak*, is made with dates and walnuts, a combination that works well and is used in the popular sweetmeat *halwa tamr*, which is simply made of pressed dates and crushed walnuts rolled into balls. The Jewish communities make a date and raisin paste, *harosset*, to celebrate Passover, and dates are often married with raisins again in fruit compotes. Fresh and dried dates are quite often added to rice with nuts, or cooked with vegetables such as spinach and pumpkin. Fresh, sour dates are poached and preserved in syrup; the thick date syrup can be used as a sweetener in the preserves of other fruit and vegetables, such as turnips.

The Bedouin and the marsh Arabs of southern Iraq pound semi-dried dates to a pulp and spread it on fish before roasting it over charcoal. Dates are also pulped and puréed and spread out thinly to dry in the sun to make the ubiquitous leathers (p96–8), which are chewed as a snack or added to winter stews for flavour. In some of the desert villages, the sap of date palms is used as a crude sweetener and a fermented drink is made from the fruit. And in parts of the Gulf and the UAE, the flowers of the date palms are sold in the markets to be used as a dip for bread, made by pounding the flowers with a small dried fish.

The fat, moist, dark dates of Iran are the best I have ever tasted. They are sweet and fruity and simply melt in the mouth.

Semi-dried harvested dates

Throughout the Middle East, a common way to eat dried dates as a sweetmeat is to remove the stone and replace it with a blanched almond, a walnut half or rose-flavoured almond paste. However, the Iranians go one step further and set the stuffed dates in a fudge-like mixture, which is garnished with ground pistachios and almonds for colour, hence its name, *ranginak*, which means 'colourful'. In the following recipe, if the dates are really moist and sweet, you can omit the sugar.

RANGINAK
(STUFFED DATE FUDGE CAKE)

Makes 12–16 (depending on the size of slices)
Preparation time 25–30 minutes
Cooking time –

75g (3oz) walnuts, halved
450g (1lb) moist dried dates, with stones removed
225g (8oz) butter
2 tablespoons sugar
225g (8oz) plain flour
1 tablespoon ground almonds
1 tablespoon ground pistachios

Place half a walnut inside each date and close it up again. Lightly grease a shallow dish or baking tin and place the stuffed dates in it, packing them in together.

Melt the butter with the sugar and stir in the flour. Cook it gently until it turns golden, then pour it slowly over the dates, filling all the gaps.

Leave the mixture to set, then sprinkle the ground nuts over the top and cut the fudge cake into squares to serve as a sweetmeat with tea or coffee.

In Turkey, this dish of grains with nuts is sometimes called 'Arab pilaf', because of the dates (which the Turks love but don't grow). Believed to be of Bedouin origin, it is a fairly versatile dish as it can be made with rice or bulgur, sometimes coloured with saffron and, occasionally, pepped up with chillies. My favourite way is with bulgur and lots of dates for their sweet, fruity flavour. With its use of two principal staples, wheat and dates, this simple dish captures the essence of the Middle East.

ARAP PİLAVI
(BULGUR WITH NUTS AND DATES)

Serves 4
Preparation time 5 minutes (+ soaking of dates if necessary)
Cooking time 35 minutes

Salt
450g (1lb) bulgur, rinsed and drained
2 tablespoons clarified butter (ghee)
2 tablespoons pine nuts
2 tablespoons pistachios
3 tablespoons blanched almonds, kept whole or split in half
110g (4oz) soft dried dates (soak them in water if hard), roughly chopped

Bring a pan of water to the boil, stir in some salt, and toss in the bulgur. Cook it vigorously for about 10 minutes, then drain.

Meanwhile, in a wide, heavy-based pan, melt the clarified butter and stir in the nuts. When they begin to brown, add dates and cook for a minute or two.

Splash in a little water (about 2 tablespoons) to keep the dates moist and, once it has bubbled up and been absorbed, tip in the bulgur, quickly tossing it about so that it is well mixed and doesn't stick to the bottom. Season if necessary and turn off the heat.

Cover with a clean tea towel and a lid, and leave to steam for about 20 minutes. If you like, melt a little extra clarified butter and pour it over the bulgur, then toss with a fork. Serve hot with yogurt or kebabs.

A popular sweet in the Middle East: dates stuffed with almonds

Arap pilavı

APRICOT

(MISHMISH) *Prunus armeniaca*

Fresh apicots

Dried fruit, Turkey

It is believed that the apricot originated in China and travelled westwards with the silk merchants, reaching Iran in the second or first century BC. Its botanical name is misleading, indicating the fruit is of Armenian origin, which is what the Greeks believed. At the end of the apricot season, villages in Anatolia are transformed into a feast of colour as the bright orange fruits are laid out on the flat roofs to dry in the sun. Dried apricots are so appreciated in the Middle East that, when they are stuffed with blanched almonds or almond paste, some Muslims regard them as a gift from Allah.

HOW IT GROWS

The apricot, which belongs to the rose family and is related to the plum, cherry, peach and almond, grows in warm temperate climates. In the Middle East, the trees grow mainly in central Anatolia in Turkey, in Isfahan in Iran, and on the oasis of al-Ghuta in Syria. Apricots come in a variety of colours, from white, orange and pink to grey and black, and in differing sizes, some as small as a berry, others as large as a peach.

APPEARANCE AND TASTE

A ripe, fresh, orange-yellow apricot is rather special. The taut skin, often tinged with rosy-red and dappled, is slightly furry and soft, like high-quality velvet or moleskin, and the juicy, golden flesh is delicate and sweet, like a fragrant honey. In Iran, they are known as *zardaloo*,

Treated dried apricots

which means yellow plum. The white apricots, like white peaches, are often tinged with pink and both their fragrance and their taste is delicately perfumed. Most commercial apricots end up dried and, if they have been dried in the sun, are full of that unmistakable apricot flavour, with an almost caramelised taste, and they look burnt. The ubiquitous orange dried apricots have been treated with sulphur dioxide to retain the bright, appealing colour.

MANUFACTURING

Throughout the Middle East, long thin strips of pressed, dried apricot, called 'apricot leathers', are sold in the markets. These 'leathers' come mainly from Turkey and Syria, where the washed and stoned fruit is puréed, spread very thinly on trays and then left in the sun to dry. 'Leathers', which are made

out of all kinds of fruit, such as mulberries, plums, apples and grapes, are popular as a chewy snack, or melted down and used to flavour stews and sauces, or diluted and made into a chilled drink. Apricot 'leathers' are regarded as a luxury amongst the Bedouin who are reputed to have a sweet tooth.

BUYING AND STORING

Sadly many commercial fresh apricots are disappointing as they are picked before they have fully ripened and the flesh can be sponge-like and tasteless, leaving you to wonder why on earth people go on about them. If you are lucky and do find ripe, juicy ones, eat them straight away and enjoy them, as they don't keep. Sun-dried apricots keep for about six months, stored in an airtight container in a cool, dry place.

Unsulphered dried apricots

CULINARY USES

Fresh apricots are usually eaten as they are. Occasionally, they are cooked in meat stews and, in Iran and Turkey, they are made into a syrupy jam. Dried apricots are stuffed with almonds or almond paste as a sweetmeat, and they are used in a number of puddings and compotes, and in rice dishes and stews. In Turkey, they are poached in a scented syrup and filled with clotted buffalo cream in the delicious dessert, *kaymaklı kayısı*. In Syria, dried apricots are poached and puréed, then mixed with chopped nuts and rose water and served as a special dish for *Ramadan*.

This is a delicious fruity, aromatic dish of Arabic origin. Traditionally, the dried apricots were soaked and puréed before being added to the stew but more modern versions found in Turkey, Iran and North Africa use whole apricots. Try to find the sharp-tasting, naturally sun dried apricots for the right flavour.

MISHMISHIYA
(LAMB AND APRICOT STEW)

Serves 6
Preparation time 40 minutes
Cooking time 1½ hours

1 kg (2¼ lb) lean shoulder of lamb, cubed
2 teaspoons ground cinnamon
1 teaspoon ground coriander
1 teaspoon ground cumin
½ teaspoon chilli powder
225g (8oz) dried apricots
A knob fresh ginger (about 2½ cm (1 in)
3–4 cloves garlic
2 tablespoons olive oil with a little butter
2 onions, chopped
2 pinches saffron fronds or about 2 teaspoons powdered saffron
About ½ tablespoon flour
Salt and freshly ground black pepper

Toss the meat in the ground spices and leave to sit for about 30 minutes.

Pour boiling water over the apricots and leave them to soak for 30 minutes, then drain. Reserve the soaking water, top it up with ordinary water to make

Apricots ripening on tree

Drying apricots in the sun on a roof top, Cappedocia, Turkey

roughly 600ml (1 pint), and purée a third of the apricots in about half of this water.

Using a pestle and mortar, grind the ginger and garlic to a paste.

In a heavy-based pan, heat the oil with the butter and fry the onions until soft. Stir in the saffron fronds and add the spiced meat. Turn the pieces of meat over quickly so that the spices don't burn and stir in the ginger and garlic paste.

Sprinkle with flour (about ½ tablespoon) and cover with the remaining water and puréed apricots. Stir well and bring to the boil, then turn the heat down and simmer gently, with the lid on, for about 1 hour, turning the meat from time to time.

Add the apricots and continue to cook for about 30 minutes, until both the apricots and meat are tender. Season well with salt and pepper.

Dried apricots are often cooked in syrup and preserved in jars but in this delicious Turkish recipe they are filled with a clotted cream made from buffalo milk (*kaymak* in Turkish, *eishta* in Arabic) and served chilled as a delightful winter or spring treat.

KAYMAKLI KAYISI

(APRICOTS FILLED WITH CLOTTED CREAM)

Serves 6
Preparation time 5 minutes +
   6–8 hours' soaking of apricots
Cooking time 15–20 minutes

225g (8oz) dried apricots, soaked
   for at least 6 hours or overnight
175g (6oz) sugar
1 tablespoon orange blossom
   water
175g (6oz) kaymak or clotted
   cream
A few fresh mint leaves

Drain the apricots and reserve 250ml (9fl oz) of the soaking water. Put the water into a heavy-based pan with the sugar and bring the liquid to the boil, stirring all the time.

Boil the liquid for a few minutes, then stir in the orange blossom water and the apricots. Bring the liquid to the boil once more, reduce heat and poach the apricots gently for 10–15 minutes. Turn off the heat and leave the apricots to cool in the syrup.

Lift the apricots out of the syrup, slit each one open with a knife and fill with a teaspoon of *kaymak* or clotted cream. Place them on a plate, spoon some of the syrup around them and put them in the fridge to chill.

Serve chilled, decorated with the fresh mint leaves.

Kaymaklı kayısı

The thin sheets of compressed dried apricot are extremely popular in Turkey and Syria. Traditionally, the peasant woman would crush the apricots with their feet, remove the kernels, then spread the apricot pulp out to dry in the sun. More modern methods employ machines to do the puréeing, but with a spell of hot summer weather apricot leather, *amardine*, can be made at home and kept in the refrigerator or freezer. Intensely fruity, the leather is dissolved in water and sweetened to make a refreshing drink, or added to stews. The dissolved, sweetened mixture can also be gently cooked to form a thick cream which is chilled and spooned over yogurt or served as a pudding with blanched almonds and clotted cream.

AMARDINE

(APRICOT LEATHER)

Makes 2 leathers
Preparation time 1–2 days
Cooking time –

Roughly 900g (2lb) fresh apricots,
   peeled and stoned
110g (4oz) sugar

Prepare two large, rimmed baking trays with a sheet of plastic wrap pulled tight over the edges (you may need to secure it with tape).

Whiz the apricots in a food processor to form a purée. Add the sugar and blend until the mixture is very smooth. Now empty the purée onto the baking trays, spreading it thinly and evenly.

Apricot leather

Cover the trays with muslin cloth, pulled tight and fastened with tape to prevent it from touching the purée, and place them outside in the sunlight until the purée is dry and pliable enough to peel off the plastic underneath. Depending on the heat of the sun, this might take two days – be careful not to let the fruit dry out and become hard.

Roll up the leather in the plastic wrap and twist the ends to seal. Store it in a cool, dry place, in the refrigerator or freezer.

CHERRY

(KARAZ) *Prunus avium*

The word 'cherry' is derived from the ancient Greek name *kerasos*, which probably came from the Black Sea port Kerasanda (modern-day Giresun in Turkey), meaning 'place of plentiful cherries', as it was surrounded by cherry forests. The wealthy Roman general Lucullus is thought to have brought cherries, or cherry trees, back to Rome from this port, which was then known as Kerasunt, after defeating the Pontic king Mithridates around 70 BC. Cherries were then spread across Europe by the Roman legions and even today their variety names – for instance, Black Tartarian, Circassian, and Turkey Heart – reflect their origins. Both the sweet cherry, *Prunus avium*, and the sour cherry, *Prunus cerasus*, are native to the eastern Mediterranean region, particularly to Turkey, Syria, and Iran.

Fresh sweet cherries

HOW IT GROWS

There are a number of species of cherry which belong to the Prunus genus, which includes apricots, plums and almonds, all of which are native to western Asia. The white blossom of the cherry tree appears in April or May and the fruit usually matures in June. As the fruit grows at the top of the trees, which can reach 20m (65ft) in height, tall ladders made out of chestnut wood are used for harvesting. The fruit has to be picked quickly, so groups of women and children climb up and fill the wicker baskets that have been strapped to the ladders until the cherry orchards have been cleared.

Wild cherries, best left to ripen on the tree

APPEARANCE AND TASTE

As one would expect, sweet cherries are sweet and juicy and sour cherries generally need sweetening. Most of the sweet cherries in the Middle East are small and round and a deep red or black when ripe. Sour cherries are slightly smaller, firmer and light red in colour. In Syria, you also get sour cherries that are black and in Turkey there are sweet cherries that are white. Dried sour cherries are considerably smaller than fresh ones and their flavour and colour are intensified.

BUYING AND STORING

Ripe sweet cherries don't last long and are best eaten fresh. Sour cherries are delicious fresh too, but they are usually preserved in syrup to be used throughout the year until the next cherry season. Dried sour cherries keep for about a year in an airtight container.

MEDICINAL AND OTHER USES

'If the mulberry didn't follow me, I would turn people into my stalk', the sweet cherry says in Turkish lore, as sweet cherries are packed with vitamins and help stimulate the metabolism, so are regarded as 'thinning'. The dried cherry stalks, believed to contain diuretic properties, are used to make a herbal tisane to lower high blood pressure. The resin of cherry trees, cherry gum, is diluted with vinegar to soothe skin rashes and to treat coughs and colds. Bees use it to seal their hives and, at one time, it was used as a stiffener by textile manufacturers. The strong, deep red wood of the cherry tree was once used to make fine furniture and musical intruments.

Cherries and cucumbers in a market

Ground *mahlab (malep)*

CULINARY USES

Generally ripe sweet cherries are eaten fresh as a snack or dessert but sour cherries are often poached with sugar or cooked with meat or poultry to give a tart, fruity flavour. Both sweet and sour cherries are made into jams and puddings, such as the popular summer syrupy bread pudding that can be made with cherries, mulberries, peaches, or apricots. Sour cherries are boiled with sugar and strained to make a fruity syrup which is used as the basis of a cool, refreshing drink. Sour cherries are also preserved whole in syrup or poached, puréed and dried into 'leathers'. They are dried whole and used to flavour stews and rice dishes in Syria, Turkey and Iran. The kernels of the *mahlab (malep* in Turkish) cherries are ground to a powder and used to flavour breads and biscuits.

The following medieval Arab dish is made with sour cherries, which lend a lovely fruity flavour to the meatballs. Traditionally, the meatballs are served on pieces of flat bread and the cherry sauce is spooned over them.

LAHMA BIL KARAZ
(MEATBALLS WITH CINNAMON AND CHERRIES)

Serves 6
Preparation time 25–30 minutes
Cooking time 25 minutes

450g (1lb) lean lamb or veal, passed through the mincer 2 or 3 times
1 teaspoon ground cinnamon
½ teaspoon ground cumin

Black cherry kernels

½ teaspoon ground cloves
Salt and freshly ground black pepper
Sunflower oil for frying
1 tablespoon clarified or ordinary butter
225g (8oz) fresh sour cherries, stoned, or dried cherries, soaked overnight
1–2 tablespoons sugar
1 teaspoon ground cinnamon

Put the minced meat into a bowl and squash it with your knuckles, then knead it vigorously, slapping it into the bowl, until it becomes smooth and pasty. Add the spices and seasoning and knead again.

Take walnut-sized pieces out of the bowl and roll them into balls. Heat up enough sunflower oil to cover the base of a pan and fry the meatballs in it, until they are brown all over, then remove and drain on kitchen paper.

Melt the butter in a heavy-based pan and add the cherries. Cook for a minute, then add a little water to stew them. Stir in the sugar and cinnamon, bring to the boil, then pop in the meatballs and simmer for about 20 minutes or until they are cooked and the cherries are soft.

Crush most of the cherries and bubble up the sauce to caramelise it, adding a little more water if necessary. Serve the meatballs on flat breads or with rice.

Lahma bil karaz

Throughout the Middle East, dried fruit and nuts are often employed in the stuffing of meat and poultry. Sometimes they are combined with rice or bulgur, and sometimes they are bound with a tart fruit molasses or tomato paste, as in this Iranian recipe, which is also ideal for turkey.

Cherry juice seller in traditional Ottoman costume, Istanbul, Turkey

MORGH TU-POR
(CHICKEN WITH DRIED FRUIT STUFFING)

Serves 6
Preparation time 40 minutes
Cooking time approximately
1 hour 30 minutes

1 free-range, organic chicken, approximately 2kg (4½lb)
Salt
½ onion
2 pinches saffron pistils
1 teaspoon sugar
75g (3oz) butter
Juice of 1 lemon

For the stuffing:
2 onions, chopped
2 tablespoons olive oil
50g (2oz) walnuts, chopped
50g (2oz) pistachios, chopped
50g (2oz) dried barberries
75g (3oz) dried cherries
110g (4oz) dried prunes, chopped
110g (4oz) dried apricots, chopped
Salt
3–4 tablespoons tomato paste

Preheat the oven to 180°C/350°F/gas mark 4.

First prepare the stuffing. Fry the onions in the olive oil until they begin to turn golden, then stir in the walnuts and pistachios. Fry for a minute, then add the dried fruit. Season with a little salt and stir in the tomato paste. Bind it together well, then leave to cool.

Rub the chicken lightly with salt, inside and out, and fill it with the stuffing. Block the cavity with half an onion and hold it closed with a skewer, or sew it up with a poultry needle and string. Lay a large sheet of foil, big enough to form a package over the chicken, in a baking dish and place the stuffed chicken on it.

Using a pestle and mortar, grind the saffron pistils with the sugar and pour over a little boiling water to extract the colour. Melt the butter in a pan, stir in the lemon juice and the liquid saffron and pour it over the chicken.

Fold the foil over the chicken in a tight parcel and place it in the oven for about 1 hour. Open the foil, baste the chicken with the juices, and roast uncovered for a further half-hour, until the chicken is cooked and golden.

A tall glass of ice-cold, deep-red cherry juice is a refreshing drink in Turkey and Iran. Every bar, café, teahouse, and caravanserai has bottles of ready-made cherry juice to serve with ice. But, if you have the pleasure of tasting the home-made syrup poured over ice and diluted with a little water, it will transport you through centuries of delightful hospitality.

SHARBAT-E ÂLBÂLOO
(CHERRY SYRUP)

Makes 1 bottle
Preparation time 3 hours
Cooking time 35 minutes

450g (1lb) sour cherries, washed and stoned
900g (2lb) sugar
225ml (8fl oz) water

Place the cherries in a deep, heavy-based pan, cover with the sugar and leave to stand for 2–3 hours to draw out the juice.

Add the water and bring the mixture to the boil, stirring until the sugar has dissolved. Reduce the heat and simmer for 10–15 minutes. Strain the mixture through a muslin cloth, press all the juice out of the fruit, and return the strained liquid to the pan. Boil gently for a further 10 minutes until the syrup is thick, then leave it to cool in the pan.

POMEGRANATE

(ROMAN) *Punica granatum*

With its leathery skin and jewel-like seeds, the pomegranate has the appearance of a fruit that has an ancient history – the dinosaur of the fruit kingdom. Like the fig and the grape, it has been so intricately woven into the tapestry of the Middle East that it appears in myth and legend. The goddess Aphrodite is said to have planted a pomegranate tree in her birthplace in Cyprus, the fruit is depicted in Egyptian tomb murals that date back to 1547 BC, and it is mentioned in the Old Testament.

The Romans called the pomegranate, *Malum punicum*, apple of Carthage, or *Malum granatum*, apple with grains, and it featured in a Latin proverb: 'Omni malo punico inest granum putre' – 'In every pomegranate is a rotten pip'. The fruit was consumed in vast quantities by the Romans. The juice was fermented and made into wine, Nero's favourite digestive drink was made from pomegranates and quinces, and the fruit was dipped in the salty sea and dried in the sun to preserve it for winter.

Later, in medieval times, Islamic mystics believed that pomegranates could 'raise' the soul and purge it of rage, hatred and envy. During the period of the Ottoman Empire, there were sweet and sour pomegranates, as well as white pomegranates, which had white skins and pink, sweet grains, and 'black' pomegranates from Baghdad, which had a purple skin and large sour grains. Once used as a souring agent before the arrival of lemons, sour pomegranates are still grown for their juice, which is used to make a refreshing drink.

Fresh eating pomegranates

HOW IT GROWS

The pomegranate is the fruit of a small bush-like tree that grows wild in its native habitat in the forests in northern Iran, to the south of the Caspian Sea and in Azerbaijan. It thrives in hot, arid regions and is cultivated in Iran, Turkey, Iraq, and in the eastern Mediterranean. The small leaves have a scarlet edging, and when the tree flowers it bursts into colour with tiny vermilion blooms. The fruit starts off pale green, like small bobbles, then gradually swells and the skin becomes leathery and coral red. The fruit matures in the late autumn.

APPEARANCE AND TASTE

In the Middle East, there are several varieties of pomegranate, both sweet and sour. Generally they are round, the size of a tennis ball or bigger, with pink, leathery skin which conceals the treasure of translucent ruby seeds inside. The seeds of a ripe, sweet pomegranate, the 'eating' variety, are fruity and juicy but the pith surrounding the clusters of seeds is very bitter. The seeds and juice of sour pomegranates are sour, or sweet-sour, to taste.

Pomegranates, not yet fully ripened

BUYING AND STORING

In the Middle East, fresh pomegranates come into season in the autumn and last for a few months. Both sweet and sour varieties are sold in some Middle Eastern stores but most of the pomegranates available in the supermarkets are sweet and come from elsewhere, such as Spain. They don't have the same intensity of colour and taste. The dark pomegranate syrup or molasses (*pekmez* in Turkish, *dibs* in Arabic, *robb* in Farsi) is sold in jars in Middle Eastern and wholefood stores and keeps for months. If you want to make an authentic *fesenjân*, you will need to look for the tart, black *robb-e anâr* from Iran. The dried seeds can be found in some Middle Eastern stores.

MEDICINAL AND OTHER USES

The Prophet Muhammad commanded: 'Eat the pomegranate, for it purges the system of envy and hatred.' Certainly, the pomegranate is believed to cool and cleanse the system and aid digestion. Hippocrates recommended drinking pomegranate juice to reduce fever and, some time later, the dried skin and flowers were used as astringents. A Turkish pharmacist who died in 1417 recommended crushing sweet and sour pomegranate grains with sugar to reduce anxiety. At the beginning of the twentieth century, the bark and root of the pomegranate tree were ground to a powder and sold as a remedy against tapeworms. But the most ancient use of the pomegranate was as a natural dye, found in the leathery skin and bark, used to tan leather and to colour cotton and wool a reddish brown.

CULINARY USES

Fresh, ripe sweet pomegranates are generally eaten as a dessert fruit or squeezed for their refreshing juice to quench thirst in the middle of the day. The fresh seeds are used in a few salads and are often added to fruit compotes and sprinkled over puddings for colour and texture. The seeds taste so sweet and are so delightful to look at, they are sometimes sprinkled with rose water, decorated with blanched almonds and served chilled as a dessert. The juice of sour pomegranates was used liberally before lemons took over, but it is still used to add to marinades and soups, to make salad dressings and a tangy

Pomegranate leather

sorbet, and to make a tart, fruity sugar syrup which is the basis of a refreshing sherbet drink. The juice of both sweet and sour pomegranates is reduced to a thick, dark syrup or molasses, which is used in sweet and savoury dishes, such as soups and stews, and in *muhammara* (p136), a red pepper and walnut dip. Like all the other fruit molasses, it is also mixed with *tahini* to make a thick, sweet paste to eat with bread or to use as a dip. Sour pomegranate molasses is particularly important in the *fesanjân* dishes of Iran, as the syrupy sharpness combines with the ground walnuts to produce a magnificent sauce. Dried wild pomegranate seeds, with their tart flavours, are scattered over some *tahini* dishes and *hummus*.

The *fesenjân* dishes of Iran are unique with their rich, dark, textured sauces made of ground walnuts and tart pomegranate syrup. For an authentic taste, you really need to use the Iranian pomegranate syrup, *robb-e anâr*.

The most common *fesenjân* dishes are made with dark meat, such as wild duck and other game birds, but there are also *fesenjân* dishes made with meatballs, fish, and aubergines.

KHORESHT-E FESENJÂN
(DUCK WITH WALNUTS AND POMEGRANATE SYRUP)

Serves 2–3
Preparation time 25 minutes (+ 1–2 hours' simmering of stock)
Cooking time approximately 1 hour 20 minutes

1 wild duck, jointed into 6 pieces (keep the carcass for stock)

For the stock:
1 onion
A few celery leaves
A few peppercorns
Salt and freshly ground black pepper
175g (6oz) walnuts, ground or finely chopped
2–3 tablespoons olive oil
1 onion, chopped
3 tablespoons pomegranate syrup
2 tablespoons sugar or honey

Put the duck carcass and the onion, celery leaves, and few peppercorns into a pot. Cover with water and simmer for an hour or two to make a light stock. Then season with salt and strain it.

In a heavy-based pan, fry the walnuts in a little of the olive oil, until they begin to darken and give off a lovely, nutty aroma, then put them aside.

Fry the onion in the rest of the olive oil, until they begin to colour, then add the duck joints to the pan. Brown them on all sides, then turn off the heat and remove the skin from the joints.

Pour in enough of the stock (about 500ml/18fl oz) to just cover the duck, bring it to the boil, then cover the pan, reduce the heat and simmer for about 20 minutes.

Stir in the ground walnuts and continue to cook gently for a further 20 minutes.

Add the pomegranate syrup with the sugar, and cook for another 15–20 minutes, until the duck is tender. Season and serve with plain rice.

In Turkey and Iran, pomegranate seeds are often added to salads and fruit compotes for a light, refreshing bite. The following salad is from Iran, but variations of it, particularly with grated fresh coconut, are served with grilled meat, or as a *meze* dish, in Turkey.

KHIYAR-O ANÂR
(POMEGRANATE AND CUCUMBER SALAD)

Serves 4
Preparation time 20–25 minutes
Cooking time –

3–4 pomegranates
1 long cucumber
1 pink or white onion
Juice of 1 lemon
A small bunch of fresh mint, chopped, or 1 teaspoon dried mint
Salt and freshly ground black pepper

Split open the pomegranates and take out all the seeds. Remove any of the bitter membrane.

Peel the cucumber, cut it into quarters lengthways, then hold it together and slice it finely.

Cut the onion into quarters and slice it finely, so the pieces are much the same size as the cucumber.

Put the pomegranate seeds, cucumber and onion into a bowl, dress with the lemon juice and toss in the mint. Leave to sit for about half an hour, and season before serving.

Left: Pomegranate seeds
Right: *Khiyar-o anâr*

Currants

Dried green grapes

GRAPE

(EINAB) *Vitis vinifera*

The vine and its fruit have been celebrated in food and wine since ancient times. There are paintings of different vines on the walls of early Egyptian tombs, the Bible mentions cultivated vineyards from the time of Noah, who was reputed to have planted vines in the foothills of Mount Ararat when the Great Flood subsided, and the seafaring Phoenicians brought the vine to Greece. As the frontiers of the Roman Empire advanced, the cultivation of the vine spread; it also moved in the opposite direction to parts of India and China where the winters were cool. The Greeks, Romans and ancient Persians cultivated vines for the fresh fruit, for making wine, and for a variety of grape products, all of which are still in production in the Middle East today.

There are thousands of grape varieties but only a few of these are commercially important, mainly for wine, though some are grown specifically for currants, raisins and sultanas. Turkey still ranks as one of the leading table-grape producers in the world. Currants, raisins and sultanas are all forms of dried grape, most of which originally came from the Mediterranean, the Middle East (mainly Turkey), and western Asia (Afghanistan); the leading producer today is California. The leaves of the vine, poached and stuffed, are popular throughout the Middle East.

HOW IT GROWS

The original grapevine, *Vitis vinifera*, was indigenous from the south-east region of the Black Sea coast and the southern region of the Caspian Sea to Afghanistan, where it still grows. This vine, and its many cultivated successors, is a climbing plant that needs support and a cool winter but, like the olive and the almond, it can grow in conditions with poor soil and low rainfall. The vines that grow around Damascus are particularly famous.

APPEARANCE AND TASTE

The ripe, fresh eating grapes of the Middle East are usually round or oblong and vary in depth of colour from black through purple, pink, red and white to green and yellow. Whether they are as small as a berry or as large as a plum, fat

Sultanas

or thin, they are nearly all fleshy, juicy and sweet. The exception is the Iranian sour grape, which is really an immature green grape, valued for its tart flavour in summer stews. Fresh vine leaves picked in the early summer are quite tender but the later leaves can be large and tough, so they need to be blanched in boiling water before being used. Generally, they have a pleasing, almost malty taste. Raisins range in colour from pale or golden to dark brown, almost black, and some are sweet, others sour. The most popular raisins in the Middle East are seedless and well flavoured, dried from the yellow Thompson seedless grapes (also known as Oval Kishmish or Sultanina) and from the Smyrna Sultana, which is a pale yellow, seedless grape with a good flavour. Sultanas are usually larger than raisins, while the currants are so tiny they are called *kuş üzümü*, 'bird grape' in Turkish. Dried from the small, black Zante grape, currants are often quite hard when sold but plump up when soaked or cooked.

BUYING AND STORING

Fresh grapes of all kinds should be bought ripe, on the bunch, and eaten fairly quickly. The Iranian sour grapes are sold fresh and dried in some Iranian or Middle Eastern stores in the early summer. Outside the vine-growing regions, the leaves are

Large raisins

usually preserved in brine and sold in packets, tins, or jars which are available in a variety of Mediterranean and Middle Eastern stores, wholefood shops, and supermarkets. They will need to be rinsed well before use. Raisins, sultanas and currants, on the other hand, keep for a long time. If they have been semi-dried, they will still be quite moist, perfect for snacking on, but they are mainly sold for cooking and need to be poached or reconstituted in water to soften and plump them up. All of them keep well in an airtight container in a cool, dry place.

MANUFACTURING

A grape syrup or molasses (*dibs* in Arabic, *pekmez* in Turkish) is made by boiling up the juice extracted from the fresh fruit. It is sold in its refined form in jars throughout the Middle East and can be found in a crude, almost fermented form in villages. It is used as a sweetener for sweet and savoury dishes or mixed with *tahini* to spread on bread. Like apricots, carob, and mulberries, fresh grapes are also pressed, puréed and dried into leathers to chew or use in cooking. Verjuice, the juice of unripe grapes, is bottled and

Harvesting of grapes by Egyptian worker, Jordan Valley

used as a souring agent in cooking and dressings, just like vinegar. In some parts of the Middle East, grapes are grown for making a variety of red, white, and rosé wines, most of which remains in the country of origin, and some fairly refined vinegars are made from fermented wine. Fresh grapes, raisins and currants are also employed in the making of Turkish *raki*, which is a distilled alcoholic drink, flavoured with aniseed, that turns cloudy when water is added.

CULINARY USES

Generally bunches of fresh, ripe, sweet grapes are sold to be eaten as fruit. They are so sweet and delicious, there is little else you would want to do with them. In Iran, though, they are used to make the wonderful pickled delicacy, *torshi-ye angoor*, which consists of huge, sweet, fleshy white and black grapes, symbolising night and day, preserved in a syrupy vinegar to be consumed on *Shab-e Yaldâ*, the festival of the longest night. Also in Iran, the sour grapes, thinned from the crop of green grapes, are added to summer dishes, such as *khoresht-e-bâdenjân*, a delicious stew made with aubergines and lamb. Fresh vine leaves are often served with *tabbouleh* (p180), an Arab salad of bulgur and mint, or with a similar Turkish salad, *kısır*. The fresh or preserved leaves are usually stuffed with an aromatic rice mixture and served cold, or stuffed with a mixture of rice

and lamb and served hot. The tiny black currants are often added to stuffings, rice dishes, and *köfte*, Turkish meat- or fish balls. Generally sultanas, raisins, and currants are used quite liberally to give a burst of fruity sweetness to a number of meat, poultry, vegetable and rice dishes, as well as to numerous puddings. Sultanas, raisins, and currants are all included in the remarkable grain, pulse and dried-fruit pudding, *aşure*, otherwise known as 'Noah's pudding'.

Raisins

Preserved vine leaves

According to legend, when the Flood subsided, Noah gathered up all the stores of grains and dried fruit on the Ark and made this pudding. Traditionally, it is made in large quantities, offered to friends and neighbours, and eaten on the tenth day of *Muharram*, which is the first day of the Muslim calendar, to mark the martyrdom of the Prophet's grandson. It can be made with wheat or barley and requires a lot of advance preparation.

AŞURE
(NOAH'S PUDDING)

Serves 12 or more
Preparation time 24 hours
Cooking time approximately
 1 hour

*225g (8oz) whole barley, with
 husks removed, and soaked for
 24 hours in plenty of water*
*50g (2oz) haricot beans, soaked
 for 8 hours, or overnight, and
 cooked until tender*
*50g (2oz) skinned broad beans,
 soaked for 8 hours, or overnight,
 and cooked until tender*
*50g (2oz) chickpeas, soaked for 8
 hours, or overnight, and cooked
 until tender*
*50g (2oz) short-grain rice, washed
 and drained*
*110g (4oz) dried apricots, cut in
 half*
110g (4oz) sultanas
110g (4oz) raisins
50g (2oz) currants
450g (1lb) sugar
*2 tablespoons cornflour, mixed to
 a loose paste with a little water*
110ml (4fl oz) rose water

To garnish:
A handful dried figs, sliced
A handful dried apricots, sliced
*A handful sultanas, soaked in
 water*
A handful pine nuts
*Fresh seeds of half a
 pomegranate*

Aşure

In a large, deep pot, cook the barley in its soaking water, topping it up if necessary, until it is tender (about 45 minutes). Add the cooked beans, chickpeas, and the rice. Bring the liquid to the boil, then reduce the heat and simmer for 10–15 minutes.

Meanwhile, soak the dried fruit in boiling water for 5–10 minutes, drain and then add to the pot. Simmer the dried fruit with the barley and pulses for about 10 minutes, then gradually add the sugar, stirring all the time, until the mixture thickens.

Spoon a little of the hot liquid into the cornflour paste and tip it into the pot. Bring the liquid to the boil again, stir in the rose water, then reduce the heat and simmer for a further 10–15 minutes.

Tip the mixture into a large serving bowl, or spoon it into individual bowls, and leave to cool. Scatter the garnishing ingredients over the top and serve at room temperature.

Stuffed vine leaves are a classic delicacy. They are popular everywhere in the Middle East and, with the spread of the Ottoman Empire, they became widely known in the Balkans and in parts of North Africa. In Turkey cold vine leaves stuffed with aromatic rice are called *yalancı yaprak dolması*, meaning 'false' or 'lying', as they contain no meat. With their delicate spicy aroma, pierced by the sharp taste of lemon, these cold stuffed vine leaves are particularly exquisite. They can be made with fresh or preserved vine leaves and in Iraq they are often made with chard or spinach leaves.

WARA EINAB
(VINE LEAVES STUFFED WITH AROMATIC RICE AND HERBS)

Serves 6
Preparation time roughly 40
 minutes (+ 20 minutes' soaking
 of leaves)
Cooking time approximately
 1 hour

*Roughly 30 fresh or preserved vine
 leaves (and a few extra to line
 the pan)*
2 tablespoons olive oil
2 onions, finely chopped
2 cloves garlic, finely chopped
2–3 tablespoons pine nuts
1 teaspoon sugar
½ teaspoon ground cinnamon
½ teaspoon ground allspice
1 tablespoon dried mint
*225g (8oz) short-grain rice, well
 rinsed and drained*
*Salt and freshly ground black
 pepper*
*A small bunch fresh mint, dill, and
 parsley, finely chopped*

For the cooking liquid:
150ml (5fl oz) olive oil
150ml (5fl oz) water
Juice of 1 lemon
1 teaspoon sugar

If using fresh vine leaves, plunge them into boiling water to soften, then drain and refresh with cold water. If using preserved vine leaves, put them in a bowl and pour boiling water over them. Soak them for about 15 minutes, making sure the water gets in between the layers. Drain the leaves, then soak them in cold water, and drain again. This gets rid of the salt.

Heat the oil in a heavy-based pan and stir in the onions. When they have softened, add the garlic, pine nuts and sugar. Fry for a minute or two, until they begin to

colour, then stir in the spices and mint, followed by the rice and seasoning.

Pour in enough water to just cover the rice and bring to the boil. Reduce the heat and simmer for about 10 minutes, until the water has been absorbed – the rice should be soft on the outside but firm in the middle. Using a fork, carefully toss in the fresh herbs and leave to cool a little.

Place a vine leaf, vein side up, on a plate or board. Put a heaped teaspoon of the rice at the bottom of the leaf, near where the stem would have been, in the centre. Fold the stem edge over the filling to seal it in, then fold both of the side edges in towards the middle and roll the leaf up like a small fat cigar. Squeeze it lightly in the palm of your hand, to fix the shape, then repeat the process with the other leaves.

Line the bottom of a shallow pan with the extra vine leaves, then pack the stuffed leaves, side by side, on top. Mix together the ingredients for the cooking liquid and pour it over the stuffed leaves.

Place a plate on top of the leaves to prevent them from unravelling, then put the lid on and simmer gently for 1 hour, topping up the liquid if you need to. Leave the stuffed leaves to cool in the pan. Serve cold with wedges of lemon to squeeze over them.

PULSES, CEREALS & GRAINS

Chickpeas

CHICKPEAS

(HUMMUS) *Cicer arietinum*

Like lentils and beans, chickpeas are a staple of the Middle East, constantly referred to as 'the food of the poor'. They were first grown in the Levant and ancient Egypt, from where they spread throughout the Middle East and North Africa to India. Wherever the Arabs travelled, they took chickpeas with them, so they later became incorporated into the cuisine of places such as Sicily and Spain. The botanical name *arietinum* comes from the seeds, which are curled at the sides and look like a ram's (*aries* in Latin) skull. The Arabic word for chickpea is *hummus*, which is also the name given to the famous Middle Eastern dish of cooked chickpeas crushed with olive oil, *tahini*, lemon juice and garlic.

HOW THEY GROW

Chickpeas are cultivated all over the Middle East, particularly in Egypt, where they are a staple crop. The plants are small and bushy, bearing pods that contain two or three seeds. The harvested pods are dried and threshed to release the chickpeas, which are further dried in the sun to rid them of any moisture.

APPEARANCE AND TASTE

Dried chickpeas are small and hard, about the size of a pea, pale tan in colour, and wrinkled from drying in the sun. They have thick, fibrous skins which become apparent with soaking and cooking and are removed in cold water before the chickpeas are added to dishes. When cooked they have a slightly earthy taste with a meaty texture that is ideal for absorbing strong flavours. Roasted chickpeas look like hazelnuts and are eaten salted as a nibble, or they are coated in sugar and eaten like sweets. Fresh chickpeas, which have a lemony taste, are brilliant green and eaten raw or cooked at the beginning of the season in late spring.

BUYING AND STORING

Dried chickpeas are available in Middle Eastern and Asian stores, wholefood shops, and most big supermarkets. If stored in an airtight container, they will keep for a year or more. Cooked chickpeas, preserved in brine, are available in tins in the same places but, even after a lot of rinsing, they have a slightly salty, metallic taste and, as they have been cooked until they are soft, they don't really absorb the flavours of a dish.

CULINARY USES

Before being used, dried chickpeas must be soaked in plenty of water for at least 8 hours, during which time they will almost double in size. For all dishes, apart from *falafel*, they must be cooked in water for about an hour, until they are *al dente*. For purées, such as *hummus*, they need to be cooked a little longer, until they are soft. Once cooked and drained, they are put into a bowl of cold water so that the loose skins float to the top; the remaining skins have to be rubbed off with one's fingers. Chickpeas are used extensively in soups, rice dishes, and stews, such as *dfeena*, an Egyptian speciality consisting of beef, a calf's foot, eggs in their shells and haricot beans, as well as chickpeas. It is also a popular Sabbath meal in Jewish households. Chickpeas are tossed into hearty gypsy salads with onions, peppers, tomatoes and cheese. They are crushed and bound into *hummus*-style garlicky dips with olive oil and lemon – variations include *tahini*, yogurt, crushed nuts, tomato paste, the pounded flesh of smoked aubergines, and red pepper paste. Puréed chickpeas are sometimes bound with mashed potato to make the Armenian dish *topik*, which is an unusual parcel stuffed with currants, nuts and spices. You can roast your own cooked chickpeas by drying them on kitchen paper for about 1 hour, tossing them in a hot, oiled heavy-based pan until they are browned and crisp, then sprinkling them with salt.

Camels are still sometimes used to transport household goods and dried ingredients, including spices and pulses

Sicak humus

This recipe is a speciality from the east of Turkey, particularly popular with the people who live in the mountains, where the air is cold. It is served by itself or as part of a hot *meze* spread, with plenty of fresh bread to scoop it up.

SICAK HUMUS
(HOT CHICKPEA PURÉE)

Serves 4–6
Preparation time 10 minutes (if using an electric mixer) + 8 hours' soaking of the chickpeas and 1½ hours' cooking
Cooking time 25 minutes

450g (1lb) dried chickpeas, soaked, cooked, and drained with skins removed
Roughly 110–150ml (4–5fl oz) olive oil
Juice of 2 lemons
2–3 cloves garlic, crushed
1–2 teaspoons cumin seeds
2 tablespoons light or dark tahini
Roughly 425g (15oz) thick, strained yogurt
Salt and freshly ground black pepper

For the top:
2 tablespoons pine nuts
Roughly 40g (1½ oz) butter
1 teaspoon Middle Eastern red pepper (p152)

Preheat the oven to 200°C/400°F/gas mark 6.

Pounding the chickpeas by hand is laborious, so if you have an electric liquidiser or food processor, whiz all the *humus* ingredients together. Season well and spoon into an oven-proof dish.

In a flat heavy-based pan, roast the pine nuts until they are browned. Quickly add the butter and allow it to melt before stirring in the red pepper. Spoon the melted butter over the top of the *humus* and bake it in the oven for about 25 minutes, until it has risen slightly and most of the butter has been absorbed. Serve hot with lots of crusty or flat bread.

Also known as *ta'amia*, these spicy balls can be made with dried white broad beans or chickpeas, or both. In Egypt, where they are claimed as a national dish, they are usually made with broad beans, but in Syria, Lebanon and Jordan, *falafel* are commonly made with chickpeas. They are eaten for breakfast, lunch or as a snack, tucked into the pocket of pitta bread with pickles, *tahini*, yogurt, *hummus*, or *baba ghanoush* (p82).

FALAFEL
(SPICY CHICKPEA BALLS)

Serves 8–10 people
Preparation time 25 minutes + soaking time
Cooking time 5–10 minutes

225g (8oz) dried chickpeas, soaked for 24 hours
225g (8oz) dried white broad beans, soaked for 24 hours
Salt and freshly ground black pepper
1 teaspoon bicarbonate of soda
1 teaspoon ground coriander
2 teaspoons ground cumin
2 teaspoons ground or flaked Middle Eastern red pepper (p152)
1 large red onion, very finely chopped
5–6 cloves garlic, crushed
A bunch fresh flat-leaf parsley, finely chopped
A bunch fresh coriander, finely chopped
Sunflower oil for deep-frying

Rinse and drain the chickpeas and beans. Pat them dry with a clean tea towel, then grind them in a food processor until they form a fine paste. Season with salt and pepper, then add the bicarbonate of soda, coriander, cumin and the Middle Eastern red pepper. Grind the paste once more. Tip into a big bowl, add the rest of the ingredients, and knead thoroughly.

Take small lumps of the mixture in your hands, shape them into flat rounds about 5cm (2in) in diameter and 2cm (¾in) thick, and place them on a plate. In a wide pan, heat enough oil for deep-frying, then fry the *falafel* in batches until they are crisp and brown all over. Drain them on kitchen paper and serve hot, as above, or with lemon wedges to squeeze over them and a cucumber and tomato salad.

BROAD BEANS

(FUL) *Vicia faba*

Broad beans (or fava beans) are among the oldest food plants. They are legumes of such antiquity that there is an Arab saying, 'Beans have even satisfied the Pharaohs.' However, they were treated with suspicion in ancient times, associated with the dead and eaten at funeral feasts. Although broad beans have long been a part of the diet of the Middle East, they are by no means the only bean in culinary use. The black-eyed bean (*Vigna unguiculata*) and members of the haricot bean family (*Phaseolus vulgaris*), such as the fresh long green beans and the pinky-beige, speckled barlotti beans, are also prized. Like chickpeas and lentils, beans have traditionally been regarded as a staple food of the poor, but they are so versatile and tasty the rich have never been able to resist them, hence the Egyptian proverb, 'The man of good breeding eats beans and returns to his breeding.'

Fresh broad beans

Egyptian brown beans need a long soaking and long, slow simmering. Beans should only be seasoned with salt once they are cooked, otherwise they don't soften. They should be tender, not soft and squidgy, almost meaty in texture, each with its own distinctive character. And, no matter how you cook them, there is no escaping the fact that beans do cause a bit of wind.

BUYING AND STORING

The season of fresh broad beans is short – just a few months in the summer. They are best eaten fresh, for if they are stored for a few days, the sugars in the beans turn to carbohydrate which alters the taste and texture. Fresh barlotti and other haricot beans are also best eaten soon after picking. Dried beans, on the other hand, store for a long time. In the markets of the Middle East, the dried beans have been picked from the year's crop, which means they look appetising, require less soaking, and taste fresh once cooked. In the supermarkets, wholefood shops and Middle Eastern stores, all of which sell a wide range of dried beans, they might be as much as two or three years old, so they will need longer soaking and, once cooked, may be tough or taste a little woody. It's worth checking the expiry dates on the packets. Most beans are available in tins but, as with chickpeas, they are often too soft, even mushy, and taste of the tin.

Fresh barlotti beans

HOW THEY GROW

The primitive broad bean was small, similar to the horse bean, which is grown only as a fodder crop. Nowadays, a range of broad beans are grown, varying in size, shape and colour. They thrive in most climates and are harvested in the summer.

Dried broad beans

APPEARANCE AND TASTE

There are two types of broad bean in the Middle East: the large, fresh green bean, called *ful akhdar* in Arabic, which can be eaten fresh or dried (*ful nabed*), and the small brown bean, *ful baladi*, which is eaten only dried. The very young fresh broad beans are green and tender and can be eaten raw or cooked lightly with or without their pods. The more mature beans are shelled before they are cooked or dried. Dried broad beans are brown in colour unless they have been skinned and split, in which case they are pale green, cream or white. The small variety of broad bean, the Egyptian brown bean, is round and dusty brown in colour. Fresh beans are favoured in season, but the dried beans, which have greater nutritional qualities can be enjoyed all year round. All dried haricot beans and the white and brown broad beans require lengthy soaking. This can be reduced by first blanching the beans in boiling water for 2 minutes, then soaking them for 2 hours. They need to be covered with a lot of water as they swell and almost double in size. Cooking times differ from bean to bean – haricot beans may take 1–2 hours, black-eyed beans only half an hour, and the

Sacks of black-eyed beans

CULINARY USES

Like lentils and chickpeas, all beans are used extensively in traditional peasant soups and stews. Fresh green beans, or young broad beans in their pods, are generally cooked lightly in olive oil or added to summer vegetable stews, but dried beans are employed in a variety of exciting ways. There is a magnificent, nourishing soup called *âb gooshte fasl*, which comes from the Persian *âbgoosht*, a name given to lamb-based soups. It calls for beans and lentils, vegetables and dried fruit, spices and herbs, all cooked slowly in a large cauldron, enriched with the sheep's head and feet. Another Persian invention is *âsh-e nazri*, a huge, bean-filled soup served at prayer meetings. It is provided for, and made by, a community wishing for the recovery of a sick child, or the safe return of a loved one who has gone on a long journey.

Broad beans marry deliciously with olive oil, either on their own or with other ingredients like artichoke hearts and dill, and they are popular mashed or puréed, known as *besara* in Egypt (*fava* in Turkey) and served with olive oil as a *mezze* dish. They are often added to rice dishes and feature in *fistuqia*, a medieval dish in which the beans are cooked with rice and yogurt. Popular in Jewish communities is an unusual dish of ancient origin called *mefarka*, a combination of broad beans, minced beef, spices and thyme, all bound together by eggs gently stirred into the dish, which is then turned out onto a plate and served cold.

Perhaps the best known of all broad bean dishes is *ful medames*. Made with small brown beans, the dish is traditionally cooked in a pear-shaped, earthenware pot, called a *damassa*, which is buried in the ashes of a fire or set over glowing coals, and left to cook overnight. In Iraq, large brown beans are used in a dish called *badkila*, which is similar to *ful medames* and is often served in the street for breakfast

This is a great winter soup. In Iran it is served with bunches of fresh herbs, radishes and pickles to pass around. Traditionally, it is a soup served in the bazaars, late at night or early in the morning, complete with every Westerner's nightmare: sheep's head, feet and bobbing eyes.

ÂB GHOOSHTE FASL
(IRANIAN BEAN SOUP)

Serves 4–6
Preparation time 20 minutes (+ 6 hours' soaking of the beans)
Cooking time approximately 2 hours

75g (3oz) dried, skinned broad beans, soaked for 6 hours
50g (2oz) dried white haricot beans, soaked for 6 hours
50g (2oz) dried black-eyed beans, soaked for 2 hours
50g (2oz) yellow split peas
450g (1lb) lamb, cut into small pieces
1 onion, coarsely chopped
110g (4oz) dried prunes, with stones removed
4 tomatoes, skinned and chopped
3–4 potatoes, peeled and cut into large dice
1–2 teaspoons ground cinnamon
1 teaspoon ground coriander
1 teaspoon ground turmeric
Salt and freshly ground black pepper
A bunch of fresh parsley, chopped

Put the beans, split peas, lamb and onion into a deep saucepan and cover with about 1.8 litres (3 pints) of water. Bring the water to the boil, remove the scum, then cover and simmer for about an hour, until the beans are tender.

Add the prunes, tomatoes, spices and potatoes. Cook for another hour, until everything is tender; add the parsley and season to taste.

Egyptian brown beans

Although basically a peasant dish, this simple salad of brown beans has become an Egyptian national dish, claimed by the Christian Copts, who regard themselves as representatives of the ancient Pharaohs. Also popular in Syria, Lebanon and Jordan, it is eaten in the street and in the fields, in primitive homes and in luxurious mansions, in rural villages and in expensive restaurants. It is often sold in the street for breakfast, sometimes tucked into Arab flat bread with a *tahini* dressing and sliced

Ful medames

tomato and onion. Some cooks add red lentils, carrots or tomatoes for colour, *bastirma* (p198) is occasionally added for flavour, and it is commonly served with hard-boiled eggs, olives, pickles and lemon to squeeze over it, or lime in the Arabian Gulf. Traditionally, the plain, cooked beans are spooned into bowls and everyone helps themselves to olive oil, lemon, parsley, cumin and seasoning, whatever they feel like. For the purposes of this book, though, I have prepared them as a salad.

FUL MEDAMES
(EGYPTIAN BROAD BEAN SALAD)

Serves 4
Preparation time 8 hours' soaking of the beans
Cooking time 1½–2 hours

225g (8 oz) Egyptian brown beans, soaked for at least 8 hours, or overnight
2–3 tablespoons olive oil
Roughly 1 teaspoon cumin seeds
2 cloves garlic, crushed
Juice of 1 lemon
Salt and ground black pepper
A bunch fresh parsley, chopped

In a heavy-based pan, gently simmer the brown beans in plenty of water for about 1½ hours, or until they are tender but not too soft.

Drain them and, while they are still warm, toss them in the olive oil, cumin seeds and garlic. Add the lemon juice and season to taste.

Toss in the parsley, serve warm or cold, and pass around pickles, olives, and hard-boiled eggs.

LENTILS

(ADAS) *Lens culinaris*

First cultivated in Egypt, lentils are legumes of antiquity, their name derived from the Latin, *lentus*, meaning slow. Lentils have stirred up mixed emotions. The Egyptians believed they could enlighten the minds of children and make them cheerful. The Persians classified them as a 'cold' food, implying that they slowed the metabolism and had a calming effect. And the Romans maintained that lentils encouraged a mildness of character. One Roman general blamed his Persian defeat on lentils. His troops had been uncharacteristically slow-witted and sluggish because they had run out of their wheat supplies and had been forced to eat lentils. Along with beans and chickpeas, they have long been regarded as a food of the poor but they have also always been enjoyed by people of all classes.

Lentils, nuts and seeds displayed at a market stall

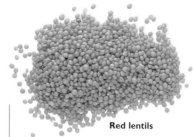

Red lentils

HOW THEY GROW

The *Lens culinaris* is an annual plant which grows to about 40cm (16in) in height, with short, broad seed pods each containing two seeds. Ranging in size from tiny to small, the husked and unhusked seeds vary in colour. Generally, they are dried before use.

APPEARANCE AND TASTE

The best-known lentils of the Middle East are the tiny red variety, sometimes known as Egyptian lentils. When the husks are removed, they are pinkish in colour. Also popular are the small pale yellow lentils, the bright orange ones, the brown ones, and the larger, matt-green ones. A little soaking in water helps to tenderise the lentils and shorten the cooking time, but the yellow, orange and red lentils rarely need this. All lentils need to be cooked in lots of fresh water, but their cooking time and texture vary according to the soil they have been grown in and how much time has passed since they have been dried. When cooked, lentils should have an earthy texture, a sprout-like taste, and a nice bite to them, unless they have been specifically cooked to a pulp. They are filling and nourishing for, apart from soya beans, they contain more protein than any other vegetable or pulse.

BUYING AND STORING

A number of Middle Eastern or Asian lentils are available in most supermarkets nowadays. Otherwise, they can be found in wholefood shops and Middle Eastern and Asian stores, where they are often sold in large quantities and need to be picked over for tiny stones and grit.

CULINARY USES

Popular and important for their nutritional value, lentils can be married with a variety of spices and ingredients to make filling, tasty dishes. They are cheap and frequently used in stews and soups, such as *shourba bilsen*, a thick lentil and coriander soup from Yemen, and in rice dishes such as the Iranian *addas polow*, made with green lentils, rice, sultanas, dates and crispy fried onions, served at *nazr* (thanksgiving ceremonies). Again in Iran, cooked lentils, lamb and fried aubergines are all pounded together to make a kind of porridge called *haleem bâdenjân*, which is blended with *kashk* (p125) and garnished with chopped walnuts and crispy fried onions.

A medieval Persian recipe, *shula kalambar*, calls for brown lentils to be cooked with spinach and spices, ingredients readily available in the street, and used to heal the sick. An unusual Arab dish, *majroush*, is made with rice, spices and yellow or brown lentils, which are pounded

Green lentils

Brown lentils

together to make a paste or dip for bread. A medieval Arab dish of the poor, called *mujaddara* (*mujadarra*), is popular today in every household. It consists of brown lentils and rice cooked together, sometimes flavoured with cumin, coriander, or mint, topped with browned and caramelised onions and served with yogurt. Similarly, the Lebanese make a simple green (sometimes brown) lentil and bulgur dish, called *imjadra*, which is topped with fried onions and melted butter and is served with yogurt.

In Turkey, the green lentils are cooked with carrots in one of the sumptuous olive oil dishes, *zeytinyağlı havuç*. The Egyptians also cook red lentils with onion and spices in a dish called *masafi*, which looks like an Indian dhal. This lentil dish, which is cooked until all the water has been absorbed and the lentils appear pulped, is used as a bed for meat and vegetable stews. Sautéed simply in clarified butter and spices, lentils are often served with *rishta* (p125) or meat dishes, which can be padded out to make something more substantial by frying peppers, aubergines, courgettes, carrots, or slices of *sujuk* (p166) or *basterma* (p198) with the lentils. And simple salads of lentils tossed in olive oil and lemon juice, often flavoured with garlic, cumin, parsley, mint or dill, padded out with chopped onions or tomatoes, and garnished with black olives, are served as *mezze*, or with meat dishes, such as kebabs.

This medieval dish is reputed to be a descendant of the 'mess of pottage' with which Jacob bought Esau's birthright and, among Christian communities, it has traditionally been served during Lent. The name *mujaddara* comes from the Arabic word for smallpox, as the dots of lentils in the rice resemble pockmarks on a face. Aside from its less-than-appetising name, it is a popular dish throughout the Arab world. In Egypt it is called *megadarra* and, in Lebanon, it is known as *mudardara*.

MUJADDARA
(LENTILS WITH RICE)

Serves 4–6
Preparation time 15 minutes
Cooking time 25–30 minutes

225g (8oz) brown lentils
Roughly 3–4 tablespoons olive oil
2 onions, finely chopped
1 teaspoon ground cumin
1 teaspoon ground coriander
225g (8oz) long-grain rice, well rinsed
Salt and freshly ground black pepper
A knob of butter
2 onions, cut in half and sliced

Put the lentils into a large pan. Cover with just enough water and boil them for about 15 minutes, until they are just tender, then drain and refresh them.

In the same pan, heat the olive oil and fry the chopped onions with the cumin and coriander until brown. Stir in the lentils and the rice, add the seasoning, and cover with just enough water.

Bring the water to the boil and simmer gently for about 15 minutes, until the rice has cooked and almost all the water has been absorbed.

Turn off the heat, cover the pan with a clean tea towel followed by the lid, and leave the rice and lentils to steam for a further 15 minutes.

Meanwhile, heat a little extra olive oil with a knob of butter in another pan and fry the sliced onions, until they are well browned and almost caramelised.

Tip the rice and lentils onto a serving dish and spoon the onions and oil over the top. Serve immediately with thick, creamy yogurt.

The mild *zeytinyağlı* vegetable dishes favoured by the Ottomans were designed to be cooked in lots of olive oil and served cold, so that the vegetables were beautifully tender and the flavoured oil could be fully appreciated. However, this dish defies the rule as it crops up in different parts of Turkey, Syria and Lebanon, served both hot and cold, sometimes spicy and accompanied by yogurt.

ZEYTİNYAĞLI HAVUÇ
(CARROTS AND GREEN LENTILS IN OLIVE OIL)

Serves 4
Preparation time 15 minutes (+ 1 hour's soaking)
Cooking time approximately 45 minutes

75g (3oz) large green lentils, soaked for 1 hour
4–5 tablespoons olive oil
1 onion, halved and sliced
2–3 cloves garlic, chopped
1 teaspoon coriander seeds
3–4 carrots, peeled and sliced
1 tablespoon tomato purée
1 teaspoon sugar
Roughly 225ml (8fl oz) water
Salt and freshly ground black pepper
A bunch fresh dill and mint, chopped
Wedges of lemon to serve

Drain the lentils and put them in a pan, covered with plenty of water. Boil them for about 15 minutes, until they are tender but not soft, then drain and refresh them.

In a wide pan, heat the oil and stir in the onion. When the onion begins to colour, stir in the garlic, coriander seeds, and the carrots. Cook for a few minutes, then add the lentils.

Stir in the tomato purée and sugar, followed by the water. Mix well and bring the liquid to the boil, then cover the pan and simmer gently for about 35 minutes, until the carrots are tender. Take the lid off, season to taste and continue to simmer for a further 10 minutes, until most of the liquid has gone.

Toss in most of the herbs and serve immediately with yogurt, or leave it to cool in the pan and garnish with the rest of the herbs. Serve with lemon to squeeze over it.

Yellow lentils

Zeytinyağlı havuç

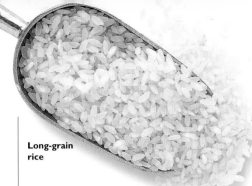

Long-grain rice

RICE

(ROZ) *Oryza sativa*

Rice was already established in northern India, China and South-East Asia by about 2000 BC, but it didn't make an impact in the Middle East until much later. The ancient Greeks and Romans imported rice, but it was expensive and mainly used for medicinal purposes. The Turkic tribes probably brought rice to Persia some two thousand years ago but it wasn't grown in Egypt until the sixth or seventh century AD. During the Ottoman times, there was such a demand for rice, it had to be imported. The long-grain variety came overland from India and, after the Ottoman conquest of Egypt in 1517, the short-grain was bought by sea from the Nile delta, making rice a luxury like sugar, which was also imported from Egypt. Rice was thus used sparingly, reserved mainly for extravagant feasts and wedding ceremonies.

In the Middle East today, rice is part of everyday fare in the cities but in most rural areas, apart from the rice-growing regions of southern Iraq, it is still used sparingly, bread and wheat being the cheaper staples. Light, nourishing, often elaborate, and cooked with pride, rice continues in its role as the food of feasts and hospitality. Cooked simply in clarified butter, it is reputed to have been a favourite dish of the Prophet Muhammad. The traditional method of cooking rice in the Middle East is called *pilaf* (or *pilau*), which originates from the medieval Persian word *pulaw* (*polow* in modern Iran). Descriptions of this technique first appeared in the Arabic books *Kitab al-Tabikh al-Baghdadi, Kitab al-Tabikh al-Warraq* and *Kitab al-Wulsa lla'L-Habib*, written in Baghdad and Syria in the thirteenth century. The Persians were particularly imaginative with their elegant and artistic pilafs bursting with colourful fruits such as sour cherries, barberries, mulberries, and pomegranates, recipes which still exist in modern Iran. When the Arabs conquered Persia, they adopted these creative pilafs and spread them throughout the region, so that variations crop up all over the Middle East, each with a national stamp.

HOW IT GROWS

Descended from a wild grass that probably originated in the Himalayas, cultivated rice gives higher and better yields than wheat or barley. In the Middle-East, the rice is mainly grown in shallow water, fed by rain or by drainage systems. Old methods of sowing the rice in nursery beds, transplanting plants by hand, and reaping with a sickle are still in use. In the rice-growing communities, the irrigated rice can be grown on the same land year after year, sometimes yielding two harvests annually. It grows mainly along the Caspian littoral in the north of Iran, in parts of Anatolia and Syria, in the southern marshlands of Iraq, and in Egypt.

APPEARANCE AND TASTE

Generally white rice is grown and used in the Middle East. Some grains are long and scented, others are short, stubby and starchy. The long, fragrant grains, used for pilafs, have a good flavour and texture when cooked, absorbing the flavours of the other ingredients. There are many different types, some requiring longer cooking, but all absorb the cooking liquid and expand greatly. The Arabic name for plainly cooked rice is *ruzz mufalfal*, meaning 'peppered rice', which doesn't imply that the rice is flavoured with pepper but that the cooked, plump grains should be separate like individual peppercorns. The short grains, used mainly for stuffings and puddings, have less flavour and are more

Short-grain rice

Harvesting rice, northern Iran

glutinous, but still retain a bite when cooked. Rice is also ground into a fine, white flour, which is particularly used for the traditional milk and rice puddings of the Middle East.

BUYING AND STORING

The harvested grain contains little moisture, which is further reduced by drying, so as long as it is stored in a cool, dry, dark place, rice can keep for anything between three and ten years. For savoury dishes, it is important to use a fragrant long-grain rice but, apart from the small quantities found in Middle Eastern stores, the rice from Iran, Turkey, Egypt and other countries is not exported. However, American long-grain and Basmati rice make excellent substitutes in most dishes. Sweet-rice dishes require a stubby, short-grain rice, for which a standard pudding rice can be substituted. Rice flour (not ground rice) is sold in Middle Eastern stores and wholefood shops.

CULINARY USES

In the Middle East, rice is not the main staple crop (wheat is) but it is the everyday food of the cities. It is the key element in a wide variety of dishes based on the traditional *pilaf* (*pilau*) – a method of cooking rice, often with other ingredients, with each grain remaining separate. Spices, nuts, dried fruit, meat and vegetables may be cooked or steamed with the rice, but plain rice (*ruzz mufalfal* in Arabic, *sade pilav* in Turkish, and *chelow* or *katteh* in Farsi) can also be cooked this way. Rice can be tinted gold with saffron, tinged pink with tomatoes, or scented with sweet fruit and spices. It is often served in a mound, as a meal in itself, or as an accompaniment to a dish. Some recipes call for it to be tipped out of the pan, upside down, in a layered mould, like in the Palestinian speciality, *makloub* (p131). A medieval speciality, called *seleq*, still popular in Saudi Arabia today, consists of rice cooked in milk until it resembles a soft cream; this is served as a bed for a whole roasted lamb or kid. Typical *pilafs* include lentils, broad beans, black-eyed beans, pine nuts, almonds, herbs and spices, chicken, noodles, aubergines, spinach, chickpeas and lamb.

A classic Persian speciality is the *khoresht*, a sour-tasting, thin vegetable or fruit stew, sometimes containing a little meat, which is served with, or spooned over, plain rice (*chelow*) as standard fare in every Iranian household. The Iranians also make a traditonal baked rice dish, *tahcheen*, which can be layered with meat or vegetables, with a yogurt-enhanced crusty bottom. Regarded as rather special, the *tahcheen* dishes are often served on festive occasions. Turkey is also known for its elaborate *pilafs*, such as *perdeli pilav*, which is often served at weddings and consists of chicken, carrots, almonds and currants cooked with rice and encased in a pastry dome. The Turks also cook a wide variety of ingredients with the rice, rather than adding them in afterwards, and they make a number of *pilafs* using fish, such as anchovies, and shellfish. In the Arabian Gulf, fish and shellfish are also added to the rice dishes called *birian*, which, with the use of turmeric, ginger, and curry powder, are more akin to an Indian *biryani*. The Turks, the Syrians, the Kurds and the Armenians all make *pilafs* with bulgur too, particularly in the countryside where wheat is the cheaper grain. And the Bedouin make a simple, tasty bulgur or rice dish combining dates and almonds.

Short-grain rice is often pounded with minced lamb or beef to make meatballs and it is employed in the famous *koofteh Tabrizi*, a mammoth stuffed meat dumpling from Tabriz and Azerbaijan. One of the principal uses of short-grain rice is in the stuffed dishes called *dolma* in Turkey, *dolmeh* in Iran, and *mahshi* in the Arab world, which are thought to have originated in Ottoman Turkey but are now

Using oxen to till a rice paddy, Turkey

popular throughout the Middle East. The rice is combined either with spices, herbs, currants and pine nuts, known as a 'false' filling, or with spices, minced meat and occasionally yellow split peas, and then used to stuff a variety of fruit and vegetables, such as aubergines, quince, apples, peppers, vine leaves, cabbage leaves, courgettes and their flowers, as well as whole lamb, kid, pigeons or poultry. Short-grain rice is also used to make the ever-popular sweet rice puddings which, at the time of the Romans, were only made to settle upset stomachs. The rice puddings of the Middle East, such as the Iranian *shollehzard*, are thick and creamy, usually flavoured with saffron, rose water or spices, and served chilled. Rice flour is used to give thickness and substance to the equally popular milk puddings, such as the traditional *muhallabia* (p187), the famous chicken breast pudding, *tavuk göğsu* (p62), from Ottoman Turkey, and the Iranian *fereni*, a delicate, rose-flavoured rice cream. In Syria and Lebanon, the birth of a son is traditionally celebrated with *meghlie* (p185),

a spicy pudding made with rice flour and flavoured with ginger, aniseed, cinnamon and fennel.

Methods of cooking rice

To make a perfect *pilaf*, the grains of rice are thoroughly washed, sometimes soaked, to remove the starch, then the rice is covered with just enough water (usually 1 cup of rice to 2 cups of water) and cooked in an open pot, until the grains are al dente and almost all the water has been absorbed. The pot is then covered with a clean cloth, followed by the lid, and the rice is left to steam for a further twenty minutes off the heat. In Iran, the rice is cooked and drained first, then butter, or a mixture of yogurt and beaten egg, is added to the pot. The drained rice is tipped over this, together with any additional flavourings, such as meat, fruit, or vegetables, covered, and left to steam over a low heat for about twenty minutes. The melted butter or yogurt at the bottom of the pot forms a golden brown crust, called *tahdeeg*, meaning 'bottom of the pot' which is a traditional feature of Persian rice and highly relished.

Rice flour

This rice dish from the Arabian Gulf can be made with mussels, scallops, or squid. In the style of an Indian *biryani*, it also has echoes of India in its use of spices: turmeric, ginger, fenugreek, and even curry powder. As the population of the Arabian Gulf is heavily expatriate, and the Gulf has a history of trade with India, the flavours of this dish are not surprising.

MAYGOO POLOW
(RICE WITH PRAWNS)

Serves 3–4
Preparation time 5–10 minutes
Cooking time approximately 30 minutes

225g (8oz) long-grain rice, well rinsed
Salt
1 tablespoon clarified butter (ghee)
1 onion, sliced
A knob of ginger, sliced into small, thin sticks
1 teaspoon turmeric
1 teaspoon ground fenugreek
1 teaspoon curry powder
225g (8oz) fresh prawns, shelled
A small bunch of fresh coriander, chopped

Put the rice into a pan and cover with just enough water. Sprinkle in a little salt and bring the water to the boil. Cook the rice for about 10 minutes, until it is tender but not fully cooked, with a bite to it, and the water has been absorbed.

In another pan, heat the clarified butter and stir in the onion.

Once it begins to colour, stir in the ginger, and cook for a minute or two, before stirring in the spices.

Quickly toss the prawns in the spices and tip the rice into the pan with a little extra salt. Reduce the heat to very low, cover the pan with a clean tea towel and the lid, and leave to steam for 10–15 minutes.

Toss in some fresh coriander and tip the rice onto a serving dish.

Literally translated as 'laid on the bottom', *tahcheen* is a classic Persian dish served on special occasions like weddings and festive days. Traditionally, the dish was made in a wide-bottomed pan which was placed in the hot coals of a baker's oven, where it would bake for many hours so that a thick, crusty layer formed on the bottom. Lamb or chicken can be used in this recipe.

TAHCHEEN
(IRANIAN BAKED RICE)

Serves 4–6
Preparation time approximately 30 minutes (+ 1 hour soaking the rice and 1 hour marinating the chicken)
Cooking time 30–40 minutes

2 pinches saffron fronds
A sprinkling of sugar
175g (6 fl oz) yogurt
2 eggs
1 onion, grated
Salt and freshly ground black pepper
1 small roasted chicken, the meat stripped off and cut into pieces
450g (1lb) long-grain rice, washed and soaked in salted water for about 1 hour
Roughly 100ml (3½fl oz) olive oil
Roughly 50g (2oz) butter, cut into pieces

Sacks of grains, pulses, dried fruit and spices in a open-air market, Turkey

Tahcheen

In a small bowl, grind the saffron with the sugar. Add a few drops of boiling water and mix well.

Mix the yogurt and egg together, beat in the grated onion and season with salt and pepper. Stir the saffron mixture into the yogurt, and marinade the chicken pieces in it for 1–2 hours.

Meanwhile, fill a large saucepan with water and bring it to the boil with a little salt. Toss in the drained rice and cook for about 5 minutes, until the grains are soft on the outside but firm in the middle. Drain and rinse under lukewarm water.

Remove the chicken from the marinade, then mix half of the cooked rice with the remaining yogurt mixture. Heat the oil in the bottom of a heavy-based pan and spread the rice and yogurt mixture across the base and up the sides. Lay the chicken on top, followed by the rest of the rice, or arrange the rice and chicken in alternate layers. Dot the butter on top.

Poke a few holes through the rice, then cover the pan with a clean tea towel and the lid. Keep it on a high heat for a minute or two, then reduce to the lowest heat level and leave the rice to steam for about 30 minutes. Alternatively, bake it in a low oven, about 160°C/325°F/gas mark 3 for 30–40 minutes.

Spoon the cooked rice onto a serving dish and arrange the chicken on it with thick wedges of crispy bottom. If you prefer, you can turn the pan upside down onto a serving dish to turn the rice out in a mound.

WHEAT

(QAMAH) *Triticum*

Dried whole wheat

The ancient civilisations of Mesopotamia, Syria, Palestine, and Asia Minor subsisted mainly on wheat and barley (*Hordeum vulgare*), making them the oldest cultivated cereals. First was barley, which up until classical times was the staple grain in the eastern Mediterranean region, including Egypt, where it was used to make a kind of porridge and bread, and was malted for beer. Gradually wheat took over, probably because the natural gluten found in wheat produces a better, lighter bread, but barley and millet remained the cheap staples for slaves and the poor. The ancient Egyptians were the first sophisticated bread-makers, using different kinds of wheat, but the Romans were the first to distinguish between 'hard' and 'soft' wheat – the 'hardness' indicating a higher proportion of gluten which gives bread a superior texture. The most important types of wheat cultivated today belong to the species *Triticum aestivum*, which is used for bread, and *Triticum durum*, which in its coarsely ground form is known as semolina. Finely ground, it is used for pasta. Traditional grinding stones, also known as saddle stones, depicted in ancient Egyptian paintings and on Assyrian reliefs, are still used in some villages but most of the wheat is ground into flour at mills or factories.

APPEARANCE AND TASTE

Once stripped of their bran coats, the dried wheat grains are tan-coloured and look a bit like large, fat grains of brown rice with a slit down one side. Whole immature wheat grains that are still green can also be eaten. Known as *freek*, they are usually roasted and then cooked like mature grains of wheat; they have a delicious smoky flavour.

Just after harvesting, some of the wheat is parboiled, drained, dried and rubbed to remove the bran, then crushed into coarse, medium, or fine grains, called *burghul* (bulgur). The colour of bulgur varies from light to dark brown to grey, and it resembles hard pellets. These have to be soaked in boiling water, or boiled, before eating. The resulting taste is distinctly nutty with a delightful springy texture.

The hard durum wheat is coarsely milled to produce the brittle grains of semolina which, when cooked, have a pleasantly light and grainy texture. Semolina can be further ground to a fine flour which is used for pasta, or it can be processed to make couscous, which is available in Lebanon, but is generally eaten in North Africa. The hard-wheat flours used for bread and pasta are usually white, with a superior taste and texture when they have been stone-ground.

HOW IT GROWS

Along with barley, wheat was probably cultivated around 6000 BC and, over the centuries, it has developed so much that it can adapt to most soils and climates. Like many other grasses and cereals, the wheat ear is formed like a tower with each storey containing two to five flowers, some of which develop into grains covered with bearded or beardless husks. To separate the grain from the husk and the ear, the harvested wheat is threshed, which is still done by traditional methods using oxen in some poorer parts of the Middle East.

Harvesting wheat in the plains of Anatolia, Turkey

BUYING AND STORING

Whole-wheat, semolina and good-quality, stone-ground, hard-wheat flours are available in wholefood stores and some supermarkets. Kept in airtight containers in a cool, dry place, they store quite well. Bulgur is becoming increasingly available in the same outlets, as well as in Middle Eastern stores. If well stored, it keeps for a long time. *Freek* is available only in Middle Eastern stores.

CULINARY USES

Wheat grains

Boiled wheat, or sometimes bulgur, is used in some festive sweet puddings in the Middle East, particularly amongst the Lebanese Maronites and the Sephardic Jews. The fragrant dish *belila* made with wheat or barley, is often served to celebrate happy occasions in Jordan, Lebanon and Syria, while the Sephardic Jews traditionally serve it to celebrate the cutting of a baby's first tooth. Another famous wheat pudding, also made with barley, is *aşure* (p109) which, in Muslim communities, is served to commemorate the martyrdom of the Prophet's grandson on the tenth day of *Muharram*, the first month of the Muslim calendar. It is also the dish that, according to legend, Noah prepared with all the provisons that were left on the ark when the flood subsided. Wheat or barley is traditionally used to make the ancient dish *harrisa* or *harriseh*, which is a porridge-like soup made with meat. It is particularly popular amongst the Kurds and Armenians, who eat it

Fine-grain bulgur

as a hearty winter breakfast and in Syria and Lebanon, it is made when a sheep is slaughtered for special occasions, such as Assumption Day among Christians. The same dish is known as *haleem* by the Iranians, who claim that it became the Prophet Muhammad's favourite dish when the Arabs conquered Persia.

Bulgur

Bulgur is usually served like rice with meat or vegetables in it. The Kurds often eat it cooked plain and served in a mound with the centre hollowed out, into which thick yogurt is spooned and melted clarified butter is poured over it. Bulgur is also used in some meatballs, particularly the traditional *kibbeh* of Lebanon and Syria, known as *kubba* in Iraq, which sometimes contain potatoes or pulses pounded with the bulgur instead of meat. And it is the basis of two distinct herb salads, the *tabbouleh* (p181) of the Arab world and North Africa, and *kısır* from southern Turkey. Generally, the coarse grade of bulgur is used for rice dishes, soups and stews, the medium grade is used in *kibbeh* and stuffings, as in the Egyptian dish of pigeons stuffed with bulgur and raisins, and the fine grade is used for salads.

Kishk

In the wheat-growing areas of Lebanon, Syria, Turkey, and Armenia, a preserved food is made of yogurt and bulgur, which is mixed together and spread out on a wide tray to dry for several days in the sun. As the bulgur soaks up the

moisture, the mixture is rubbed between the palms, daily, to break it up until it resembles tiny grains, which are then spread out on clean cloths to dry in the sun. Commonly known as *kishk* (*tarhana* in Turkish), these fermented, dried grains are used to flavour and thicken stews and soups, or to make a sort of porridge for breakfast. The word *kishk* originally comes from the Persian word *kashk*, which referred to cracked wheat or barley, but in modern Iran it refers to dried buttermilk which is formed into balls or crushed into a powder and used in much the same way as *kishk*. Two medieval culinary manuals, the Arab *Wulsa* and the Egyptian *Kanz*, refer to recipes using *kishk*.

Semolina

Semolina is used in the popular Syrian dish *ma'mounia*, which is like a sweet, cinnamon-flavoured porridge. It is also used in a variety of breads and cakes to give them a light texture, such as in the Turkish dessert *Revani*, a semolina cake soaked in syrup. And it is used in some traditional *halwa* or *helva* dishes, in which the semolina is cooked with butter and sugar and ingredients such as pine nuts, until the grains turn golden.

Flour

Wheat flour is the main flour used for risen loaves and flat breads but a few bread doughs are made with barley or maize. Similarly, wheat is used in all flat

Coarse bulgur

bread or pastry doughs employed in *sanbusak* (p141) or *börek*, and in the numerous sweet pastries. Wheat flour is also used to make the Middle Eastern pasta which has been in existence since ancient times. Medieval culinary manuals refer to fresh noodles as *lakhsha*, a Persian word, and to dry noodles as *itriyya*. By the thirteenth century, the word *lakhsha* was replaced by *rishta* (*reshteh* in Farsi) also a Persian

Semolina

word which is what the noodles are called today. Although cheap and simple to make, *rishta* is not considered a dish of the poor but, instead, is regarded as rather grand.

Also popular in parts of the Middle East is the Turkish pasta dish *mantı*, which is thought to have originated from the Chinese noodle dough, *mantu*, and travelled across Central Asia to Anatolia with the Turkic-speaking peoples. *Mantı* dough can be filled with meat, nuts or chickpeas, shaped like ravioli and boiled, or it can be filled and shaped into little open parcels and baked in stock in the oven. However it is cooked, *mantı* is always served with garlic-flavoured yogurt, often topped with melted butter, thyme and Middle Eastern red pepper (p152). Different types of pasta, such as the small teardrops used in some soups and rice dishes, are manufactured in Turkey and among the Jewish people, who are proud of their *calsones*, which are rather like cheese-filled ravioli.

Rishta noodles

The Lebanese and the Syrians both claim *kibbeh* as their national dish. Basically, *kibbeh* are meatballs or patties and, once again, each country in the Middle East has its own version. The following Lebanese recipe for bulgur and lamb *kibbeh* would take a long time to prepare if we used the traditional method of grinding everything by hand but with an electric mixer it doesn't take very long at all.

KIBBEH
(BULGUR AND LAMB PATTIES)

Serves 6
Preparation time 20–25 minutes + 20 minutes' soaking of bulgur
Cooking time 3–5 minutes

Muslim farmers, Yemen

225g (8oz) bulgur
450g (1lb) lean lamb, cut into small chunks
1 big onion, grated
1 teaspoon ground allspice
1 teaspoon Middle Eastern pepper (p152) or ground paprika
1–2 teaspoons salt
Sunflower oil for frying
A small bunch fresh flat-leaf parsley
Lemon wedges

Rinse the bulgur, put it into a bowl and cover with just enough boiling water. Leave it to soak for 20 minutes, then squeeze out any excess moisture and put it into a food processor. Blend it to a pasty mixture and pop it into a bowl.

Put the lamb into the food processor, blend it to a paste, and add it to the bulgur. Add the onion, spices and salt to the lamb and bulgur and, using your hands, knead them all together.

Divide the mixture into batches and blend each batch in the food processor. Knead it all together one more time, then shape the mixture into little balls (dip your hands in cold water from time to time as the mixture is sticky), and flatten each ball in the palm of your hand.

Heat some sunflower oil in a heavy-based frying pan and fry the *kibbeh* over a moderate heat until browned. Drain on kitchen paper and serve hot with fresh parsley and lemon to squeeze over them.

Puddings often play a significant role in the Middle East. They are not just delights for those with a sweet tooth, but are served to celebrate a birth or a marriage, to commemorate the death of a religious figure or to mark a religious event. In Syria and Lebanon *belila*, also known as *qamhiyya*, is traditionally made with young green wheat or barley, and is served at happy events such as the New Year. Often the cooked grains are bathed in syrup and served in individual bowls, allowing each person to sprinkle the nuts and cinnamon on top. This fragrant pudding is offered to nursing mothers as it is believed to enrich their milk and, in Sephardic communities, it is served to celebrate the cutting of a baby's first tooth.

BELILA
(WHOLE-WHEAT IN A FRAGRANT SYRUP WITH NUTS)

Serves 10–12
Preparation time 20 minutes (+ soaking overnight)
Cooking time approximately 1 hour

450g (1lb) whole-grain wheat, soaked overnight, drained and rinsed, with bits of husk removed
450g (1lb) sugar
Juice of ½ lemon
3 tablespoons rose water
110g (4oz) raisins, soaked in water for 20 minutes
2 teaspoons ground cinnamon
110g (4oz) pistachios, coarsely chopped
110g (4oz) blanched almonds, coarsely chopped

Put the wheat into a heavy-based pot with plenty of water. Bring to the boil, then reduce the heat and simmer for about 1 hour, or until the wheat grains become tender and burst open (add more water if necessary). Drain and tip the cooked grains into a serving bowl.

Put the sugar into a heavy-based pan with roughly 600ml (1 pint) of water. Bring to the boil, stirring all the time. Add the lemon juice and rose water, then reduce the heat and simmer for 10–15 minutes, until the syrup coats the back of the spoon. Stir in the raisins at the end.

Pour the hot syrup over the cooked wheat. Sprinkle the top with cinnamon and nuts, and serve hot or cold, spooned into individual bowls or cups.

Kibbeh

NUTS & SEEDS

CHESTNUT

(KASTANA') *Castanea sativa*

Whole chestnuts

The chestnut tree, often referred to as Spanish, is of west Asian origin. Around 300 BC, the Greek writer Xenophon described how Persian nobles gave their children chestnuts to eat to fatten them up. The best chestnuts are thought to have come from Sardis in Asia Minor, not far from modern-day Izmir in Turkey, and the Greeks took them from there to Europe. Wild chestnuts, which are slightly smaller than the cultivated variety, were often regarded as a staple for the poor. They contain more starch and less oil than other nuts and, therefore, provide nourishment during the winter, often used instead of potatoes. In the Mediterranean regions, where the chestnut trees grow, the shiny brown shells are split and the nuts are roasted over charcoal grills in the streets. The strong, flexible bark and branches of the chestnut tree are used to make orchard ladders and domestic tools.

Roasted chestnut seller, Istanbul, Turkey

CULINARY USES

Chestnuts mainly feature in the cooking of Turkey, Syria, Lebanon and the Palestinian territories. An old substitute for potatoes, chestnuts are sometimes cooked with lamb in a hearty stew. They feature in *makloub*, a stunning, moulded rice dish thought to be Palestinian. And they feature in a number of dishes from Istanbul and Bursa in Turkey, particularly in stuffed cabbage leaves, *lahana dolması*.

HOW IT GROWS

Like almond trees, chestnut trees grow in a temperate climate and are happiest in the Mediterranean region. They are medium-sized, hardy trees and live for a long, long time. Their fruit is round, green and spiky, with a leathery inner shell that preserves the vitamins in the kernel, which ripens in October and November. The best chestnuts grow around Bursa in Turkey.

APPEARANCE AND TASTE

Enclosed in hard, shiny brown shells, chestnuts are pale beige in colour. They are meaty nuts that dry well and can be preserved in syrup. Roasting brings out the best flavour, which is mild and distinct, with a slightly floury texture.

BUYING AND STORING

Fresh chestnuts are easily available in season. The shell should be hard and unbroken. In a cool, dry place, they keep for a few months. Dried chestnuts are available in some supermarkets and specialist shops and should be stored in an airtight container. The syrupy preserves, in the style of *marrons glacés*, are available in Middle Eastern and Mediterranean stores.

This is a winter dish from Bursa, the first seat of the Ottoman dynasty, which lies at the foot of the ancient Mount Olympus. The chestnuts from the surrounding groves are roasted over braziers in the streets, poached in syrup, or wrapped in cabbage leaves. Boiled fresh or dried chestnuts can be used, but the flavour and texture of roasted chestnuts are best. Occasionally the stuffed leaves are served hot with an egg and lemon sauce, but usually they are eaten cold with a *tahini* dressing, or simply with lemon to squeeze over them.

Dried chestnuts

LAHANA DOLMASI
(STUFFED CABBAGE LEAVES WITH CHESTNUTS)

Serves 4–5
Preparation time approximately 1 hour
Cooking time 25 minutes

1 green cabbage to give roughly 16–20 leaves
2 tablespoons olive oil
1 onion, finely chopped
1 teaspoon ground allspice
1 teaspoon ground cinnamon
75g (3oz) short-grain rice
Salt and freshly ground black pepper
225g (8oz) fresh chestnuts, roasted, shelled and chopped
A small bunch fresh dill and flat-leaf parsley, finely chopped
Juice of ½ lemon mixed with 1 tablespoon olive oil

Put the whole cabbage into a big pan of boiling water and cook until tender. Drain and refresh, then carefully tear off the leaves. Choose roughly 16 of the best inner leaves and cut out the base of the central vein.

Heat the oil in a pan and soften the onion. Stir in the spices and rice and pour in enough water to cover. Season with salt and pepper and bring the water to the boil. Reduce the heat and simmer until the liquid is absorbed. Gently toss in the chestnuts and herbs.

Place a cabbage leaf flat on a surface. Spoon some of the rice mixture just above the cut-away base, fold over the two sides to seal it in, then roll up the leaf from the base into a tight parcel, like a log. Repeat with the other leaves and pack them snugly into a shallow pan.

Add a little water to the lemon juice and olive oil and pour it over the stuffed leaves. Place a plate directly on top, then cover the pan and cook gently for about 25 minutes. Serve hot or cold with wedges of lemon.

In Arabic the word *makloub* (*maqlubi*) means 'turned over', which is exactly what this Palestinian dish is. Popular in Syria, Lebanon and Jordan, the rice is cooked on top of layers of vegetables and meat and then turned upside down, so that the meat or vegetables are on top. All kinds of vegetables are used, but an unusual version includes chestnuts.

MAKLOUB
(PALESTINIAN RICE WITH CHESTNUTS)

Serves 4–6
Preparation time approximately 50 minutes
Cooking time 40 minutes

225g (8oz) chestnuts
2 tablespoons clarified butter (ghee)
1 onion, chopped
225g (8oz) lamb, cut into small pieces
1 teaspoon baharat (p162)
600ml (1 pint) lamb or beef stock, or water
A little oil
450g (1lb) long-grain rice, soaked in boiling water for 10 minutes and drained

Cut one or two gashes in the chestnut shells and put them in a pan of boiling water. Reduce the heat and simmer for 20 minutes. Then drain the chestnuts, remove the shells and cut in half.

Meanwhile, in a heavy-based pan, melt the clarified butter and stir in the onion. When it begins to brown, add the meat and cook it until it begins to brown. Then stir in the spices, followed by the stock. Bring the liquid to the boil, reduce the heat and simmer for about 40 minutes, until the meat is tender. Drain the meat and add water to the stock to make it back up to 600ml (1 pint).

Brush a little oil on the base and sides of a heavy-based saucepan, preferably one with sloping sides. Arrange the meat on the bottom, followed by a layer of chestnuts.

Cover with the rice, spread evenly over the top, then carefully pour in the stock, taking care not to disturb the layers. Don't stir. Put the lid on and cook it gently for about 25 minutes, until the liquid has been absorbed. Turn off the heat, cover with a clean tea towel, followed by the lid and leave to steam for a further 15 minutes.

To serve, loosen the edges with a sharp knife, then place an inverted, flat serving dish over the top of the pan and, using both hands to grasp the pan and the dish firmly together, turn them upside down. Carefully lift the pan off, leaving the rice mould with the meat on top.

Makloub

HAZELNUT

(BUNDUK) *Corylus colurna*

Wild hazel trees were probably first brought from Asia Minor and cultivated in Europe. Pliny mentions that hazelnuts came from the Black Sea coast, where most hazelnuts are still grown. In fact, Turkey is the largest producer of hazelnuts. Hazel wood is believed to contain magical and medicinal qualities and the nuts contain so much protein, they are often mixed with almonds, raisins and cinnamon and given to children as a nutritious snack.

APPEARANCE AND TASTE

Ripe hazelnuts are round and beige in colour and encased in a hard, brown shell. Like almonds, they can be eaten when they are immature and juicy, and have a milky, sharp taste. Ripe hazelnuts are dried until they are firm and quite sweet. Roasting improves their flavour and texture.

Roasted, shelled hazelnuts

BUYING AND STORING

Hazelnuts are sold in and out of their shells, chopped or ground. Shelled hazelnuts are often sold with their brown skins on; if you roast or blanch the nuts, these will rub off easily. Hazelnuts still in their shells keep fresh for longer but the shelled nuts also keep surprisingly well.

CULINARY USES

Hazelnuts feature mainly in the dishes of Turkey and Egypt. Ground hazelnuts are used in biscuits and sweetmeats, such as *helva* (or *halva*). Roasted hazelnuts combine deliciously with chocolate and are used in a range of Turkish Delights. Hazelnuts are occasionally used in rice dishes but are more commonly used in salads and sweet pastries. They are also used to make a Black Sea version of *tarator* (p209), a sauce made with nuts, garlic, bread and lemon juice, and served to accompany fish and deep-fried shellfish in Turkey, Syria, Lebanon and Egypt. As the taste and texture of hazelnuts complement fish so well, they are often fried with onions and currants and served with fish, or they are combined with pine nuts, onions, tomatoes and parsley to make an Egyptian sauce served with fried fish, such as red mullet. Again in Egypt, hazelnuts are used in the homely sweet pastry, *om Ali*. Hazelnuts are also used in *dukkah* (p163), an Egyptian spice and nut mixture served with olive oil as a dip for bread.

Whole hazelnuts

HOW IT GROWS

Indigenous to Anatolia, hazelnuts grow profusely along the Black Sea coast where 300,000 tons are harvested a year. The fruits, which ripen from late August to October, are picked and laid out to form long hazelnut carpets by the roadside, at the edges of gardens, or in any available flat space, so that the husks split and fall off and the nuts dry in the sun.

Jars of mixed hazelnuts and pistachios in honey

This syrupy bread-and-nut pudding is a homely dish in Egypt. Some families make it with thin pancakes, others with thin pastry, but the most common is with flat bread. Sheets of *fila* toasted or fried work well in this pudding, which is usually made in individual bowls.

OM ALI
(EGYPTIAN BREAD PUDDING WITH NUTS)

Serves 6
Preparation time approximately 25 minutes
Cooking time 25 minutes

Roughly 6 sheets of fila
2–3 tablespoons clarified or ordinary butter
175g (6oz) hazelnuts, almonds and pistachios, chopped
110g (4oz) sultanas
1 litre (1¾ pints) milk
300ml (10fl oz) cream
110g (4oz) sugar
1–2 teaspoons ground cinnamon

Preheat the oven to 230°C/450°F/gas mark 8.

If you prefer to toast the *fila*, pop the sheets in a slow oven for about 15 minutes, until they are crisp and brown, then crumble them. Otherwise melt the butter in a wide pan, tear the *fila* into pieces and fry them in the butter until they are crisp and brown.

Arrange the crispy *fila*, layered with the nuts and sultanas, in individual oven-proof bowls, or in a big oven-proof dish.

In a heavy-based pan, bring the milk, cream and sugar to the boil, stirring all the time. Keep boiling for a few minutes, then pour it over the layered *fila*. Pop the dishes, or dish, into the oven and bake for about 25 minutes, until the top is browned. Sprinkle the top with ground cinnamon and serve hot.

Taratorlu kabak

Steamed or fried vegetables in a crushed nut and garlic sauce, *tarator*, are popular in most regions of the Middle East. I particularly like the following Turkish *meze* recipe as the combination is light and fruity. The courgette and apple can be deep-fried or steamed.

TARATORLU KABAK
(COURGETTE AND APPLE IN A HAZELNUT AND GARLIC SAUCE)

Serves 3–4
Preparation time 20 minutes
Cooking time –

2 courgettes, partially peeled and sliced
1 apple, quartered, cored and sliced
Sunflower oil (optional)
50g (2oz) hazelnuts
2 cloves garlic
2 tablespoons olive oil
Juice of 1 lemon
2 tablespoons creamy yogurt
A small bunch flat-leaf parsley
Salt and freshly ground black pepper
A handful roasted hazelnuts, roughly chopped

Steam the courgettes with the apple for about 5 minutes, until tender, and then refresh them under cold running water. Or deep-fry them in sunflower oil, until golden.

Using a pestle and mortar, pound the hazelnuts with the garlic and bind with the olive oil and lemon juice. Beat in the yogurt and parsley and season to taste.

Arrange the courgette and apple mixture on a plate, spoon the sauce over the top and garnish with the roasted hazelnuts.

Whole dried
sunflower seeds
in their husks

SUNFLOWER SEED

(BISRA ABBAD AL-SHAMS) *Helianthus annuus*

Husked
sunflower seeds

Native to North America, sunflowers probably came to Turkey, via Spain, in the sixteenth century, along with tomatoes, peppers and corn, articles of trade with the New World. Apart from the ornamental uses of its spectacular head, it is the seeds of the sunflower that are in demand for culinary purposes. It is often thought that the flower got its name from its resemblance to the sun, but it could also have acquired the name from its ability to turn its handsome head towards the sun, so that it faces east at sunrise and west at sunset.

Sunflower seeds for sale, Iraq

HOW IT GROWS

Sunflowers grow in sunny temperate climates and can reach up to 3.6m (12ft) in height. One flower head can contain hundreds, sometimes thousands, of seeds. Sunflowers grow wild in the Mediterranean regions of the Middle East, and they are cultivated in Turkey for the seeds and oil. At harvest time the edges of country roads are strewn with the drying heads.

APPEARANCE AND TASTE

The seeds are flat and grey with a pleasant taste and a bite to them. The dried pods, which are long and black, are edible, but they are quite fibrous and chewy. As with most nuts and seeds, flavour improves with roasting.

BUYING AND STORING

The dried seeds are sold both in their pods and out, plain or roasted. They keep well in an airtight container.

MANUFACTURING

In Turkey the seeds are pressed to make a light, general-purpose cooking oil, high in polyunsaturates and without cholesterol. Tasteless, it is mainly used for frying or for salad dressings in areas where olive oil is unavailable or too expensive.

CULINARY USES

Roasted and salted, sunflower seeds are often sold to nibble on. Children love them and buy bags of them on their way home from school. They are often added to a mixture of nuts and spices or served with a glass of *rakı* (p184). They can also be added to salads, sprinkled on breads and used in some rice dishes. But the main role of sunflower seeds is in the light oil.

The following Turkish recipe is popular in the summer months, when fish is usually cooked on the outdoor grill. Surplus catch, or leftover cooked fish, will be deftly turned into aromatic or spicy balls, served with a fresh seasonal salad and rice.

BALIK KÖFTESİ
(FISH BALLS WITH CURRANTS AND SUNFLOWER SEEDS)

Serves 4–6
Preparation time approximately 30 minutes
Cooking time 10 minutes

450g (1lb) fresh fish fillets, trimmed, with bones removed
2 slices day-old bread, soaked in a little water and squeezed out
1 red onion, finely chopped
2 cloves garlic, crushed or finely chopped
2 tablespoons sunflower seeds
2 tablespoons currants, soaked in water for 15 minutes and drained
2 teaspoons tomato paste
1–2 teaspoons ground cinnamon
A bunch fresh parsley and dill, finely chopped
1 egg
Salt and freshly ground black pepper
A little plain flour for coating
Sunflower oil for frying
A lemon, cut into wedges

In a bowl, break up the fish with a fork. Add all the other ingredients and knead well with your hands. Form the mixture into balls, flatten them a little and lightly coat them in flour.

Heat up some sunflower oil in a pan and fry the fish balls over a gentle heat until they are cooked through and golden brown all over. Drain on kitchen towel and serve hot with lemon to squeeze over them.

Tahinli karnabahar salatası

Dishes that are referred to as salads in the Middle East often form part of the *mezze* spread but, increasingly, in the big cosmopolitan cities like Istanbul and Damascus, salads like this one are served as a side dish, or as the main dish for wealthy, lunching ladies. Similar salads are made with carrots, cabbage, leeks and onions. Roast the sunflower seeds in a heavy-based pan, until they brown and give off a nutty aroma.

TAHİNLİ KARNABAHAR SALATASI
(CAULIFLOWER WITH SUNFLOWER SEEDS IN A SESAME DRESSING)

Serves 3–4
Preparation time roughly 20 minutes
Cooking time –

1 small cauliflower, washed and broken into small florets
1 apple, peeled and diced
A bunch of fresh parsley, mint and coriander, chopped
2–3 tablespoons roasted sunflower seeds
1–2 tablespoons light tahini
Juice of ½ lemon
1–2 cloves garlic, crushed
Salt and freshly ground black pepper

Put the cauliflower, apple, fresh herbs and roasted sunflower seeds into a bowl.

In a small bowl, mix together the *tahini*, lemon juice and garlic with a little water, until it is the consistency of double cream. Season the dressing and pour over the salad.

Toss well and garnish with some extra roasted sunflower seeds.

Whole walnuts

WALNUT

(JAWZ) *Juglans regia*

Walnut trees have grown wild across Asia since prehistoric times and walnuts have long been regarded as the king of nuts. Their Latin name means 'Jupiter's acorn', in accordance with the ancient myth that the gods ate walnuts while men lived on acorns. The walnut tree was so highly regarded by the ancient Persians that the nuts were reserved solely for the king. And when the Persian king sent some walnut trees to the king of Greece, he too made sure that he was the only one to enjoy them.

HOW IT GROWS

Walnut trees generally grow in temperate climates. The most important species is the Persian walnut, which grows wild right across Asia but is also cultivated for its superior nuts. These trees bear green fruit with flesh surrounding a hard-shelled stone which holds the edible kernel. When it is immature and green, the entire fruit can be eaten or pickled, but as the fruit ripens, the fleshy part becomes leathery.

APPEARANCE AND TASTE

Walnut shells appear like two half-shells seamed together. They open in two halves, each one containing a half-kernel which looks a bit like a diagram of a brain. In fact, in Afghanistan, walnuts are called *charmarghz*, which means 'four brains'. The green, unripe fruit are very sour but the half-ripe nuts can be preserved in syrup. Ripe walnuts are quite oily with a strong, slightly bitter, woody taste.

BUYING AND STORING

Ripe walnuts are sometimes sold in their shells but usually they are sold shelled, in half-kernels or broken pieces. As with all nuts, walnuts in their shells store well for several months.

MANUFACTURING

Walnuts are pressed for their pungent, topaz-coloured oil. Walnut juice is used as a dark brown dye.

CULINARY USES

Walnuts are used in a variety of syrupy puddings and pastries, such as *kalburabastı*, a Turkish dish of walnut sponges soaked in syrup, and the much-loved *baklava*. It is the nut used in the Persian *fesenjân* (p104) dishes that combine crushed walnuts with tart pomegranate syrup in a sauce for duck, fish and aubergines. It is the principal flavouring and texture in *çerkez tavuğu* (p62), the delightful Circassian dish of walnuts and chicken. Walnuts are also used in savoury pastries such as the spinach pies, *fatayer bi sabanikh*, and they are pounded with red peppers in the delicious *mezze* dish *muhammara*. Crushed with garlic, bread and olive oil, walnuts are used to make a strong-tasting version of the popular sauce *tarator* (p209), which is served with fish and shellfish, such as *midye tavası*. In Istanbul, the traditional *tarator* is always made with walnuts. Chopped walnuts are stuffed into figs and baked in honey, or

Shelled walnuts

they are stuffed into tiny aubergines and pickled, and they are used in numerous spicy fruit and nut fillings for poultry and fish, particularly in the famous Turkish mackerel dish, *uskumru dolması*. Green walnuts are preserved in syrup.

This vividly flavoured and textured *mezze* dip is particularly popular in Aleppo in Syria and in Gaziantep in Turkey, the two places famous for their hot red peppers. Some variations of *muhammara* include *tahini* or white cheese.

MUHAMMARA
(RED PEPPER AND WALNUT DIP)

Serves 4
Preparation time 25–30 minutes
Cooking time –

2 red bell peppers, grilled over charcoal or roasted in the oven, with skin and seeds removed
110g (4oz) walnuts, coarsely ground
2–3 cloves garlic, crushed
1 teaspoon flaked Middle Eastern red pepper (p152), or 1 chilli, finely chopped
Juice of ½ a lemon
2 tablespoons olive oil
110g (4oz) yogurt cheese (yogurt strained overnight)
Salt and freshly ground black pepper

Remove the skin and seeds of the peppers and chop to a pulp. Using a big pestle and mortar, pound the peppers, walnuts and garlic together to make a textured paste. Beat in the

Middle Eastern red pepper, olive oil and lemon juice. Then beat in the yogurt cheese until thoroughly blended and season it to taste.

Spoon the mixture into a serving bowl and drizzle a little olive oil over the top to keep it moist. Garnish with a few extra walnuts, fresh mint, or black olives. Serve with flat breads to scoop it up.

A legacy of the Ottoman Empire, *baklava* is arguably the grandest of the Middle Eastern syrupy pastries. Certainly, it is the best known and the most misunderstood. The magnificent creation of the pastry chefs in the Topkapı Palace, the classic *baklava* was made with eight layers of a special pastry dough, using clarified butter and seven layers of nuts. In the Middle East, *baklava* is generally associated with celebrations, such as births, weddings, festivals, the Jewish *Bar Mitzvah* and *Ramadan* for the Muslims. As vast quantities are consumed, most people buy their *baklava* from the specialist pastry shops, where they will be enticed by other syrupy pastries too. However, if you use sheets of *fila*, a straightforward *baklava* is easy to prepare at home. Once again, pistachios are often regarded as the most prestigious filling, but walnuts are traditional.

BAKLAVA
(LAYERED PASTRY WITH WALNUTS AND SYRUP)

Serves 8–12
Preparation time 30 minutes
Cooking time approximately 1 hour

175g (6oz) clarified or ordinary
* butter*
100ml (3½ fl oz) sunflower oil
450g (1lb) fila

450g (1lb) walnuts, finely chopped
1 teaspoon ground cinnamon

For the syrup:
450g (1lb) sugar
250ml (9fl oz) water
Juice of ½ lemon, or 2 tablespoons
* rose water*

Preheat the oven to 160°C/325°F/gas mark 3.

Melt the butter with the oil in a pan and brush a little of it on the base and sides of a 30cm (12in) baking tin. Place a sheet of *fila* in the bottom and brush with the melted butter and oil. Do the same with half the quantity of *fila* sheets, easing them into the corners and trimming the edges if they flop over the rim.

Spread the chopped walnuts over the top sheet and, if you like, sprinkle with cinnamon. Continue with the *fila* sheets, brushing each layer with the melted butter and oil. Brush the top and, with a sharp-pointed knife, cut parallel lines right through all the layers to the bottom, making small diamond shapes. Then pop it in the oven for about 1 hour. If the top is not golden brown at the end of the hour, turn the oven up to 200°C/400°F/gas mark 6 for a few minutes.

Meanwhile, make the syrup. Put the sugar and water into a pan and bring to the boil, stirring all the time. Stir in the lemon juice, reduce the heat and simmer for 10–15 minutes – if using rose water, add it at this stage. Leave the syrup to cool.

Take the golden *baklava* out of the oven and pour the cold syrup over the hot pastry. You can zap it back into the oven for 5 minutes if you like, to help the pastry absorb the syrup, or just let it cool. Once cooled, lift the diamond-shaped pieces out of the tin and arrange on a serving dish.

Baklava

POPPY SEED

(KASHAKISH) *Papaver somniferum*

An Arab resting in the desert, title-page from *The Valley of the Nile*

The poppy was valued by the ancient Egyptians and the ancient Greeks, who grew it for opium to use as a painkiller and sleeping draught, hence its botanical name, meaning 'sleep-bearing'. Opium is derived from the alkaloids in the sap of the unripe seed pods, which also produce the medicinal derivatives morphine and codeine. With such addictive properties, the poppy was much in demand and cultivation spread to parts of Arabia and Persia, India and China. Opium-smoking, which first became fashionable in the nineteenth century, has led to bans on poppy cultivation without a permit in most countries. The east of Turkey is famed for its dark, almost black, honey made from pollen of the opium poppy. Fiery, with hallucinatory properties, it is aptly called *deli bal*, meaning 'crazy honey'.

Poppy seeds

HOW IT GROWS

Related to the wild poppies that grow all over the eastern Mediterranean, the opium poppy is cultivated in Turkey and Iran. It is an annual plant with quite thick, hairy stems, large, frilly leaves and splendid pink, white or lilac flowers. When the flowers die, they leave behind oval seed pods, which are dried and then split to release the tiny seeds.

APPEARANCE AND TASTE

The tiny seeds, which are not narcotic when ripe, are usually slate-blue or camel-brown in colour; there is also a beige variety from India. They have a crunchy texture and a mild, nutty flavour which is enhanced when they are roasted.

BUYING AND STORING

The seeds are always sold whole. Like other spices, they can be ground at home. They store well in airtight containers kept in a cool, dry place.

CULINARY USES

The seeds and leaves of the opium poppy are edible. In the Middle East, the seeds are occasionally pressed to extract a pleasantly flavoured oil, or are ground with the oil and used as a paste in some dishes. Usually, though, they are used whole, sprinkled liberally over breads and biscuits and added to pickles, salads or egg dishes for a delightful crunch. In Jewish communities poppy seeds are sprinkled over the braided egg dough *Hallah*, the Sabbath and holiday bread, as the seeds represent the manna that fell from heaven. Also in Jewish communities, poppy seeds are added to the cakes and biscuit doughs made for festival of *Purim*. In Egypt and other parts of North Africa, the sweet couscous dishes, which the Jews serve at *Hanukah*, sometimes contain poppy seeds. Believed to give strength, poppy seeds are occasionally added to honey doughs and syrups in Egypt and Yemen, and the roasted seeds are ground into some spice mixtures, particularly in Armenian communities.

Poppy seedheads

Poppy seed cakes, biscuits and pastries are specialities of the Jewish festival *Purim*, a day of jubilation commemorating Queen Esther, a Jewess who was married to a Persian king, and her outwitting of the Persian vizier Haman, who had decreed all Jews should be sentenced to death. As Queen Esther was said to have broken her three-day fast by eating poppy seeds after praying for the decree to be repealed, they have become symbolic. These little semolina cakes, which are popular in Egypt, Lebanon, Jordan, and not just amongst the Jewish communities, can be made with almonds, coconut and poppy seeds.

BASBOUSA
(SEMOLINA CAKES WITH POPPY SEEDS)

Serves 6–8
Preparation time approximately 30 minutes
Cooking time 35 minutes

110g (4oz) clarified or ordinary butter
175g (6oz) sugar
2 tablespoons poppy seeds
1 teaspoon vanilla essence
2 eggs
450g (1lb) fine semolina
1 teaspoon baking powder
½ teaspoon bicarbonate of soda
175g (6oz) strained yogurt
12 almonds, blanched and halved

For the syrup:
225ml (8fl oz) water
450g (1lb) sugar
Juice of ½ lemon

Preheat the oven to 190°C/ 375°F/gas mark 5.

First make the syrup. Bring the water and sugar to the boil, stirring all the time. Add the lemon juice and continue to boil for a few minutes, then reduce the heat and simmer for about 10 minutes, until the syrup coats the back of the spoon. Leave the syrup to cool

In a bowl, cream the butter with the sugar until light and fluffy. Beat in the poppy seeds and vanilla essence, then beat in the eggs, one at a time. Sift the semolina with the baking powder and bicarbonate of soda onto a plate, then fold it into the creamed butter with the yogurt. Tip the batter into a greased rectangular baking tin, roughly 20 x 30cm (8 x 12in), and spread it evenly. Arrange the almond halves in lines over the top, so that a nut will be in the centre of each piece when the cake is cut.

Bake it in the oven for 30 minutes, or until a skewer inserted into the cake comes out clean. Quickly pour the cold syrup over the hot cake, cut it into lozenge shapes and return it to the oven for 4–5 minutes. Serve warm or at room temperature with *eishta*, the thick cream made from buffalo milk, or clotted cream.

The pickles of Iran are both exotic and exciting, full of fruits, spices and seeds. These persimmon pickles are particularly delicious, reflecting some of the key flavours and textures of the Middle East.

TORSHI KHRAMLU
(PERSIMMON PICKLES)

Makes 2 big jars
Preparation time 30 minutes
Cooking time –

2 dried limes
3 teaspoons white mustard seeds
3 teaspoons roasted coriander seeds
3 teaspoons roasted poppy seeds
2 teaspoons black peppercorns
1 teaspoon cardamom seeds
4–6 cloves
1 teaspoon ground cinnamon
900g (2lb) ripe persimmons, cored and cut into wedges
8–10 cloves garlic, peeled
12 fresh or dried dates, pitted and halved
850ml (1½ pints) white wine vinegar
2 teaspoons salt
50g (2oz) sugar

Break the dried limes into pieces. Mix the spices together with the ground cinnamon.

Place some of the persimmon pieces in a sterilised jar with some of the lime, spices, garlic and dates. Repeat in layers.

Put the vinegar, salt and sugar in a pan and bring to the boil, stirring until the sugar is dissolved. Pour the hot vinegar over the persimmons, leave to cool and then seal the jars. Store for a couple of weeks before eating.

Basbousa

PINE NUT

(SNUBAR) *Pinus pinea*

The use of pine nuts in the Middle East goes back to ancient times, when they were included in the cornucopias of fruit placed on statues that had been erected to symbolise the wealth of a city. The medieval Arabs used them liberally in savoury dishes and confectionery, and the Ottomans acquired a taste for them in many of their lavish dishes. Today, they are one of the most widely used nuts in Middle Eastern cooking, found concealed in almost every stuffing and scattered over numerous dishes.

HOW IT GROWS

The pine nut comes from the woody cones of the umbrella-shaped stone pine, *Pinus pinea*, which grows at low altitudes and in relatively poor soil around the Mediterranean coastline. Some cones open at maturity, others remain closed for several seasons. Just as the heat of a forest fire will open the cones like an exploding grenade, heat is used to prise them open commercially.

Roasted pine nuts

APPEARANCE AND TASTE

Pine nuts are the small, edible seeds of a range of pine trees. Most of them are ivory in colour and shaped like long teardrops. They are creamy in texture with a sweet, pleasant taste of pine resin.

BUYING AND STORING

Good pine nuts are the second most expensive nut after macadamias. They are sold shelled and keep well in an airtight container for a month or two. If they are stored for too long, they go soft and rancid owing to their high oil content.

CULINARY USES

In the Middle East, pine nuts are used in puddings, fruit compotes, jams and sweetmeats such as the Turkish *un helvası*, prepared for births and weddings. They frequently pop up in rice dishes, and there is practically no aromatic rice filling or minced lamb stuffing for poultry, vegetables, and pastries such as *sanbusak* that doesn't include pine nuts. They are also added to some meat, fish or vegetable balls. Lightly roasted, they are a popular finish to many dishes, particularly sprinkled over syrupy pastries and cakes. Ground pine nuts are used in a very smooth, sumptuous version of the popular *tarator* (p209) sauce served with fish and shellfish, particularly in Turkey, Lebanon, Syria and Egypt.

Helva or *halva* made at home is quite different from the hard, manufactured blocks made with sesame seeds. It should be quite light and soft, able to be eaten with a fork. This recipe is for a popular Turkish *helva*, served at happy events such as a wedding or the birth of a child.

UN HELVASI
(FESTIVE HELVA WITH PINE NUTS)

Serves 8
Preparation time –
Cooking time approximately 50 minutes

175g (6oz) butter
175g (6oz) plain flour, sieved
1 tablespoon sunflower oil
50g (2oz) pine nuts
600ml (1 pint) milk
225g (8oz) sugar
150ml (5fl oz) water
Icing sugar for sprinkling

Melt the butter in a large, heavy-based pan. Stir in the flour to form a thick roux and cook it for a few minutes, until it begins to change colour.

Stir in the sunflower oil and continue to cook until the roux turns camel-brown and comes away from the sides of the pan. Then add the pine nuts and cook until they turn golden.

At the same time, keeping an eye on the roux, heat the milk and sugar up in another saucepan and bring to the boil, stirring all the time. Then reduce the heat and simmer for about 10 minutes, until the syrup coats the back of the spoon.

For the next stage, which requires some fast work, use oven gloves to protect your hands against the steam. Quickly pour the water into the roux and stir madly, then pour in the hot milk syrup and stir equally madly, pressing the doughy balls against the side of the pan until the mixture binds together in a thick, gooey paste. Punch the paste with the wooden spoon and flip it against the sides of the pan, cooking it until the pine nuts begin to drop out of the mixture, which should have become soft and spongy.

Reduce the heat to very, very low and cover the pan with a clean tea towel, followed by the lid. Make sure you lift the hanging flaps of tea towel up over the lid to prevent them from catching fire and leave the mixture to steam for about 20 minutes. Then turn off the heat and leave the mixture to cool.

Serve the *helva* at room temperature, by scooping it out in thin layers and sprinkling it with icing sugar.
Extolled in poems recited at the

courts of Abassid Caliphs in tenth-century Baghdad, these savoury pastries are particularly popular in Egypt, Lebanon, Jordan and Syria. The Turks make a variety of similar pastries, called *börek*, and the Jews make little filled pies called *pasteles*, which are made with the same dough. Generally the fillings are much the same – the traditional minced lamb or beef filling, called *tatbila*, with cinnamon and pine nuts, or white cheese with mint and dill, spinach with cheese or nuts and a Jewish aubergine and tomato filling called *khandrajo*. Traditional *sanbusak* are shaped like half-moons and sprinkled with sesame seeds.

SANBUSAK
(SAVOURY PASTRIES FILLED WITH MINCED MEAT AND PINE NUTS)

Serves 6 (makes roughly 30 pastries)
Preparation time roughly 45 minutes
Cooking time 40 minutes

For the filling:
1 onion, finely chopped
1 tablespoon clarified or ordinary butter, or olive oil
450g (1lb) finely minced lamb or beef
2–3 tablespoons pine nuts
1 teaspoon ground cinnamon
½ teaspoon ground allspice
Salt and freshly ground black pepper

For the dough:
110ml (4fl oz) sunflower oil
110ml (4fl oz) melted clarified or ordinary butter
110ml (4fl oz) warm water
1 teaspoon salt
450g (1lb) plain flour

For the top:
1–2 eggs, beaten
2–3 tablespoons sesame seeds
Preheat the oven to 180°C/

350°F/gas mark 4.

To make the filling, soften the onion in the butter and stir in the meat. Cook for a few minutes, until the meat changes colour, then stir in the pine nuts. Cook for another minute or two, until the nuts begin to colour, then stir in the spices and season. Sprinkle 4–5 tablespoons of water over the meat, cook it for a few minutes more, then put it aside. Now make the dough. In a large

Sanbusak

bowl, mix the oil and melted butter with the warm water and salt. Sift the flour and add it gradually to the bowl, using a knife to mix it, until it is stiff enough to use your hands. Form the dough into a soft, oily ball, adding a little extra flour if necessary. Take a walnut-sized lump of dough, roll it into a ball and flatten it between the palms of your hands. Place it on a floured surface and repeat with the rest of the dough.
Put a heaped teaspoonful of the

filling in the middle of one half of each circle, then fold over the other half to make a half-moon shape. Pinch the edges together to seal them and place them on a greased baking tray. Brush the surface with the beaten egg and sprinkle lightly with sesame seeds, then pop them into the oven for 35–40 minutes, until they are pale golden in colour. The pastries can be served hot or cold, but they are best just straight out of the oven.

PISTACHIO

(FUSTUK HALIBI) *Pistacia vera*

Whole roasted pistachios

The small tree *Pistacia vera* is native to parts of western Asia and the Levant, particularly in the area between Turkey and Afghanistan, and in Lebanon and Syria, where the highly prized nut has been eaten since about 7000 BC. The name pistachio comes from *pesteh*, the Persian word for the nut, and the genus *Pistacia* includes trees producing an edible resin (mastic).

The Romans introduced pistachio trees into Europe in the first century AD. Of all the culinary cultures in the Middle East, it is the Turkish and Iranian that make the most of pistachios. There are shops dedicated to displaying and selling them – in or out of their shells, packed in boxes, embedded in toffee or *lokum*, wrapped in cellophane, or tied up with ribbons. When they are freshly roasted and still warm, they are quite irresistible.

Slivered pistachios

CULINARY USES

As a snack, pistachios are roasted and salted and, in Iran, they are sometimes roasted in lemon juice to bring out their flavour. Ground pistachios are used to make a sweetmeat like marzipan and as the basis for a delectable, creamy, green ice cream. They are also sprinkled over a variety of biscuits and syrupy pastries for colour. Chopped pistachios feature in a variety of puddings, such as the grain-based dish *belila* (p126), given to nursing mothers and eaten to celebrate a baby's first tooth, and the wobbly, blancmange-style *balouza* and its syrupy version, *balta*. They are used in the Egyptian pudding *om Ali* (p133), in the Arab pancakes *ataif*, and in a number of rice dishes throughout the Middle East. Along with almonds and walnuts, they feature in the rice stuffing for *qouzi mahshi*, an impressive Saudi Arabian speciality of a whole roasted kid served on a tray surrounded by mountains of rice.

During the Ottoman period, pistachios were incorporated into specific syrupy pastries such as *kadaif*, a shredded pastry bathed in syrup and filled with pistachio nuts, *şöbiyet*, the diamond-shaped pastries, and *bülbül yuvası*, meaning nightingale's nests, and they were packed into the paper-thin rolls called *dürüm*. In Turkey, they are used in a highly prized *helva*, they are embedded in varieties of Turkish Delight and they are concealed in *fistikli kebabi*, a minced meat kebab, rolled like a sausage and filled with whole pistachios. In Iran, they are pounded with fresh basil to make a paste for the noodles, *rishta*, and they are ground and added to an exotic version of the spice mixture *advieh* (p168). Whole, chopped or slivered pistachios are added to numerous Iranian jams and pickles, puddings and rice dishes.

HOW IT GROWS

Remarkably, the pistachio tree grows in arid areas where no other plants, apart from shrubs, survive. Generally, the tree produces a good crop in alternate years. The small, dry fruits of the tree look like olives and grow in clusters. Inside the stone of the fruit is the kernel which is the nut that we eat. When the fruit is ripe, the shell of the kernel opens at one end, which the Iranians call *khandan* (laughing).

APPEARANCE AND TASTE

The skin of the fruit is soft and pinky-red, enveloping the hard, beige-coloured shell. Inside, the kernel is green all the way through with a distinctive taste. Some are yellowy green with a hint of red, others are almost cream-coloured, but the most highly prized are dark green. Plain pistachios are delicious, but once they have been roasted, their flavour is quite exquisite.

Shelled roasted pistachios

BUYING AND STORING

Pistachios, like pine nuts, are expensive. They are sold both in and out of their shells. Generally, if they are kept in an airtight container, the nuts in their shells will store well, but if they have already been shelled and stored badly, they tend to get soft and chewy. Ground pistachios don't keep well. They lose their flavour and begin to look dull.

Ataif is a medieval dish of pancakes dipped in syrup, sprinkled with pistachios and eaten with thick, clotted cream, *eishta*. In the tenth century a poem written about the dish was recited at a lavish banquet in honour of the Caliph Mustakfi of Baghdad, who was particularly fond of *ataif*. It is also a dish served at festivals, weddings and to break the fast of *Ramadan*. Nowadays, people often buy ready-made pancakes from the baker's and fill them with nuts, before dipping them in syrup. The following recipe is based on the medieval recipe.

ATAIF
(ARAB PANCAKES DIPPED IN SYRUP)

Serves 4–6 (roughly 16 pancakes)
Preparation time 1¼ hours
Cooking time 3–4 minutes for
   each pancake

*15g (½oz) fresh yeast, or a scant
   teaspoon dried yeast
1 teaspoon sugar
250ml (9fl oz) lukewarm water
225g (8oz) plain flour
Sunflower oil*

For the syrup:
*450g (1lb) sugar
300ml (½ pint) water
Juice of ½ lemon
1–2 tablespoons orange blossom
   water*

To serve:
*2–3 handfuls pistachios, chopped
Clotted cream*

Dissolve the yeast with the sugar in a little of the lukewarm water and leave it to froth.

Sift the flour into a bowl and make a well in the middle. Pour the yeast into the well, along with the remaining water, and beat it all together to form a smooth batter. Cover the bowl with a cloth and leave it in a warm place for about 1 hour,

until the batter rises a little and becomes bubbly and elastic.

To make the syrup, bring the sugar and water to the boil in a pan, stirring all the time. Stir in the lemon juice, reduce the heat and simmer for 10–15 minutes, until it coats the back of the spoon. Add the orange blossom water and simmer for a further 5 minutes. Leave the syrup to cool, then chill in the refrigerator.

When the batter is ready, heat a heavy-based frying pan and, using a piece of kitchen paper, rub it lightly with a little sunflower oil. Use a coffee cup, half a teacup, or half a soup ladle to measure the quantity of batter for a pancake, and pour it into the hot pan, tilting it slightly to spread the batter a little – the pancake should be quite fat and roundish.

Reduce the heat a little and fry the pancake for a minute or two, until it begins to bubble and lifts off the base of the pan, then flip it over and fry the other side.

Dip each hot pancake into the cold syrup, spread or serve with cream, and sprinkle with the chopped pistachios.

These delicious little stuffed biscuits are called *ma'amoul* by the Arabs and *menena* by the Jews. Christians regard them as an Easter speciality and Muslims eat them during *Ramadan*. Usually they are filled with walnuts or pistachios, or with a paste made of softened dates. The pistachio-filled *ma'amoul* are considered the most desirable.

MA'AMOUL
(BISCUITS STUFFED WITH PISTACHIOS)

Makes roughly 20 biscuits
Preparation time 30–40 minutes
Cooking time 25 minutes
225g (8oz) plain flour

*110g (4oz) butter
1 tablespoon sugar
1 tablespoon orange blossom or
   rose water
Roughly 1 tablespoon milk*

For the filling:
*110g (4oz) pistachios, finely
   chopped
2 tablespoons sugar
1 tablespoon orange blossom or
   rose water*

Preheat the oven to 160°C/ 325°F/gas mark 3.

Mix together the ingredients for the filling and put aside. Sift the flour into a bowl and rub in the butter until the mixture looks like fine breadcrumbs. Stir in the sugar and the orange blossom or rose water, then bind with enough milk to form a soft, malleable dough.

Take a walnut-sized lump of dough in your fingers and shape it into a little pot with thin sides. Fill the pot with the chopped nuts to about three-quarters full, then pinch the top edge together to close the opening and form a ball. Flatten the ball slightly in the palm of your hand and place it on a baking sheet with the smooth side on top.

Repeat with the rest of the dough. Prick the tops with a fork to make a pattern and pop them into the oven for about 25 minutes. When they come out of the oven, they should be soft and pale, not brown.

Leave them to cool on the baking sheet, until they have firmed up, then transfer them to a wire rack or plate. Dust them with icing sugar before serving.

Ataif

Whole blanched almonds

ALMOND

(LOZ) *Prunus amygdalus*

Almond trees have grown along the Mediterranean and in Central Asia for thousands of years. The oldest mention of their cultivation is in the Bible (Numbers 17:8) – Aaron's miraculous rod is made of almond wood. The ancient Greeks cultivated almonds and the Romans regarded them as a Greek nut. They played an important role in early Arabic cookery, not least for the milk which was extracted from them and used in puddings and drinks. The fruit of the almond trees are eaten fresh and dried. Immature almonds are eaten along with their velvety green husks before the shells harden. Often sold by street pedlars as a snack, they are dipped in salt and then popped whole into the mouth. There are old recipes for meat stews using these green almonds, but nowadays the mature, dried almonds are used instead.

HOW IT GROWS

The almond tree only fruits in temperate climates. It doesn't like frost or tropical humidity, so it only grows in western Asia and around the Mediterranean. Although it belongs to the same genus as the apricot and cherry tree, its leathery fruit is quite different: it can be eaten immature and it has a large stone and kernel.

APPEARANCE AND TASTE

Knocked off the trees in their hard, pockmarked, beige shells, whole almonds are oval-shaped, slightly swollen and about 2–3cm (1in) in length. Their ridged, cinnamon-coloured skins are very thin and can easily be removed by soaking the nuts in water. Once blanched in this way a pearly white nut with a delicate aroma, a creamy texture, and sweet taste remains. Blanched almonds can be flaked or ground to a coarse powder for different recipes. The immature green almonds, which are eaten whole, have a crunchy texture with a slightly astringent, watery nut inside. As you might imagine, they taste like young shoots, but the salt lifts and sweetens them.

BUYING AND STORING

Almonds are best bought in their shells or skins as they keep fresh longer. You can then blanch them yourself, which gives you a softer, creamier nut – the blanched ones you buy have usually dried out and can be quite brittle. The same applies to the bought flaked and ground almonds, which have usually lost a lot of their delicate flavour and moisture from sitting. Almonds in their skins, flaked, chopped and ground, are easily available in most supermarkets and wholefood shops but ready-blanched almonds are more difficult to find. As with all nuts, almonds should be stored in an airtight container in a cool, dry place, where they will keep for about 8 months.

CULINARY USES

Blanched almonds are often eaten plain or toasted as a nibble. To blanch: place the shelled almonds in a bowl and pour boiling water over them. Leave them to soak for about 5 minutes, until the skins loosen. Then drain and refresh them under running cold water and rub the skins off between your fingertips – some may be more stubborn than others. To toast: pat the blanched nuts dry, pop them on a baking tray and put them in a hot oven (200°C/400°F/gas mark 6) for about 10 minutes, until they are crisp and lightly browned, then toss them in salt and eat as a snack. Or roast them in a hot, heavy-based pan until they turn brown and glisten, giving off a lovely nutty aroma.

Blanched and flaked almonds are used in rice dishes, meat and poultry stews, vegetable and fruit stuffings, fruit compotes, such as *khoshaf*, biscuits, such as the almond bracelets *kahk bi loz* (p163), and sweets. Along with walnuts and pistachios, they are one of the nuts popular in the sweet, syrupy pastries, particularly in the Turkish speciality *sütlü nüriye*, a melt-in-the-mouth pastry filled with shaved almonds and

Assorted dried fruit and nuts

bathed in a milk syrup. Whole blanched almonds are also popular with roasted chicken and duck, such as the classic Middle Eastern roast duck with honey and almonds. Blanched almonds are coated in sugar for sweet festivals, births, circumcisions and other feasts and ceremonies. Ground almonds are used in biscuits, sweets and puddings, particularly *keşkul*, the famous almond milk pudding from the Ottoman Palace kitchens, and they are pounded and kneaded with sugar to form the paste we call marzipan, the bases of the delightful dusted almond balls, *orass bi loz*, which are coloured yellow with saffron in Iraq. Freshly ground almonds are bound with olive oil, lemon juice and garlic to make *tarator* (p209), a sauce for fish, seafood and chicken. They are also tied up in a muslin cloth and poached in water to extract their natural creamy milk, which is then used to make a delicate syrup that is diluted and served as a cool, refreshing drink.

Khoshaf

Syrupy fruit compotes are very popular in the Middle East. *Khoshaf* (*hoşaf* in Turkish) is the classic combination of dried fruit and nuts, served as a winter dessert and at ceremonial feasts.

KHOSHAF
(DRIED FRUIT AND NUT COMPOTE)

Serves 8
Preparation time 5 minutes + 48 hours' soaking time
Cooking time –

450g (1lb) dried apricots
225g (8oz) prunes
110g (4oz) sultanas
110g (4oz) blanched almonds
50g (2oz) pine nuts
225g (8oz) sugar (you can use less if you prefer)
2 tablespoons rose water
1 tablespoon orange blossom water

Put the dried fruit and nuts into a large bowl and cover with water. Add the sugar, rose water and orange blossom water and gently stir it all together.

Cover the bowl and let the fruit and nuts soak for 48 hours. During that time the water and sugar will form a golden syrup with the juices of the fruit.

Serve chilled.

The name of this recipe probably originated in Persia, where the beggars, *fuqara*, who regarded themselves as the 'paupers of God', went from house to house begging for food to be placed in the oval bowl, the *keshkul*, which was suspended on a chain from their shoulders. Hence, this

delicately flavoured dessert (*keshkul* in Arabic, *keşkul* in Turkish), which was a favourite of the Ottomans, is always served in individual bowls, sprinkled with ground nuts or grated coconut to symbolise the *keshkul* being filled.

KEŞKUL
(ALMOND CREAM)

Serves 4
Preparation time 10 minutes (+20 minutes' blanching and peeling almonds)
Cooking time 35 minutes

110g (4oz) blanched almonds
600ml (1 pint) milk
25g (1oz) rice flour
110g (4oz) sugar
1–2 tablespoons finely ground pistachios or coconut

With a pestle and mortar, pound the almonds to a smooth paste and blend with a little of the milk. In a small bowl, slake the rice flour with a little milk, then pour the rest of the milk into a saucepan. Add the sugar and bring the milk to the boil, stirring all the time.

Stir a little of the hot milk into the rice flour, then add the rice flour to the pan. Keep stirring the milk and add the almond paste.

Reduce the heat and let the mixture simmer for about 25 minutes, stirring from time to time, until it thickens. Pour the mixture into individual bowls and leave to cool.

Serve chilled with finely ground pistachios or coconut on top.

Light tahini

SESAME SEED

(SIMSIM) *Sesamum indicum*

Thought to have originated in India or China, sesame was one of the first oil-yielding plants to be cultivated in Egypt and the Near East. Often mentioned in the works of classical writers, the seeds have been crushed to a paste and used in confectionery and spice mixtures since medieval times. When sugar cane was introduced to the Arabs in the early Middle Ages, the Jews played a leading role in the ensuing sugar industry, acquiring recognition for their good cooking and confectionery, which often used sesame seeds and sesame oil. As Jews are restricted to vegetable oils in their cooking, they rely on olive oil and the pungent sesame oil for flavour. In nineteenth-century Egypt and Iraq, a Jewish house was said to be detectable from miles away, due to the strong-smelling sesame oil, *siraj*. This would explain the well-known maxim, 'Sleep in a Christian bed and enjoy Jewish food.'

BUYING AND STORING

The seeds are best bought whole and then roasted when needed. They store well in an airtight container, away from direct sunlight. *Tahini* comes in light and dark varieties, smooth and coarse. The darker, coarser version is made from roasted sesame seeds and the husks, and there are some excellent organic brands available. Sesame oil is available in Middle Eastern, Asian and Chinese shops, as well as supermarkets and wholefood shops. It needs to be stored away from the light.

CULINARY USES

Roasted seeds are used in a variety of spice mixes and blends, such as *zaatar* (p198) and *dukkah* (p163). They are often sprinkled over rice and meat dishes for a bit of crunch and nutty flavour. Similarly, they are sprinkled liberally over savoury pastries and breads such as *fatayer bi semsem*, sweet sesame rolls and *semit*, the ubiquitous bread rings, sold on every street, that would be naked without their sesame seeds. They are used in confectionery, such as the popular *simsimiyya*, made with sesame seeds, almonds, honey and cinnamon. In savoury dishes, the seeds are never a principal ingredient or flavouring, but *tahini* often is. The light *tahini*, which is cream-coloured and smooth in texture, is regarded as superior and is ideal for a number of *mezze* dishes, like *baba ghanoush* (p82) and *hummus*, whereas the coarser, darker variety, which includes the husks, is used for the

HOW IT GROWS

Sesame is an upright annual herb with deeply veined, oval leaves and white or pink flowers which form small sausage-shaped pods that contain the seeds. The seeds are harvested while they are still immature and green, as the ripened seeds have a tendency to burst out of the pods and scatter, which may be where the command, 'Open, sesame' in *Ali Baba and the Forty Thieves* comes from.

APPEARANCE AND TASTE

The tiny seeds are almost flat and teardrop-shaped, varying from pearl-coloured to brown and black. The black seeds hold more flavour but the lighter-coloured seeds are more common in the Middle East. They have a crunchy texture and a mild nutty flavour, which is enhanced when they are roasted. Although tiny, the seed is rich, containing 50 per cent oil, which is extracted by crushing it.

MANUFACTURING

Sesame seeds are crushed to make a nutty cooking oil which is high in polyunsaturated fatty acids and keeps well. As a source of oil, the sesame plant has a low yield, even lower than the olive, so the oil is valued highly. The seeds are also ground into a thick oily paste called *tahini* or *tahina* (*tahin* in Turkish), from the Arabic word *tahana*, 'to grind'. To make *tahini* the seeds are soaked before they are crushed to loosen the bran from the kernels. They are then soaked again in salted water, which causes the bran to sink to the bottom and the kernels to float to the top. The kernels are then roasted and ground to extract the thick oily cream which we know as *tahini*.

Roasted sesame seeds

Semit

delicious mixture *tahin pekmez*, which is spread on bread. *Tahini* also features in the spicy pine-nut filling for the unusual Armenian dish *topik*, and it is used in some salad dressings and sauces. Both crushed sesame seeds and *tahini* are used to make blocks of *helva* (*halva*), which is made with sugar syrup and a variety of ingredients such as nuts, chocolate and *bois de Panama*.

In Egypt, the Levant and Turkey, these bread rings, liberally covered with toasted sesame seeds, are sold in the streets. The cry of *'semit, semit!'* (*simit* in Turkish) can be heard throughout the day as the street vendors walk around with baskets or trolleys filled with the freshly baked rings or carry long wooden poles onto which the rings are threaded. Standard breakfast or snack fare, these popular rings are easy to make at home.

SEMIT
(BREAD RINGS WITH SESAME SEEDS)

Makes 8 rings
Preparation time 40 minutes (+ approximately 2½ hours' proving time)
Cooking time 25–30 minutes

10g (½ oz) fresh yeast or 7g (¼ oz) dried yeast
½ teaspoon sugar
Roughly 300ml (10fl oz) lukewarm water
450g (1lb) organic white bread flour
1 teaspoon salt
1 egg beaten with 2 tablespoons water
A shallow bowl full of sesame seeds

Preheat the oven to 200°C/400°F/gas mark 6.

Cream the yeast with the sugar in a little of the lukewarm water, until it begins to froth. Sift the flour with the salt into a large bowl. Make a well in the centre and pour in the yeast with the rest of the water and use your hands to draw in the flour from the sides.

Knead the mixture well until it forms a dough, then knead it on a lightly floured surface until it becomes smooth and elastic. Clean the bowl, add a drop of sunflower oil to the bottom, and roll the ball of dough in it. Cover the bowl with a damp cloth and leave the dough for an hour or two to prove and double in size.

Punch the risen dough and knock it back into an elastic ball. Divide the dough into 6 or 8 pieces (or more if you want smaller rings) and shape each piece into a ring, roughly 18cm (7in) in diameter. Brush each ring with the beaten egg, dip it into the bowl of sesame seeds, then place it on an oiled baking tray.

Cover with a damp cloth again and leave the rings in a warm place for about half an hour to double in size. Bake in the oven for 25–30 minutes, until the rings are golden-brown and sound hollow when tapped on the bottom.

Mixed with lemon juice, the sesame paste *tahini* makes a lovely dressing for salads and a tangy sauce for baked chicken or fish, as in this dish, found throughout the Middle East. Trout, sea bass and red mullet work well, as do haddock fillets.

Semit seller

TAJIN SAMAK BI TAHINA
(FISH BAKED IN *TAHINI*)

Serves 4–6
Preparation time 15 minutes
Cooking time approximately 30 minutes

300ml (10fl oz) light tahini
150ml (5fl oz) lemon juice
150ml (5fl oz) water
2 cloves garlic, crushed
Salt and freshly ground black pepper
1–2 tablespoons olive oil
2 onions, halved and sliced
1 teaspoon cumin seeds
1 whole fish, weighing roughly 1kg (2¼lb), gutted and cleaned
A small bunch fresh flat-leaf parsley, finely chopped

Preheat oven to 160°C/325°F/gas mark 3.

In a bowl, beat the *tahini* with the lemon juice and water to form a smooth, creamy sauce, then beat in the garlic and season to taste.

Heat the oil in a pan and fry the onions with the cumin seeds, until they are golden brown.

Spread half of the onions in the base of an dish, add the fish and cover with the remaining onions.

Pour the *tahini* sauce over the fish and bake in the oven for about 30 minutes, until the flesh flakes easily. Serve hot with parsley sprinkled over it.

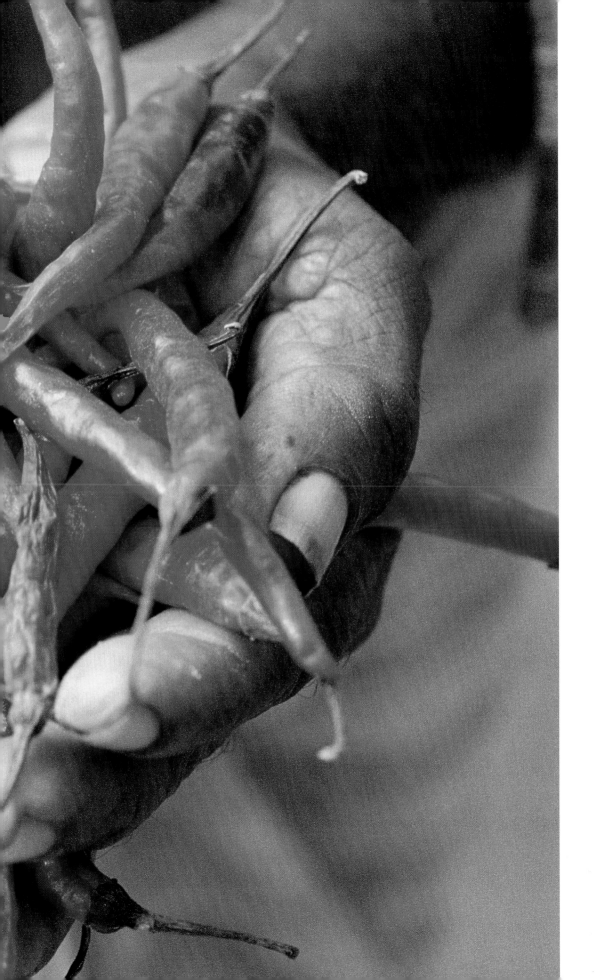

FLAVOURINGS

DILL

(SHIBIT) *Anethum graveolens*

Dill plant with flowers

The ancient Romans regarded dill as a symbol of vitality. The ancient Greeks used it as a cure for hiccups. And both the Romans and the Greeks are reputed to have drifted into peaceful slumber by wrapping fresh, aromatic dill leaves around their heads. The ancient Persians believed that 'you are what you eat', which, similar to the yin and yang theory of ancient China, led to the consumption of 'cold' foods to cool the blood and relieve fever, and 'hot' foods to warm the blood and reduce melancholy or sickness. During the Ottoman period, this theory was also put into practice and dill, which was regarded as 'warming', played an important role balancing the 'cooling' vegetables such as marrows, courgettes and broad beans.

Fresh dill

HOW IT GROWS

Indigenous to western Asia, dill belongs to the parsley family and is closely related to fennel. It is an annual herb that can grow up to 1m (3ft) in height, with thin, feather-like leaves, crowned with clusters of tiny, yellow flowers and flat, oval fruits. When the fruits have ripened and turned yellow-brown, the seeds are extracted and dried.

APPEARANCE AND TASTE

Although the long, green, feathery fronds of fennel and dill look very similar, they taste quite different. Fennel has an anise flavour whereas dill is more akin to caraway. The flat, oval seeds are light brown with a warm aroma.

BUYING AND STORING

The fresh leaves should be bought on the stalk and kept in a plastic bag in the refrigerator or, like flowers, left to stand in a glass of water. They don't last long and, if left in plastic, they begin to turn a bit like pond weed. Dried dill leaves are available but they smell and taste like dried, cut grass. The seeds store quite well in an airtight container in a cool, dry place.

MEDICINAL USES

Dill has been cultivated for its medicinal qualities for a long time. It is believed to lower cholesterol and to stimulate the production of breast milk in nursing mothers. An infusion of the seeds in water is used to cure hiccups, flatulence and stomach complaints, and is often given to infants to soothe colic and induce a restful sleep.

CULINARY USES

Fresh dill is particularly popular in Turkey and Iran, where it is often combined with mint to balance cooling vegetables. It is the favoured herb in the splendid Ottoman olive oil dishes, such as *zeytinyağlı enginar* (p221), artichoke hearts in olive oil. Dill is nearly always used in broad bean dishes such as *fava*, a purée of broad beans, and *bâghâli polow*, an Iranian rice dish with broad beans. Dill is also used to flavour yogurt dips, cucumber and yogurt salads, cheese pastries, such as *sigan böreği*, and rice dishes. It is often used with fish, particularly in dishes that are served cold. In Iraq, it is combined with yogurt to flavour an Assyrian soup made with rice and vegetables. Both the dill fronds and the seeds are used in preserves and pickles.

During his reign of the Ottoman Empire, Mehmet the Conqueror filled the kitchens of the Topkapı Palace in Istanbul with chefs who specialised in just one thing, such as the *börekçi*, the maker of savoury pastries. Even to this day, there are specialist pastry-makers throughout the Middle East and the Turks excel at it. The variety of *börek* is immense. Some are fried and others are baked or steamed; different types of pastry dough are used, but perhaps the most common are the ones made with paper-thin sheets of *yufka* (known as *fila* in the rest of the Middle East). Filled with minced meat, spinach, or cheese and herbs, these pastries are particularly popular when rolled into the shape of a cigar, *sigarı böreği*. If kept covered with a damp cloth in the refrigerator, they can be made in advance and fried at the last minute. For this recipe, I have used *fila* (sold as *filo* or *phyllo*) rather than any other pastry as it is more readily available outside the Middle East, and for the cheese I have used feta, which works well as a substitute for the Turkish white cheese – the latter is a great deal creamier and comes in different grades of texture and saltiness, depending on the region it is from.

SİGARA BÖREĞİ
(CHEESE-FILLED PASTRY CIGARS)

Makes approximately 30
Preparation time 25–30 minutes
Cooking time 15–20 minutes

450g (1lb) feta cheese
4 eggs
A large bunch of fresh dill, mint
 and parsley, chopped
Roughly 8 sheets of fila pastry
Sunflower oil for frying

Mash the cheese with the eggs in a bowl and beat in the herbs. Cut the *fila* into long strips, approximately 8cm (3in) wide.

Take one strip and spoon a little of the cheese on to the end nearest to you. Fold the corners over the filling and roll it up into a tight cigar, until you are almost at the other end. Dip the far end into a cup of water,

then seal up the cigar. As you prepare the cigars, keep them under a damp cloth so they don't dry out.

Heat up enough sunflower oil for deep-frying in a shallow pan. Fry the cigars in batches, until they are golden brown. Drain them on kitchen paper and serve while they are still warm

Sigara böreği

In Iran there are two superb rice dishes flavoured with dill. One, *baghali polow*, consists of the classic combination of broad beans and dill. The other, *sheveed polow*, is simply a dish of plain rice flavoured with dill, which is often served with preserved, salted fish from the Caspian Sea. The same combination is enjoyed along the Black Sea coast of Turkey, where the mackerel and anchovies are hung up to dry for dishes such as this.

SHEVEED POLOW
(RICE WITH DILL)

Serves 4–6
Preparation time approximately 2
 hours' soaking
Cooking time 50 minutes

450g (1lb) long-grain rice, well
 washed and drained
1–2 teaspoons salt
A big bunch of fresh dill, chopped
50g (2oz) butter, cut into pieces

Put the rice into a pan with the salt and enough water to just cover it, then leave it to soak for about 2 hours.

Bring the water to the boil and stir in the dill. Reduce the heat and simmer for about 10 minutes, until the water has been absorbed.

Scatter the pieces of butter over the rice, then wrap a clean tea towel around the lid and place it over the pan.

Reduce the heat to very, very low and leave the rice to steam for about 40 minutes. Turn off the heat and let the rice stand for 5 minutes before opening the lid. Slide a knife down the sides of the rice to ease it away from the edges, then tip it upside down onto a serving plate. Serve immediately with preserved or fresh fish.

RED PEPPER

(FILFIL AHMAR HALABI) *Capsicum frutescens*

Oiled red pepper

Middle Eastern red pepper is difficult to define. Is it a chilli or not? During the sixteenth century, sweet and chilli peppers came from the New World to Constantinople, from where they spread throughout the regions of the Ottoman Empire. Among them were long red peppers whose pungent flavours were instantly incorporated into the cooking of the empire, not least in Hungary, where the first peppers were called 'Turkish peppers', the most likely ancestors of Hungarian paprika. Middle Eastern red peppers do come from the same family as the chilli, and some would regard them as such, but in the Middle East the dried, ground spice is ranked in a class of its own, varying in strength from region to region, getting hotter the further south you go. It is such a popular spice that strings of dried red peppers hang from doorways or balconies, like bright decorations, and large sacks of red pepper flakes and powder are found in every market.

BUYING AND STORING

Whole dried red peppers and the flaked or ground spice are available in Middle Eastern stores but make sure they are deep red in colour. If they have begun to turn brown, they will taste stale. The whole peppers can hang in your kitchen for almost a year but the flaked and ground spice must be stored in an airtight container and, even so, will begin to lose its intensity after six months.

HOW IT GROWS

Like all chillies, the red pepper is a perennial with sharp-tasting fruits. It can be cultivated in most regions of the Middle East but the bulk of it is grown in Gaziantep, Maraş and Urfa in southern Turkey, and in Aleppo in northern Syria, hence its other names: 'Antep' (from Gaziantep) and 'Aleppo' pepper.

Red peppers drying

APPEARANCE AND TASTE

The fresh peppers are long, thin, and horn-shaped, similar in appearance to the Guajillo chillies of Mexico. They are rarely eaten fresh, but are hung up on strings to dry before being crushed or ground and used as a spice. Hotter than paprika and milder than cayenne, the spice is surprisingly rich and fruity. The best-quality red pepper is deep red and flaked, and is rubbed with oil so that it keeps fresh and imparts its flavour. The flakes can also be roasted until dark, almost black, and oiled for a rich, nutty flavour that packs a punch.

CULINARY USES

Middle Eastern red pepper has many uses, but the one that sets it apart from other chillies is its liberal use as a condiment. In Syria and Turkey, bowls of it are often put on the table, alongside dried thyme, or oregano, and *sumac*, ready to be sprinkled over *mezze* dips, yogurt dishes, kebabs, grilled fish, and salads. It is added to rice dishes, soups, stews, and egg dishes and it is often used to fire up meatballs and grilled meats, such as *Adana kebabı*. In Turkey, it is often combined with melted butter to drizzle over yogurt and meat dishes.

Ajvar

This is one of the most popular ways of cooking liver in the Middle East. The liver of goats, sheep, lambs and chickens can all be cooked in the same way. The depth of fieriness and the addition of other spices may vary from region to region, but the red pepper remains a constant.

KIBDAH MAKLIYA
(LAMBS' LIVER SAUTÉED WITH RED PEPPER)

Serves 4
Preparation time 15 minutes
Cooking time 4–5 minutes

2–3 tablespoons olive oil
2 cloves garlic, chopped
1 teaspoon cumin seeds
2–3 tablespoons flour
450g (1lb) lambs' liver, cut into thin strips, with ducts and tough skin removed
2 teaspoons Middle Eastern red pepper
Salt
1 lemon, cut into quarters

Heat the oil in a heavy-based frying pan and stir in the garlic and cumin seeds.

Tip the flour onto a plate and quickly toss the liver in it so that it is lightly coated. Add it to the pan and sauté lightly, until just cooked.

Sprinkle with the red pepper and season with salt, then serve immediately with lemon to squeeze over it.

A dish of Arab origin, *ajvar* is popular in Syria and Iraq, and in south-eastern Turkey (where it is called *acvar*). It is served warm with yogurt or lemon and lots of fresh bread.

AJVAR
(WARM GRILLED PEPPER AND AUBERGINE SALAD)

Serves 3–4
Preparation time 25–30 minutes
Cooking time 5 minutes

1 red bell pepper
1 fat aubergine
1 red onion, roughly chopped
2 cloves garlic, roughly chopped
A scant teaspoon sugar
2–3 tablespoons olive oil
1–2 teaspoons Middle Eastern red pepper
Juice of 1–2 lemons
1–2 teaspoons vinegar
A bunch fresh flat-leaf parsley, roughly chopped
Salt and freshly ground black pepper

Place the pepper and aubergine directly onto a gas flame, or over a charcoal grill, and burn the skin all over. Pop them into a plastic bag to sweat for a few minutes and then hold them under running cold water while you remove the burnt skin.

Put the pepper onto a board, cut it in half, remove the stalk, seeds, and pith, and chop it to a pulp. Cut the stalk of the aubergine and chop the flesh to a pulp.

In a flat pan, sauté the onion and garlic with a little sugar in the olive oil, until they just begin to take on some colour. Stir in the red pepper and add the pulped sweet pepper and aubergine.

Beat in the lemon juice and vinegar, stir in most of the parsley, and season to taste. Serve warm with the rest of the parsley and fresh flat bread.

CHILLI

(FILFIL HAR) *Capsicum frutescens*

Green chillies

Chillies are found in dishes all over the world, yet they are relatively new to most continents. First cultivated in Mexico as early as 7000 BC, chillies didn't reach Europe until Columbus brought them back to Spain at the end of the fifteenth century. The Portuguese then took them to India, Asia and Africa, and the Ottomans, who dominated the political stage with Spain in the sixteenth century, spread them around their vast empire. There are many different types of chilli, and only the very hot varieties are covered in this section.

HOW IT GROWS

All chillies fall into the *Capsicum* genus, which belongs to the *Solanaceae* family that includes the tomato and aubergine. The two major varieties are *Capsicum annum*, which is an annual bush bearing larger, milder-tasting fruit, and *capsicum frutescens*, which is a taller perennial with smaller, sharper, often fiery-tasting fruit. Generally, the unripe fruits are green and the mature fruits are red. The mature fruits are usually dried in the sun.

APPEARANCE AND TASTE

In the Middle East, the hot chillies can be either red or green, long or short, but are always thin and fiery. They should not be confused with the milder, fruity flavoured Middle Eastern red pepper (p152), which, although a member of the chilli family, is often not regarded as such and is mainly used in its dried form. All chillies contain capsaicin, found in the seeds, ribs and skin, which makes them hot and mouth-tingling. Some are perfumed, sweet and fiery, others burn like hell-fire.

Right: Hot green chillies, cucumbers and tomatoes, Turkey

Left: Chilli powder

BUYING AND STORING

When buying fresh chillies, look for firm, shiny ones. Dried chillies can be bought whole and store well in airtight containers. Crushed and ground dried chillies lose their flavour after a few months.

CULINARY USES

Generally, the young, green chillies are used fresh – chopped or sliced into stews and a few salads, such as çingene pilavı, a Turkish gypsy salad of onions, peppers, chillies, grated white cheese and herbs, or fried and grilled whole in a variety of kebabs. The two Arab dishes *samak harra* and *battata harra* are well known for their chilli content. The small, fiery green chillies are pickled in vinegar and salt. Red chillies are used fresh too but, more often, they are dried and ground to intensify the flavour and then used in hot pastes, marinades and winter stews. In Yemen, chillies are used to make *bisbas*, a fiery paste made with chillies, garlic and salt, similar to *harissa*, which is used in North Africa, Jordan and its neighbouring countries. Both *bisbas* and *harissa* are used to flavour soups and stews, or as a dip for bread; only a small amount is needed. Chillies have the ability to cool down the system in hot weather and heat it up in the winter. If you find them insufferably hot, don't try gulping down water; the only things that will soothe your throat and tongue are milk and yogurt.

Chillies and çarliston peppers in the market

The spices used in this popular Arab dish vary in Syria, Egypt and Lebanon, but the chillies are always there. Serve it with a salad or one of the many yogurt dishes to put out the fire.

BATTATA HARRA
(HOT SPICY POTATOES)

Serves 4
Preparation time 20 minutes
Cooking time 20 minutes

4 tablespoons olive oil
450g (1lb) new potatoes, peeled and diced
3 cloves garlic, crushed
2–3 hot chillies, chopped
1 teaspoon cumin seeds
Salt
Juice of ½ lemon
A small bunch fresh coriander, chopped

Heat the olive oil in a heavy-based frying pan and add the potatoes.

Fry until browned and crispy, then stir in the garlic, chillies and cumin seeds.

Fry for a minute or two longer, then season with salt, refresh with lemon juice, and sprinkle the coriander over the top. Serve hot with grilled or roasted meat, poultry or fish.

Each region has its preferred chilli paste or relish. In Turkey and Syria, the hot, dried red chilli peppers are soaked and pulped to a paste, and sometimes they are roasted before being soaked to give them a rich flavour. In Yemen, the hot paste *bisbas* is made with fresh or dried chillies which are ground to a pulp with garlic and salt. A similar paste called *shatta* is used in other parts of the Middle East, and the North African relish *harissa*. Stored in the refrigerator, *harissa* keeps for a long time if it is always covered with a layer of oil. It is excellent added to stews, spread on bread, or stirred into yogurt to make a dip.

HARISSA
(CHILLI RELISH)

Makes 1 medium-sized jar
Preparation time 10–15 minutes
 (plus 1 hour for soaking)
Cooking time –

225g (8oz) dried red chilli peppers, soaked in water for 1 hour
1 whole head of garlic, peeled
1 tablespoon coriander seeds, ground
1 tablespoon dried mint
1 tablespoon salt
A small bunch fresh coriander leaves
A little olive oil

Drain the chilli peppers, cut off the stalks and remove the seeds.

Fresh chillies

Using a pestle and mortar, pound the chillies to a paste with all the other ingredients (or whiz them in an electric mixer), adding enough olive oil to make a thick paste.

Spoon the relish into a jar and keep it in the refrigerator.

Battata harra

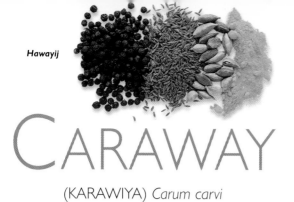

Hawayij

CARAWAY

(KARAWIYA) *Carum carvi*

Originally from the temperate areas of Asia, including the regions now known as Iran and Turkey, caraway has been used for culinary and medicinal purposes for over 5,000 years. Believing the aroma kept lovers from straying, the ancient Egyptians, Greeks and Romans used caraway to make love potions. The name comes from the ancient Arabic *karawiya*, which is still the word used for it in the Arab world today.

HOW IT GROWS

The biennial plant is cultivated for its seeds, which are the split halves of the dried fruits. It grows up to 60cm (2ft) in height with light green feathery leaves, which have a mild caraway flavour.

APPEARANCE AND TASTE

The dried seeds are dark brown with light brown, almost green, ridges. They are hard, sometimes bow-shaped, with pointed ends and are no bigger than 4–7mm (¼in) long. They have a warm, sweet aroma with a slightly spicy, pungent taste.

BUYING AND STORING

Dried seeds and ground caraway are available in most supermarkets and Asian stores, but, as with most spices, it is best to buy the seeds and grind them yourself. Both the dried seeds and the ground spice should be stored in airtight containers in a cool, dark place.

MEDICINAL USES

Apart from its role in ancient love potions, caraway is believed to 'spring-clean' the body. Chewed or infused, it is reputed to freshen the breath, aid digestion, relieve flatulence and colic, activate the kidneys, and reduce nausea.

CULINARY USES

Caraway is mainly used to flavour breads, buns, and biscuits. The seeds are sometimes used with vegetables such as carrots, leeks and cabbages, and in vegetable stews and dishes. Caraway is included in many versions of the Iranian spice mixture *advieh* (p168), and it is one of the main ingredients in *hawayij*, a peppery spice mixture from Yemen. To make a small quantity of *hawayij* to add to soups and stews, just grind to a powder 6 teaspoons black peppercorns, 3 teaspoons caraway seeds and 1 teaspoon cardamom seeds, and blend them together with 2 teaspoons ground turmeric.

In Yemen, the stews are often quite fiery, either from chillies or from one of the many hot spice mixtures prepared in every home. The use of *hawayij* gives this stew an enjoyable kick. Traditionally, it would be served with plain rice or flat bread.

AKUW'A
(YEMENI OXTAIL STEW)

Serves 5–6
Preparation time 25 minutes
Cooking time 3½–4 hours

2 oxtails, jointed
4–5 tomatoes, skinned and chopped
6 small onions, peeled and left whole
4–5 cloves garlic, peeled and left whole
2 teaspoons hawayij
Salt

Caraway seeds

Wash the oxtail joints and put into a large pot. Cover with cold water and bring to a slow simmer. When the water is boiling gently, skim the top, and add the tomatoes, onions and garlic.

Stir in the *hawayij*, season with salt, then cover the pan and simmer gently for about 3 hours, until the meat is so tender it is practically falling off the bone and the liquid has reduced.

Serve hot with plain rice or flat bread to mop up the sauce.

In Turkey, cooked vegetables are mashed to a pulp and then beaten, or served, with yogurt to make the delectable *ezme* dishes for the *meze* table, such as the following carrot dish.

HAVUÇ EZMESİ
(CARROT PURÉE WITH CARAWAY SEEDS AND YOGURT)

Serves 4
Preparation time 15 minutes (plus 15 minutes – steaming)
Cooking time –

4 large carrots, peeled and steamed until soft
2 tablespoons olive oil
Juice of ½ lemon
1 teaspoon caraway seeds
Salt and freshly ground black pepper
4 heaped tablespoons thick yogurt
2–3 cloves garlic, crushed
A small bunch fresh mint or dill

In a bowl, mash the carrots with a fork and blend with the olive oil, lemon juice and caraway seeds (or whiz them all together in an electric mixer). Season to taste, then spoon the mixture onto a serving dish, leaving a well in the middle. Beat the garlic into the yogurt, season to taste and spoon into the well. Sprinkle the mint or dill on top.

Havuç ezmesi

CAROB

(KHARRUB) *Ceratonia siliqua*

Often referred to as locust beans, these pods which are rich in sugar, have been used as a source of food since ancient times. In the Bible, the reference to John the Baptist surviving in the desert off locusts and honey may, in fact, refer to these nutritious locust beans rather than the insect. In some parts of the Middle East, Africa and Asia, carob pods are used primarily as animal fodder, but in the eastern Mediterranean region they have been cultivated for culinary purposes since the ancient Greeks first prized the pods as a sweetmeat and used the seeds as a weight for gold. The modern-day word 'carat' derives from the Greek *keration*, which means 'little horn', and is the name given to the carob seed.

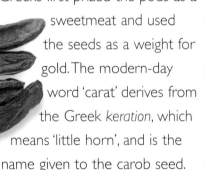

Carob pods

Gold Souk, Saudi Arabia

HOW IT GROWS

The large, leathery pods are the fruit of an ancient evergreen tree, *Ceratonia siliqua*, which is cultivated and grows wild in the eastern Mediterranean region. When the pods ripen they become full of a sweet gum. They are picked and pressed to extract the sticky juice, *dibs kharrub*, which is used for culinary purposes

APPEARANCE AND TASTE

The ripened pods are long, brown and leathery, containing a sticky, dark gum which has a distinctive fruity smell and tastes like caramel. The thick molasses extracted from the pods is almost black in colour, like treacle. Broken carob pods, called kibble, are roasted and ground to produce a brown powder which resembles powdered chocolate.

BUYING AND STORING

As carob powder has a fat content of only 0.7 per cent, compared to the 25–50 per cent of chocolate, it is often sold as a chocolate substitute in the 'health' stores of the West. Otherwise carob pods and powder are available in Middle Eastern stores. As there is not a huge demand for carob, it is best to use or chew the pods fairly quickly, as they may not be at their freshest. Carob powder stores in an airtight container for about six months and the molasses, which is sold in jars, keeps well in a cool, dark place.

Jar of thick, fruity carob molasses

CULINARY USES

Generally the pods are chewed as a snack, the powder is used in biscuits, and the molasses is used like honey on bread, or in sweet pastries. Like most of the fruit molasses made from grapes, mulberries, dates and pomegranates, carob molasses is sometimes used to give a fruity sweetness to stews, sweetmeats, and a few *mezze* dishes, such as *nazuktan*, made with smoked aubergine pulp and crushed almonds. And like the grape and date molasses, it is delectable when bound with *tahini*, in equal quantities, to form a moreish paste that can be spooned onto bread and eaten as a snack or for breakfast. The same paste can be used as a filling in some flat-bread doughs, which are then baked in the oven, or it can be pepped up with lemon and mint to make a Turkish savoury dip, *tahin tarama*.

Tahini mixed with a fruit molasses, in equal proportions, is a very popular combination in Turkey, Syria, Lebanon and Jordan. It works particularly well with grape, date, and carob molasses. The Turks take this delicious combination one step further and present it as a *meze* dip, mixed with lemon juice and mint.

TAHİN TARAMA
(*TAHINI* DIP WITH CAROB AND MINT)

Serves 3–4
Preparation time 5–10 minutes
Cooking time –

4 heaped tablespoons smooth tahini
3–4 tablespoons carob molasses
Juice of 1 lemon
½ tablespoon dried mint

Carob pods in a basket

In a bowl, combine the *tahini* with the carob molasses.

Beat in the lemon juice, followed by the mint, and adjust the flavour according to your taste – a little more lemon, a little more mint – it is completely up to you. (If the *tahini* you use is particularly thick, you might need to add a tiny bit of water to thin it down.)

Serve with bread to scoop it up.

The following *mezze* is another one of those dishes that pops up in different parts of the Middle East under different guises. The Arabs and the Turks can make anything with the cooked flesh of a grilled or baked aubergine and this dish, which is found in southern Turkey, Syria, and Jordan, is just one of the fine examples.

NAZUKTAN
(AUBERGINE PURÉE WITH ALMONDS AND CAROB SYRUP)

Serves 4
Preparation time 25–30 minutes
Cooking time –

2 aubergines
Juice of ½ lemon
2 tablespoons carob molasses
2–3 cloves garlic, crushed
1 teaspoon Middle Eastern red pepper (p152) or 1 mild red chilli, chopped
3 tablespoons almonds, roasted and chopped
A small bunch of fresh mint, chopped
3 tablespoons thick creamy yogurt
Salt

Grill the aubergines over charcoal, or directly over a gas flame, until they are soft. Slit them open, scoop out the hot flesh and put it into a bowl.

Using a fork to break up the aubergine, mix it with the lemon juice, carob molasses, and garlic.

Add the red pepper, chopped almonds, and mint, and bind with the yogurt. Season to taste and garnish with a few whole roasted almonds and mint.

Tahin tarama

CINNAMON

(QIRFA) *Cinnamomum verum*

Cinnamon sticks

Cinnamon has long been used as a spice and flavouring. Arab traders supplied the ancient Greeks and Romans but never revealed their source. Instead, they made up fantastic stories about the dangers of collecting cinnamon: they had to enter valleys infested with poisonous snakes and the bark burst into flames under the sun. However, the Arabic writers of the twelfth to fifteenth

Cinamon bark

centuries put an end to the secrecy, revealing the true source as Ceylon. This led to the Portuguese occupying Ceylon for its wild cinnamon at the beginning of the sixteenth century, followed by the Dutch in 1636, who inherited the monopoly in cinnamon and began its cultivation.

HOW IT GROWS

Cinnamon is the dried bark of an evergreen tree of the laurel family. It is indigenous to Sri Lanka, which is the largest producer. The tree grows to a height of 10m (33ft), but some cinnamon cultivators grow straight shoots in a bush form and harvest them when they are 1.5–1.8m (5–6ft) high. To get the cinnamon we cook with, the outer bark is stripped off the tree and dried in chunks, while the inner bark is prised off in sections, scraped clean, cut into equal sizes, rolled into scrolls by hand and then dried in the sun.

APPEARANCE AND TASTE

Cinnamon is sold as loose chunks of crude bark or as brittle cinnamon sticks which look like delicate, tan-coloured scrolls. It is also sold as quillings, which are like offcuts of the inner bark, and in powder form. The bark should smell of cinnamon, and the warm, sweet aroma is intensified when it is ground.

BUYING AND STORING

Cinnamon sticks are easy to grind so, as with most spices, it is best to store them in an airtight container and grind them when you need them. Ready-ground cinnamon doesn't retain its fresh, warm, spicy aroma for long.

MEDICINAL USES

An infusion of cinnamon in hot water is drunk to relieve nausea and for stimulating the digestion. A few drops of cinnamon bark oil in hot water make a pleasant, spicy inhalation for head colds.

CULINARY USES

In the Middle East, cinnamon is used to flavour biscuits, sweetmeats, puddings, savoury rice and meat dishes. It is often sprinkled on top of milk puddings, such as the Turkish chicken breast pudding, *tavuk göğsu* (p62), and on top of milky drinks, such as *salep* (p178), made from ground orchid root. It is the favoured spice to combine with nuts, so it's used in the fillings of a number of syrupy pastries, such as *baklava* (p137) and *konafa* (p47). The Iranian *khoresht* is often spiced with cinnamon, and in Lebanon, Syria and Turkey, cinnamon is one of the only spices, along with allspice, used to flavour meat, particularly lamb. It is the principal flavouring in *ma'mounia*, a sweet semolina porridge served for breakfast, and it is often the main spice, along with allspice, to be used in the dried fruit and rice stuffings for meat and poultry, and in the meat and rice stuffings for vegetables and fruit, such as *dolmeh sib* (p182) or *dolmeh beh*, the stuffed apples and quinces of Iran. Cinnamon sticks are used to flavour soups, stews and some pickles, such as the Turkish sweet and sour pears, *armut turşusu*. Cinnamon is one of the main spices in the ubiquitous Arab spice mix, *baharat* (p162), which also includes ground cloves, cumin, coriander and paprika, and is always combined with cardamom seeds in the Iranian spice mixture, *advieh* (p168).

Ground cinnamon

Spiced fruit and vegetables are popular as a snack, or as part of a *mezze* spread. Unlike pickles, they are not usually made from immature fruit with the intention of preserving it, but with ripened fruit to be eaten that day or week. This recipe comes from Bursa, which lies beneath the snow-capped peaks of Mount Olympus, surrounded by lush fruit orchards.

ARMUT TURŞUSU
(SWEET AND SOUR PEARS)

Serves 6
Preparation time 10 minutes
Cooking time 30 minutes

300ml (10fl oz) white wine or
*   cider vinegar*
100ml (3½fl oz) water
175g (6oz) honey
2 cinnamon sticks
6–8 allspice berries
A pinch of saffron fronds
3 large fresh pears, peeled, cored,
*   and cut in half vertically with*
*   the stalks left on*
A handful of walnuts, blanched
*   and skinned*
A small bunch of fresh mint
*   leaves*

Put the vinegar, water, honey, cinnamon, allspice and saffron into a big, heavy-based pan and bring it to the boil, stirring all the time until the honey has dissolved.

Reduce the heat, put in the pears and poach them gently for about 25 minutes, until they are tender. Remove the pears with a slotted spoon and place them on a dish.

Add the walnuts to the vinegar syrup and let it bubble for about 5 minutes to reduce and thicken it. Spoon it over the pears and leave to cool.

Serve the pears with plenty of fresh mint leaves.

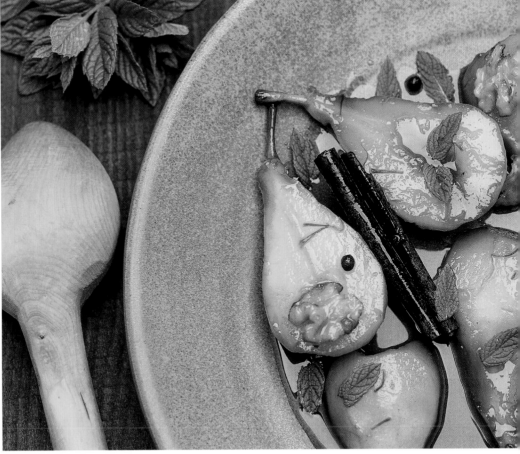

Armut turşusu

Rice dishes with chicken or lamb are popular throughout the Middle East. Rice dishes made with the livers are particularly favoured, especially on festive occasions when a hen or sheep is slaughtered and all the parts are consumed. The livers of both can be used for the following dish, an Istanbul speciality, which is eaten on its own with yogurt, or served with a plain kebab.

İÇ PİLAVI
(AROMATIC RICE WITH CHICKEN LIVERS AND PINE NUTS)

Serves 4–6
Preparation time 15 minutes
Cooking time 40 minutes

1–2 tablespoons clarified butter
*   (ghee) or olive oil*
1 onion, chopped
2–3 tablespoons pine nuts
2 tablespoons currants, soaked in
*   water for 15 minutes and*
*   drained*
1 teaspoon ground allspice
½ teaspoon ground cinnamon
350g (12oz) long-grain rice,
*   soaked in water for 15 minutes*
*   and drained*
Roughly 700ml (1¼ pints) chicken
*   stock or water*
Salt and freshly ground black
*   pepper*
225g (8oz) chicken livers, trimmed
*   and cut into small pieces*
A small bunch of fresh parsley and
*   dill, finely chopped*
A handful of roasted pine nuts

Melt the clarified butter in a heavy-based saucepan and stir in the onion and pine nuts. When they begin to brown, add the currants, then stir in the spices and rice.

Pour in the stock or water, season with salt and pepper, and bring the liquid to the boil. Turn down the heat and simmer gently for about 15 minutes.

Meanwhile sauté the chicken livers in a little extra clarified butter.

When all the liquid has been absorbed by the rice, toss the chicken livers and herbs through it, then cover the pan with a clean tea towel, followed by the lid, and leave it to steam, off the heat, for a further 15–20 minutes.

Tip it out onto a serving dish, using a fork to make sure it is well mixed, and garnish with a few roasted pine nuts.

Ground coriander

CORIANDER

(KUZBARA) *Coriandrum sativum*

Baharat mix

The coriander plant was cultivated in ancient Egypt for medicinal and culinary purposes and the seeds were found in the tombs of the pharaohs. Used as a spice since classical times, the seeds were likened to the colour of manna in the Bible. The fresh leaves are used widely in the Middle East by the Iranians, the Circassian communities, and in the Arab regions, where they are sometimes referred to as 'Arab parsley'. Coriander is also one of the bitter herbs eaten at the Jewish Passover.

Coriander

HOW IT GROWS

Also known as cilantro, coriander is related to parsley. It is an ancient annual herb from the carrot family. Native to southern Europe and the Middle East, this pretty plant can grow up to 60cm (2ft) in height, with a long, thin stem and lots of wide, floppy, scalloped leaves two-thirds of the way up. The upper leaves are small and thin, resembling sparrows' claws, leading up to the delicate, pinkish-white flowers at the top. The seeds are picked when ripe and then dried for use.

APPEARANCE AND TASTE

The whole coriander plant has a distinctive spicy, citrus aroma. Although the large, bright green, scalloped leaves look a bit like flat-leaf parsley, they are quite different in aroma and taste. Coriander leaves are soft and floppy with a fresh smell and a bitter, fruity taste, with a hint of orange peel and ginger. The small, golden seeds have a warm, sweet aroma, which is intensified when roasted, with a slightly peppery, woody taste.

BUYING AND STORING

Unless you grow coriander yourself, the flowers and roots are rarely available, so it is the large green leaves and the seeds you will find. Sold in bunches, the stems can be floppy but check that the leaves are fresh-looking. Coriander droops quickly and should be kept in water, like cut flowers. The seeds should be whole and gold in colour, with a distinctive aroma. They keep well in an airtight container in a dry, cool place and can be dry-roasted for a more pungent, nutty flavour or ground to make your own powder. Ready-ground coriander loses its aroma and flavour quickly.

CULINARY USES

All parts of the coriander plant are used. The root can be used in spicy soups and stews and the small, upper leaves and flowers are delicious in salads, but in the Middle East it is the lower leaves and the seeds which are the most commonly used. The leaves are used in salads, rice dishes and stews in Iran and the Arab regions. The well-known Circassian dish, *Çerkez tavuğu* (p62), made with chicken, walnuts and coriander, is traditionally made with fresh coriander. Both the leaves and the seeds are used in pickles, such as the stuffed baby aubergine pickle of Iran and Turkey.

The aromatic seeds and the ground spice are used in vegetable stews, meatballs, and some cakes and breads, such as the medieval savoury bracelets *kahk*. The seeds are roasted and crushed in the delicious Egyptian speciality *dukkah*, which is an appetising dip made with nuts and spices. The seeds are often ground and used in an Arab condiment called *taqlia*, which consists of ground coriander mixed with fried, crushed garlic and salt which is added to some meat and chicken dishes. And the seeds are ground and used in the Iranian spice mixture *advieh* (p169), and in the ubiquitous Arab spice mixture, *baharat*.

To make a basic *baharat* mixture, grind together 2 tablespoons black peppercorns, 1 tablespoon coriander seeds, 1 tablespoon broken cinnamon bark, 1 tablespoon cumin seeds, ½ tablespoon cloves, ½ tablespoon cardamom seeds, 1 whole nutmeg, and mix it all with 2 tablespoons ground paprika.

Coriander seeds

Dukkah

This loose, dry mixture of nuts and seeds is an old Egyptian favourite. Crushed to release the flavours, rather than ground, the mixture is used as a dip for bread which has first been dipped in olive oil. Served for breakfast, or as a snack or *mezze* dish, the recipe varies from family to family. It is served in a shallow bowl placed beside a bowl of olive oil to make the dipping swift and easy. A humble street version of *dukkah*, consisting of dried mint, salt and pepper, is sold in paper cornets, like *zaatar*, ready to be sprinkled on bread.

DUKKAH
(EGYPTIAN CORIANDER AND SESAME SEED DIP)

Makes roughly 400g (14oz)
Preparation time 25–30 minutes
Cooking time –

A handful of hazelnuts, roasted
225g (8oz) sesame seeds, roasted
110g (4oz) coriander seeds, roasted
50g (2oz) cumin seeds, roasted and ground
A scant teaspoon salt

Using a pestle and mortar, pound the roasted seeds and nuts with the ground cumin and salt. The mixture should be finely crushed and dry, not worked into a paste.

Serve with bread and olive oil, or keep in an airtight container for a maximum of a month.

These traditional spice bracelets are mentioned in the medieval cookery manual, *Kittab al-Wulsa Ila'L-Habib*. Mainly flavoured with coriander, they are sprinkled with sesame seeds and *mahlab* (p100), ground black cherry kernels, and are eaten for breakfast or as a snack during the day. In Yemen and Egypt, a little chilli powder is also sometimes added to the dough.

KAHK
(SPICE BRACELETS)

Serves 6
Preparation time approximately 2½ hours
Cooking time 1 hour 20 minutes (plus 1–2 hours, cooling and drying out)

450g (1lb) strong bread flour
1 tablespoon ground coriander
½ tablespoon ground cumin
½ tablespoon salt
25g (1oz) fresh yeast, or 10g (½oz) dried yeast
½ teaspoon sugar
110g (4oz) clarified butter (ghee)
1 egg, lightly beaten
Roughly 4 tablespoons sesame seeds
1–2 tablespoons mahlab (p100)

Sift the flour with the spices and salt into a large mixing bowl.

Dissolve the yeast with the sugar in a little lukewarm water, until it begins to bubble. Melt the clarified butter and then leave to cool.

Make a well in the middle of the flour and pour in the yeast and clarified butter. Using your hand, draw the flour in from the sides and work the mixture into a dough, adding a little lukewarm water to help bind it. Knead the dough for about 10 minutes, until smooth and pliable. Take a walnut-sized lump of the dough and roll it into a thin cigarette, about 10cm (4in) long, then bring the ends together, pressing them firmly, to make a bracelet. Repeat with the rest of the dough.

Brush the tops with the beaten egg, sprinkle with sesame seeds, and place the bracelets on an oiled baking tray. Leave in a warm place for 1–2 hours, until they have risen. Meanwhile, heat the oven to 180°C/350°F/gas mark 4.

Sprinkle the risen bracelets with *mahlab* and place them in the oven for 20 minutes. Reduce the heat to 150°C/300°F/gas mark 2 and bake them for an hour. Turn off the heat and leave them to cool and dry out in the oven. They should be firm and golden.

SAFFRON

Saffron

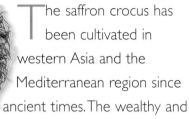

(ZAFFARAN) Crocus sativus

Safflower

The saffron crocus has been cultivated in western Asia and the Mediterranean region since ancient times. The wealthy and noble used saffron as a delicate scent in their banqueting halls and to colour their food and dye their clothes. Cleopatra is said to have used saffron for her complexion and Nero is reputed to have ordered the streets of Rome to be sprinkled with saffron water before he entered it. Saffron travelled to India from Persia and then to Spain with the Arabs. It is not to be confused with safflower, a plant related to the thistle and sunflower, which is often called 'poor man's saffron' as the deep orange-red flowers also yield yellow and red dyes. It is used as a cheap substitute for saffron, which is the only spice to be measured by the carat for it is worth its weight in gold.

HOW IT GROWS

Native to Persia and Asia Minor, the *Crocus sativus* is cultivated in Iran and Turkey, where it still grows wild. The best and most fragrant saffron is reputed to come from the sunny plateau of central Iran. Saffron is contained in the orange-red stigmas of this perennial bulb which flowers for only two weeks in October. The pretty lavender flowers are picked by hand in the early hours of the morning, before they wilt under the sun, and the delicate stigmas are skilfully prised out of each one and dried. Each crocus bulb produces only one or two flowers and each flower contains three stigmas, so it takes a staggering number of flowers, roughly 80,000, to obtain 450g (1lb) of dried saffron.

APPEARANCE AND TASTE

The dried stigmas appear in a tangle of wiry threads, about 2cm (1in) long, the texture of straw. The overall colour is burnt orange with tinges of red and yellow. The deeper the colour, the better the quality. It is mildly pungent and delicately perfumed with a slightly bitter taste. The threads turn tomato-red when soaked in water and impart a glorious yellow colour.

BUYING AND STORING

The dried stigmas are sealed in containers to prevent them from bleaching. As they are so expensive, they are sold in small quantities. This doesn't matter, though, as only two pinches are required for any one dish. Saffron needs to be stored away from direct light and the colour, flavour and fragrance deteriorate on keeping. Ground saffron is also available but it is really only useful for colour as it is easily adulterated and has virtually no fragrance or flavour.

Baskets of freshly picked crocus flowers

MEDICINAL USES

Medicinally, saffron was regarded as a tonic for the heart and melancholy, and a cure for fevers. It is also believed to be an aphrodisiac, while a hint of saffron in bed is reputed to have a soporific effect.

CULINARY USES

Saffron's primary role in the Middle East is a culinary one. Yellow being a happy colour, saffron dishes are often reserved for festive occasions. The strands can be added directly to a dish or soaked in warm water to extract their colour and fragrance. For some cakes and breads, the strands are ground to a fine powder with a little sugar. Throughout the Middle East, saffron is used to colour and flavour savoury rice dishes, milk puddings, and a delicious, creamy ice cream. The Turks make a saffron rice pudding called *zerde*, usually served at weddings, and the Iranians have *shollehzard*, also a saffron-flavoured rice pudding, which is served on the

Liquid saffron

anniversary of the death of a member of Prophet Muhammad's family. Of all the countries in the Middle East, saffron is most used in Iran, where it is added to many savoury and sweet dishes.

Desserts do not play a big role in the cuisine of Iran; fresh fruit is preferred instead, followed by coffee and sweetmeats. The milky puddings and rice desserts are generally reserved for raising spirits during bereavement or for inducing an appetite in an ill person. The following pudding is traditionally served to commemorate the martyrdom of the Prophet's grandson, Imam Hassan – a Shi'ite tradition which is also practised by many Sunni Muslims. Known as Imam Hüseyin to the Turks, the same occasion is marked by serving the grain and dried fruit pudding aşure (p109).

SHOLLEHZARD
(SAFFRON RICE PUDDING)

Serves 6–8
Preparation time 5 minutes
Cooking time approximately 45 minutes

110g (4oz) pudding rice, washed and drained
Roughly 1.8 litres (3 pints) water
175g (6oz) sugar
2 pinches saffron pistils, ground with a little sugar and soaked in 1–2 teaspoons tepid water
2 tablespoons rose water
2 tablespoons sunflower oil
Ground cinnamon
Pistachio slivers

Put the rice in a pan with the water and bring it to the boil. Reduce the heat and simmer, until the rice is very soft (approximately 25 minutes).

Stir in the sugar, saffron and rose water, and continue to simmer until the sugar has dissolved.

Stir in the oil and simmer for a few more minutes, then tip the rice into a serving bowl, or individual bowls. Leave to cool and set, then decorate with ground cinnamon and pistachio slivers, if you like.

In southern Iraq, Al Iraq, the main date- and rice-growing region of the country, the word for rice is *timman*. The plain steamed rice is similar to the *chelow* of neighbouring Iran and the rice dishes are like the Iranian *polow*, but the distinctly spicy flavours are reminiscent of the Arabian Gulf.

Timman z'affaran

TIMMAN Z'AFFARAN
(IRAQI SAFFRON RICE)

Serves 5–6
Preparation time 25 minutes
Cooking time approximately 45 minutes

2 pinches saffron threads
½ teaspoon sugar
2 tablespoons rose water
850ml (1½ pints) beef or chicken stock
450g (1lb) long-grain rice, washed and soaked in cold water for about 20 minutes
Salt
2 tablespoons clarified butter (ghee)
110g (4oz) blanched almonds
1 onion, chopped
225g (8oz) minced beef
1–2 teaspoons baharat (p162)
2 tablespoons sultanas

Grind the saffron threads with the sugar, add the rose water and leave to steep to extract the colour.

Pour the stock into a heavy-based pan, bring it to the boil, and stir in the saffron. Drain the rice and toss it into the stock with some salt (if the stock is well seasoned omit the salt). Reduce the heat and simmer, uncovered, for about 15 minutes, until almost all the water has been absorbed.

Meanwhile, heat the clarified butter and stir in the almonds. Cook until golden brown, then remove from the pan.

Add the onion to the pan and fry until it begins to colour. Stir in the minced beef and cook until well browned. Add the *baharat* and sultanas, cook for a minute, then season with salt.

Tip the meat mixture onto the rice and carefully fold it through until they are well mixed. Cover the pan with a clean tea towel, followed by the lid, turn off the heat and leave the rice to steam for about 20 minutes. Pile the rice mixture onto a serving dish and garnish with the golden almonds.

CUMIN

(KAMMUN) *Cuminum cyminum*

Cumin seeds

Cumin has been grown in Egypt, Arabia, and the Mediterranean regions since ancient times. In the Bible, there are references to the harvested plant being threshed to extract the seeds. The Romans used cumin frequently, often as a substitute for pepper. And Pliny's remark on the spice speaks for itself: 'When one is tired of all seasonings, cumin remains welcome.'

HOW IT GROWS

Cumin is the seed-like fruit of a pretty little annual herb of the parsley family, thought to be native to the Nile Valley. The plant grows to about 30cm (1ft) high with small flowers that range from white or pink to mauve.

APPEARANCE AND TASTE

Cumin seeds are camel-coloured with a greenish tinge. They are small and elongated, about 5–6mm (¼in) long, and look very similar to caraway seeds. They are slightly bitter, with a distinctive warm taste and aroma which are deliciously enhanced when the seeds are roasted. Less common is the black cumin seed which is known as 'black cumin', a name also attributed to the unrelated nigella seed.

BUYING AND STORING

Whole cumin seeds are often sold with tiny flecks of dried stalk, left from the threshing and drying process. When you open a new packet, they should have a distinctive, spicy aroma and they keep well in an airtight container, stored in a cool dry place away from the light. The ready-ground spice loses its flavour quickly so it's best to grind your own.

MEDICINAL USES

Cumin is regarded as a dependable cure for gastro-intestinal complaints. A hot infusion with the seeds is drunk to aid the digestion and to calm flatulent colic.

Ground cumin

CULINARY USES

As the belief that cumin calms flatulence is widespread in the Middle East, it is added to many pulse dishes, such as the Egyptian *ful medames*. It is also used in a variety of meat, vegetable, egg and rice dishes. It is the principal flavouring in *maqaniq* and *sujuk* (two slightly different air-dried sausages made with minced lamb or beef and spices), and it is used in the fenugreek and red pepper paste that coats the air-dried beef fillet called *pastırma* in Turkey and *basterma* in Syria and Lebanon (p198). Ground cumin is also one of the main spices in the Arab spice mixture, *baharat* (p162), and the Iranian spice mixture, *advieh* (p169). And, along with spices like coriander, it is used in some bread doughs, like the medieval savoury bracelets *kahk* (p163).

Hard-boiled eggs are a great favourite on pilgrimages and picnics, and for festivals such as *Mulid el Nabi*, which celebrate the birth of the Prophet. But they are not just plain hard-boiled eggs, they are flavoured with spices, coloured with saffron, or cooked gently with onion skins to the ancient recipe *beid hamine*, until the egg yolks are so creamy they melt in the mouth and the whites turn beige. In the following

Sujuk (sucuk in Turkish) hanging in the market, Istanbul

medieval recipe from Egypt, which is as popular in the home as it is on the street, the hard-boiled eggs are fried quickly in olive oil and then dipped in cumin or mixed spices.

BAID MUTAJJAN
(FRIED HARD-BOILED EGGS WITH CUMIN)

Serves 3–6
Preparation time 10 minutes
Cooking time 4–5 minutes

2 teaspoons ground cumin
2 teaspoons ground coriander
A scant teaspoon ground cinnamon
Salt
6 freshly cooked hard-boiled eggs
3 tablespoons olive oil

Mix the spices together with some salt. Shell the eggs while still warm and heat the oil in a frying pan.

Fry the eggs lightly, rolling them about in the pan to make sure they are evenly coated, then dip them immediately into the spices. Eat while still warm.

The cured, horseshoe-shaped sausages hanging in the markets and charcuteries of the Middle East are generally made from beef or lamb and heavily spiced with garlic, red chilli pepper, and cumin. They are delicious sliced and grilled, or cooked with beans in a stew. The following Anatolian dish is traditionally made in an earthenware pot, a *güveç*, and left to cook slowly in the ashes of a fire or the cooling bread ovens. More conventionally, it can be made on top of the stove, or in the oven. Turkish *sucuk* and Arab *sujuk* and *maqaniq* are available in some Middle Eastern stores.

GÜVEÇTE SUCUK
(SPICY SAUSAGE WITH BLACK-EYED BEANS)

Serves 4–6
Preparation time 20 minutes (plus 6 hours' soaking)
Cooking time approximately 45 minutes

1–2 tablespoons clarified butter (ghee)
1 onion, halved and sliced
2–3 cloves garlic, roughly chopped
1 teaspoon sugar
1 teaspoon cumin seeds
1 teaspoon coriander seeds
1 cumin-spiced sucuk, sliced
110g (4oz) black-eyed beans, soaked for 6 hours
5–6 tomatoes, skinned and chopped
Salt and freshly ground black pepper
A bunch of fresh flat-leaf parsley or coriander, chopped

In a heavy-based pan, melt the clarified butter (or ghee) and stir in the onion, garlic, and sugar. When they begin to colour, stir in the seeds, followed by the sliced *sucuk*.

Cook for a minute or two to release some of the flavours from the *sucuk*, then stir in the beans and tomatoes. Pour in enough water to just cover the beans, put on the lid and simmer for about 30 minutes, until the beans are tender and the liquid has reduced. Alternatively, cook it in the oven (on 180°C/350°F/gas mark 4) for 30–40 minutes.

Season to taste and toss in the fresh herbs.

Güveçte sucuk

**Cardamom
pods**

CARDAMOM

(HAIL) *Elettaria cardamomum*

CULINARY USES

In some parts of the Arab world, the seeds are used solely as a digestive, or as a flavouring in coffee. In Iran, the pods are often infused in tea and coffee. When the whole pods are added to a dish for flavouring, they are not meant to be eaten – the husk-like shell is tough and indigestible. The seeds are used for flavouring some sweet biscuits and pastries, such as the chickpea shortbreads, *nân-e nokhodchi*, and the almond pastries, *ghotâb*, from Iran. They are used in some puddings and sweetmeats, such as *al-salooq* from the Arabian Gulf, and, mixed with other spices, they are added to meat stews, particularly the Yemeni dishes *akuw'a* (p156), oxtail stew, and *kirshuh*, liver and kidney stew. The traditional Iranian spice mixture, *advieh*, which varies

Known as the 'queen of spices', black pepper being the 'king', cardamom is one of the most ancient of all spices, used by the early Egyptians and the ancient Greeks and Romans. With a long history as a prized article of trade, cardamom reached Europe through the old caravan routes. It was of such value that cardamom seeds were sent to family and friends as an invitation to a wedding ceremony. Even today, in the Middle East cardamom is the third most expensive spice after saffron and vanilla.

HOW IT GROWS

Cardamom is the dried fruit of a perennial herb, which grows up to 5m (16ft) tall. It belongs to the ginger family and is indigenous to south India. The fruits, which are oblong, are picked before they are ripe and then cured by drying until they become hard and a woody green colour.

ones and the white ones, which are just green ones that have been bleached. Each fruit, or pod, contains cells which hold as many twenty small pungent black or dark brown seeds. When crushed or chewed, these seeds have a distinct, warming aroma with a lingering, almost bitter-sweet, eucalyptus-like taste.

MEDICINAL USES

An infusion of cardamom pods in hot water is drunk to soothe sore heads and stomach disorders. The seeds are also chewed to relieve heartburn and to freshen the breath.

APPEARANCE AND TASTE

There are a variety of cardamom pods but the most commonly used ones in the Middle East are the ribbed, diamond-shaped, wood-green

BUYING AND STORING

Look for whole, unbroken, green pods to get the freshest, aromatic seeds, which should be black or very dark brown. The pods keep well in an airtight container in a cool, dry place but ground cardamom loses its flavour very quickly, so it's better to grind your own.

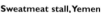

Sweatmeat stall, Yemen

**Fragrant advieh
with rose petals**

considerably from the Persian Gulf to the Caspian Sea, always includes cardamom seeds. A basic *advieh* recipe will include roughly equal amounts of cumin seeds, caraway, cardamom, cinnamon, and coriander, all ground to a powder with turmeric. For a mild *advieh*, some people add a lot of cinnamon to the mixture; for a fragrant *advieh*, saffron, dried rose petals, and pistachios might be added; and for a hearty *advieh*, the addition of black pepper and cloves to a greater amount of cumin, coriander, and turmeric gives it a spicy kick, more akin to a mild Indian *garam masala*. Cardamom seeds are also used in the Yemeni spice mixture *hawayij* (p156), a blend of pepper, caraway, cardamom and turmeric.

Fiery flavours are characteristic of Yemeni cooking. Hot chilli pastes and spicy dips, popular from sunrise to sunset, are made in every household. *Zhug* is both a paste added to soups and stews, and a dip for bread. Only a little amount is required at a time.

ZHUG
(HOT CARDAMOM AND GARLIC RELISH)

Makes 1 small jar
Preparation time 20 minutes (+ 1 hour's soaking)
Cooking time 10 minutes

*4 dried red chillies, soaked in
 water for 1 hour
1 whole head of garlic, peeled
 and roughly chopped
The seeds of 4 cardamom pods
1 teaspoon caraway seeds
1 teaspoon black peppercorns
½ teaspoon salt
A bunch of fresh coriander leaves,
 roughly chopped*

Drain the chillies and cut off the stems. Using a pestle and

mortar, pound the softened chillies to a pulp with the garlic.

Grind the cardamom seeds, caraway and peppercorns to a coarse powder and add it to the pulped chilli and garlic. Pound it all together with the salt and fresh coriander, until it resembles a coarse purée.

Tip the mixture into a small pan with about 50ml (2fl oz) water. Simmer uncovered for about 10 minutes, then leave to cool.

Spoon the relish into a jar, seal it and keep it in the refrigerator, ready to use.

A guest in an Arab home is treated like a king, offered coffee or tea, dates, sweetmeats, syrupy pastries, and digestive spices, including cardamom. The guest is not left for a moment without being offered something. The following pastries, shaped like crescent moons as a symbol of Islam, are just one of many sweetmeats offered with coffee.

AL-SALOOQ
(DEEP-FRIED CARDAMOM PASTRIES)

Serves 6
Preparation time 30 minutes
Cooking time approximately 20
 minutes

*450g (1lb) flour
1 teaspoon baking powder
1 teaspoon ground cardamom
110ml (4fl oz) melted butter or
 sunflower oil
110ml (4fl oz) milk, boiled and
 left to cool*
*sunflower oil for deep-frying
Icing sugar*

Sift the flour, baking powder and ground cardamom into a bowl.

Add the melted butter and, using a wooden spoon, mix into the flour until it is crumbly. Pour in the cooled milk and mix to a soft dough. Knead until smooth.

Take walnut-sized lumps of dough in your hands, roll them into fat fingers, and shape them into crescent moons.

Heat enough oil for deep-frying in a pan and fry the crescent moons, in batches, until they are golden brown. Drain them on kitchen towel and toss them into a bowl of icing sugar

Al-salooq

BAY LEAF

(WARAQ AL GAR) *Laurus nobilis*

Also known as sweet bay or sweet laurel, the bay leaf is thought to have originally come from Asia Minor. The ancient Greeks and Romans used bay leaves to crown warriors, athletes, and poets, hence the term 'poet laureate'. In Persian, the name for bay leaf is *barg-e boo*, which means 'leaf of fragrance'.

Dried bay leaves

HOW IT GROWS

The tree belongs to the family *Lauraceae*, which also includes cinnamon and avocado. It is a small tree with glossy, grass-green leaves and waxy, creamy blossoms.

APPEARANCE AND TASTE

Fresh bay leaves are shiny, slightly waxy, spear-shaped and the colour of freshly cut grass. They are slightly bitter and should be used sparingly with fish or meat. The dried, khaki-coloured leaves, on the other hand, are quite spicy without any trace of bitterness.

BUYING AND STORING

The fresh leaves will keep for a few days in a plastic bag in the refrigerator but it is best to dry them, or buy them already dried, and store them in an airtight container in a cool, dark place. They keep well for about six months and then they start to lose their flavour.

CULINARY USES

Fresh bay leaves can be used in soups and stews, if they are shredded before use, but generally it is the dried leaves that are used most. Whole or crushed, they are added to fish dishes, stews, soups, meat and poultry stocks, and marinades. For heavy lamb dishes, the leaves are crushed and fried with the meat to cut the fat and the strong muttony flavour and odour. In Turkey, the dried leaves are steeped and simmered in tea with dried figs and sugar.

In the Middle East, almost every part of the sheep is consumed. The head is usually rubbed with spices and onion juice and then roasted, or it is boiled in a simple broth, which is often used in the traditional *fatta* (p34) dishes. Your butcher should be able to prepare the head for you – you can ask him to keep the eyes, if you like.

RAS KHAROUF
(SHEEP'S HEAD SOUP)

Serves 4
Preparation time 10 minutes
  (plus 2 hours' soaking time)
Cooking time 2 hours

1 sheep's head, skinned with the
  brain removed
1 onion, quartered
Roughly 6 peppercorns
3–4 bay leaves
2 dried limes, pierced
Salt

Using a sharp knife, cut the chin muscles on both cheeks and separate the head from the jaw (you could ask a butcher to do this). Wash the head well and soak for 2 hours in salted water, changing the water once or twice.

Place the head, onion, bay leaves, peppercorns and limes in a deep pan and cover with just enough water. Bring to the boil, remove any scum, and cook for about 2 hours, until the meat comes away easily from the bone.

Lift the head out onto a board, remove all bones, and slice the meat and chop the tongue. Strain the stock, return it to the pan, then season it with salt. Add the meat and tongue and serve hot.

Bay tree

Tajin samak

Baking fish whole in the oven is one of the most popular ways of cooking fish in the Middle East. Almost any fish will do, rubbed in olive oil or clarified butter, or marinated in onion juice, and baked with bay leaves, thyme, oregano or garlic. The clarified butter, crispy roasted garlic and bay leaves give the following dish a lovely flavour.

TAJIN SAMAK
(FISH BAKED WITH BAY LEAVES)

Serves 2–4
Preparation time 10 minutes
Cooking time approximately 45 minutes

1 whole fish, such as trout, sea bass, red mullet, weighing about 1.3kg (3lb), gutted and washed
Salt
1–2 tablespoons clarified butter, melted
½ teaspoon cumin seeds
2 cloves garlic, chopped
4–5 bay leaves
Lemon wedges to serve

Preheat oven to 150°C/300°F/gas mark 2.

Make a few incisions in the skin of the fish, rub it in salt, and place it in a baking dish.

Melt the clarified butter with the cumin seeds, garlic and a few crushed bay leaves. Pour it over the fish and tuck the remaining bay leaves around it.

Bake the fish for about 45 minutes, or until it is ready, and serve hot with lemon to squeeze over it.

MINT

(NAANA) *Mentha*

Mint

Mint was grown by the Romans, who pickled it in vinegar. Similarly, a medieval Arab dressing was made with dried mint, aromatic herbs, saffron and vinegar. And the Ottomans, who categorised herbs and vegetables as 'warming' or 'cooling' to the blood, regarded mint as warming. With its refreshing and digestive qualities, mint is one of the most popular herbs in the Middle East. There are many varieties with different strengths and flavours but, apart from spearmint, which is used primarily in tea, most of the mint grown in the Middle East is interchangeable. The Arabic name for mint, *naana*, means 'gift of Allah'.

Herb seller with bundles of mint

and hairy, others are smooth and papery. Some are big and oval, others long and pointed. Some are sweet and minty, others peppery, fruity or like spearmint. Whatever the variety, all should have a clean, strong, minty aroma of their own. Dried mint is usually dark green or grass-green in colour with a more subtle fragrance.

BUYING AND STORING

Mint is sold fresh and dried but, undoubtedly, the fresh is far superior. Dried mint loses its flavour quickly and is better stored in vinegar than in an airtight container. Fresh mint can be kept for a few days in a plastic bag in the refrigerator or with the stems immersed in a glass of water.

MEDICINAL USES

A soothing herb, mint is often used in infusions to ease sore throats, bronchitis, nausea, and stomach disorders. Mint oil is used in throat lozenges, in ointments for weary limbs, and as the fresh flavour in many toothpastes.

CULINARY USES

Fresh mint is one of the most pleasing and useful herbs. In many parts of the Middle East, bowls of fresh mint leaves are passed around during or after a meal, to freshen the breath, or to aid the digestion after a heavy feast. The leaves are also infused in boiling water to make a soothing tisane. Fresh and dried mint leaves are often added to yogurt to make numerous, delectable *mezze* dishes, such as the Turkish *haydari*, a simple dip consisting of yogurt, garlic and mint, and the cool, refreshing yogurt drink, *abdug* (p43 – *ayran* in Turkey). In Iran the leaves are used to make *sharbat-e sekanjebeen*, a vinegar and sugar syrup flavoured with mint, which is used as the basis of a refreshing drink.

Throughout the Middle East, mint is added liberally to simple vegetable, pulse, and grain salads, such as *tabbouleh*, it is one of the preferred herbs for many rice dishes and, along with parsley, it is added to the various regional 'gypsy', 'shepherd' and 'country' salads, which usually consist of chillies, onions, cucumber and tomatoes. As a 'warming' herb, it is often combined with dill and used to flavour cheese-filled pastries and to balance 'cooling' vegetables such as courgettes, marrows and broad beans. In Turkey, fresh or dried mint is used to flavour bowls of *cacık*, a

Mint bush

HOW IT GROWS

Mint is a perennial herb that grows easily, both wild and cultivated, in temperate and cool climates. It is a bushy plant and can grow up to 60cm (2ft) in height.

APPEARANCE AND TASTE

Fresh mint leaves come in different shades of green. Some are tough, scalloped, textured

Dried mint

dish of yogurt and cucumber, which is often served as a refreshing accompaniment to meat dishes, or as a chilled soup. A similar dish called *mâst-o khiyâr* (p215) is made in Iran, only there it is more exotic with the addition of chopped walnuts, sultanas, chives and rose petals. Also in Iran, mint is added with parsley to the stews from the province of Mazandaran, such as *khoresht-e reevâs*, a delightful lamb stew with rhubarb. And, in the same way that melted butter and red pepper are poured over some dishes in Turkey, a condiment called *na'nâ dâgh*, which consists of dried mint stirred into melted butter or *ghee*, is poured over winter soups in Iran.

High up in the mountains of eastern Anatolia sits the little town of Bingöl, meaning 'a thousand lakes', after which this dish is named. The delicious combination of raw, fried, or steamed carrot with yogurt is found in every pocket of Turkey, but the addition of the pomegranate seeds and mint, representing the thousand lakes, places this *mezze* recipe in Bingöl.

BİNGÖL CACIK
(CARROT AND YOGURT SALAD WITH POMEGRANATE AND MINT)

Serves 4 (as part of mezze spread)
Preparation time 15 minutes
Cooking time —

600ml (1 pint) thick yogurt
2 cloves garlic, crushed
3 carrots, peeled and grated
Seeds of 1 pomegranate
A bunch fresh mint leaves, finely chopped
Salt and freshly ground black pepper

Beat the yogurt in a bowl with the garlic. Beat in the carrots with most of the pomegranate seeds and mint.

Season to taste and spoon the salad into a serving bowl, or individual bowls.

Sprinkle the remaining pomegranate seeds and chopped mint leaves over the top.

The word for rhubarb in Farsi is *reevâs*, which stems from the old Persian word *reev*, meaning 'a shining light'. Believed to cleanse the blood and purify the system, rhubarb has been used in Iranian cooking since ancient times. In Safavid times, the plant was used to thicken lamb and vegetable stews, but today finely chopped mint and parsley give substance to such stews. This pretty pink and green stew is traditionally served to aid the digestion.

KHORESHT-E REEVÂS
(RHUBARB STEW WITH MINT AND PARSLEY)

Serves 4–6
Preparation time 25 minutes
Cooking time approximately 1½ hours

2–3 tablespoons olive oil
2 onions, halved and sliced
450g (1lb) lean lamb, trimmed and cubed
A big bunch of fresh mint, chopped finely
A big bunch of fresh flat-leaf parsley, chopped finely
Salt and freshly ground black pepper
Roughly 900g (2lb) rhubarb, trimmed and chopped into 2½cm (1in) lengths

Heat the oil in a heavy-based pan and fry the onions, until they turn golden. Add the meat and brown it on all sides, then pour in enough water to just cover. Put on the lid and simmer gently for about 30 minutes.

In a separate pan, fry the chopped herbs in a little extra olive oil, tossing them all the time so that they release their flavour but don't burn. Add the herbs to the meat and continue to simmer for a further 40–50 minutes, until the meat is tender.

Season the dish, then add the rhubarb, cooking it for a few minutes so that it is hot through but not soft and mushy. Serve immediately with plain rice.

Khoresht-e reevâs

NIGELLA

(HABBAT AL-BARAKAH) *Nigella sativa*

Nigella

Native to western Asia and the Mediterranean region of the Middle East, this little black seed is sometimes mistakenly known as black cumin or black onion seed, although it has nothing to do with either and doesn't taste a bit like them. In Arabic, the nigella seed is known under two names: *habbat al-sauda*, meaning 'black seed', and *habbat al-barakah*, which means 'seed of grace'. In Farsi, it is *siâhdâneh*, which also means 'black seed' and in Turkish, it is known as *çöreotu*, as it is most commonly associated with *çörek*, a sweet bun sprinkled with nigella seeds, eaten during the Sweet Festival immediately after *Ramazan* (*Ramadan* in Arabic).

HOW IT GROWS

The *Nigella sativa* plant is a close relative of *Nigella damascena*, or love-in-the-mist, whose seeds can also be used as a condiment. It is a hardy annual herb which grows wild on the forest floors and is also cultivated for its seeds. It grows to about 60cm (2ft) in height with dense, feathery foliage and bluish-white flowers which form seed capsules. These have to be collected before they are ripe, otherwise the pods will burst open and scatter the seeds. The pods are dried whole and then crushed to release the seeds.

APPEARANCE AND TASTE

Nigella seeds look like tiny, charcoal teardrops. They are very aromatic with a slightly bitter, peppery flavour with a light floral hint. It is one of the distinct tastes and smells on bread in the Middle East.

BUYING AND STORING

The seeds are usually sold whole. They can be easily found in Middle Eastern, Indian and wholefood stores. They keep well in an airtight container in a cool, dry place.

CULINARY USES

Nigella seeds are primarily used for sprinkling on biscuits, breads, and buns, such as the Turkish *çörek*. They are used for flavouring vinegar, particularly in Iran where their distinctive flavour features in pickles and preserves such as *torshi-ye leeteh*, a pickled relish made with vegetables and herbs, and *torshi-ye meeveh*, a blend of pickled fruit and vegetables. They are sometimes roasted and crushed and added to yogurt or onion-juice marinades for lamb. They are used in some simple Armenian salads made with root vegetables, such as radishes and carrots. In some parts of the Middle East, nigella seeds are sprinkled over the everyday white cheeses and they are a feature of the Lebanese *hallumi*.

Potato salads vary from region to region but, generally, they are first cooked in oil and spices and then left to cool. Although this recipe is from the Arabian Gulf, it is similar to dishes in Egypt and Iraq.

A beautiful and fragile Nigella flower

SALATAT BATATA
(ARABIAN POTATO SALAD)

Serves 4–6
Preparation time 25 minutes
Cooking time 15 minutes

6–8 medium-sized new potatoes, boiled with their skins on until tender but firm
2 large onions, halved and finely sliced
3–4 tablespoons olive oil or sunflower oil
2 cloves garlic, crushed
1 tablespoon nigella seeds
½ teaspoon ground coriander
½ teaspoon ground cumin
1 teaspoon ground turmeric
1 teaspoon ground chilli
Salt and freshly ground black pepper
Juice of 1 lime plus extra for serving

Remove the skins from the cooked potatoes and cut them into bite-size pieces.

In a heavy-based pan, soften the onions in the oil but don't brown them. Add the garlic and nigella seeds and cook for a minute, then stir in the spices. Reduce the heat and toss the potatoes into the pan, making sure they are well-coated with oil and spices. Season to taste and spoon the mixture into a dish. Leave to cool, add the lime juice and serve with lime wedges.

Turp salatası

The following dish is Armenian. It is light and refreshing, designed to be eaten with grilled kebabs. The long white radishes, also called 'mouli', are used for this salad but carrots and celeriac work well too.

TURP SALATASI
(RADISH SALAD WITH NIGELLA)

Serves 4–6
Preparation time 25–30 minutes
Cooking time –

4 white radishes, peeled and grated
2 teaspoons nigella seeds
2 tablespoons olive oil
Juice of 1 lime or lemon
Salt
A small bunch fresh parsley or coriander, finely chopped (optional)

Put the grated radish into a bowl. Add the nigella seeds and pour over the oil and lime juice. Sprinkle with salt and mix well.

Leave to sit for about 15 minutes to let the flavours mingle, then mix it again. Toss in the herbs, if you like, and serve.

BASIL

(REYHAN) *Ocimum basilicum*

Apart from in Iran, basil is not used widely in the Middle East. The old belief that the plant breeds scorpions may account for its scant use. However, the aromatic, pungent green leaves are often chewed as an appetiser, a breath freshener, or are simply passed around in a bowl as an accompaniment to a meat dish.

Green basil

HOW IT GROWS

Originally native to India, the green-leafed plant is cultivated in Iran and some parts of the Mediterranean region. It is a pretty plant with a lovely smell and small, purple-tinged white flowers at the top of each stalk. A smaller-leafed, purple variety, which grows wild in the Mediterranean region, is used more widely in the Middle East.

APPEARANCE AND TASTE

The leaves of sweet basil should be soft and bright green with a lovely, pungent smell, particularly if you tear them with your fingers. The wild purple basil, which has a slightly spicy flavour, is similar to the cultivated dark, opal basil, but it has smaller leaves and is quite vibrant in colour.

BUYING AND STORING

Always look for fresh, soft leaves with a strong scent. Once the leaves go limp, they lose their flavour. Fresh leaves can be kept in plastic bags in the refrigerator for a day or two. They can also be preserved in oil or vinegar to impart their strong flavour. Basil loses its flavour when dried.

CULINARY USES

Both the green and purple varieties are used to flavour stews, kebabs and salads. It is one of the preferred herbs to flavour aubergines, often included in the popular stuffed aubergine pickle. In Iran, the fresh, pungent leaves are pounded with pistachios to make a kind of pesto, served with the thin noodles, *reshteh* (p125). Also in Iran, the sweet basil seeds are used to make a fragrant syrup, the basis of a refreshing sherbet drink. In Iraq, basil is added to the ubiquitous yogurt drink *abdug* (p43 – *ayran* in Turkey), which is generally flavoured with mint in other parts of the Middle East.

Purple basil

Yogurt dips, flavoured with herbs, make popular *mezze* dishes. The following recipe is from Iran, but variations of it pop up all over the Middle East.

POLOOR
(YOGURT AND CHEESE DIP WITH HERBS)

Serves 2–4
Preparation time 5 minutes
Cooking time –

110g (4oz) white cheese (feta)
110g (4oz) thick, strained yogurt
A mixed bunch of fresh basil, mint, parsley and dill
Salt (optional)

Mash the cheese in a bowl and blend it with the yogurt.

Wash the herbs and pat them dry, then chop them finely and beat into the yogurt and cheese.

Season with salt, if necessary, and serve with crusty or flat bread as a dip or spread.

This fragrant Persian dish is traditionally made at *No Rooz*, the spring festival, with the first fresh herbs of the year. The rice symbolises bounty, and the dish is often served with a herb omelette, the eggs symbolising birth, or with lightly fried fish, which symbolise freshness.

SABZI POLOW
(RICE WITH FRESH HERBS)

Serves 4
Preparation time 10 minutes (plus 3 hours' soaking of the rice)
Cooking time 35–40 minutes

1 tablespoon salt
450g (1lb) long-grain rice, well rinsed and soaked in salted water for 3 hours
Roughly 75ml (3fl oz) sunflower oil

A big bunch of fresh basil, parsley,
mint, dill, chives and coriander,
finely chopped
1 clove garlic, finely chopped
1 teaspoon ground fenugreek
2 pinches of saffron pistils
Sugar
2 tablespoons clarified butter
(ghee)

In a deep pan, bring about 2
litres (3½ pints) of water to the
boil with a tablespoon of salt.
Drain the rice and toss it into
the boiling water for 2–3
minutes. Test to see if it is al
dente, then drain it and rinse
with lukewarm water.

Heat the sunflower oil in a
heavy-based pan and sprinkle a
layer of rice across the bottom,
followed by a layer of herbs,
garlic and fenugreek. Repeat
two or three times, finishing with
a layer of rice, piled into a
conical shape.

Using an inverted wooden
spoon, poke a few holes right
through the rice to the bottom
and cover the pan with a clean
tea towel, followed by the lid –
lift any trailing flaps of towel up
over the lid. Keep the pan over a
high heat for a minute or two to
get the steam up, then reduce
the heat to very low and leave it
to steam for about 30 minutes.

Using a small pestle and mortar,
grind the saffron with a tiny
sprinkling of sugar to a powder,
then stir in a tablespoon of
boiling water. Put 2–3 spoonfuls
of the cooked rice in a bowl,
pour over the liquid saffron and
mix together.

Toss the rest of the rice lightly
and tip it onto a serving dish,
creating a mound. Sprinkle the
saffron rice over it, then quickly
melt the clarified butter and
pour it all over the rice. Serve
immediately.

Sabzi polow

ORCHID ROOT

(SAHLAB) *Orchis mascula*

Orchid roots

Orchid roots have long been thought to have aphrodisiac qualities and it is easy to see why. The root is testicle-shaped, hence the name *orchis*, meaning 'testicle' in Greek, and the Arabic for the root is *thalab* (fox), originating from *khusya th-thalb*, which translates as 'fox's testicle'. The orchid roots are ground to a powder which plays an important role as a gelatinous, thickening agent in a unique ice cream and in a hot winter drink believed to be nutritious for children.

HOW IT GROWS

The roots come from various members of the orchid family – namely *Orchis latifolca*, *Orchis militaris*, *Orchis morio* and *Orchis mascula*. These orchid plants grow in the temperate climates of the Middle East.

APPEARANCE AND TASTE

The small, dried roots are hard and bulb-shaped. They are slightly yellowish in colour, or chalky white. Often they are sold on strings, like long, beaded necklaces. The roots are ground into a fine, white, almost silky, odourless powder, also called *sahlab* (*salep* in Turkey). When blended with milk, it has a very sublte taste.

BUYING AND STORING

The dried roots, which are sold in the markets in the Middle East, are expensive and difficult to source outside the region. Ground orchid root, which is also expensive, is available in some Middle Eastern stores, but make sure you don't buy 'instant *sahlab*' which is a mixture of cornflour and orchid root used to make an inferior drink. Pure orchid root powder will keep for a only few months in an airtight container.

Sahlab

CULINARY USES

The ground orchid root, *sahlab* is used more for its properties as a gelatinous thickening agent than for its taste. Principally, it is used in a thick, hot, sweet, milky drink, topped with a sprinkling of cinnamon, which is particularly popular in Turkey where it is made in big brass or copper urns. And in Iran, Syria, Lebanon and Turkey, it is used to make a snowy-white ice cream, giving it a pleasing elastic consistency. As the creamy ice cream is spooned out it seems to stretch.

This is a lovely, thick winter drink, made with milk and flavoured with cinnamon. It is particularly popular in Istanbul and Bursa, where tea-rooms display the large copper urns in which the *salep* is made. It is also a popular drink in the ski resort Uludağ, above Bursa.

SALEP
(ORCHID ROOT DRINK)

Serves 3–4
Preparation time –
Cooking time approximately 10 minutes

1 tablespoon salep
600ml (1 pint) milk
2 tablespoons sugar
Ground cinnamon

Mix the *salep* to a loose paste with a little of the milk.

Heat the rest of the milk with the sugar in a heavy-based saucepan, stirring all the time. Just as it is about to boil, reduce the heat, and stir a little of the hot milk into the slaked *salep* paste, then tip the *salep* into the pan.

Stir vigorously until the mixture thickens, then pour it into individual cups. Sprinkle each one with cinnamon and drink while it's piping hot.

Thickened with *sahlab* and flavoured with *mastic* and orange blossom water, this snow-white ice cream is popular in the Middle East, particularly with the older generation, for whom ice cream was a special treat. Traditionally, the ice-cream sellers made it in large barrel-shaped cylinders, stirring it with a long, rotating pole around the hollow centre which was filled with ice. Nowadays, most ice creams are made commercially and there are many to choose from, but traditional ice-cream sellers can still be seen in the streets of Cairo, Damascus and Istanbul. In the regions that were once part of the Ottoman Empire, a creamy version of this classic ice cream is known as *dondurma kaymak*, from the Turkish *kaymaklı dondurma*. In Iran, a similar ice cream is called *bastani sa'labi*.

BUZA AL-HALIB
(SNOW-WHITE ICE CREAM)

Serves 6–8
Preparation time 2 minutes
Cooking time approximately 25
   minutes

3 tablespoons sahlab
1.2 litres (2 pints) milk
225g (8oz) sugar

Salep

*A small piece mastic (the size of
   half a fingernail), pounded with ½
   teaspoon sugar*
*1 tablespoon orange blossom
   water*
Pistachio nuts

Mix the *sahlab* to a loose paste
with a little of the milk. Put the
rest of the milk in a heavy-based
pan with the sugar and bring it to
the boil, stirring all the time.

Reduce the heat, add some of
the hot milk to the *sahlab* paste
and tip the *sahlab* into the milk,
stirring vigorously. Add the
ground mastic and keep stirring
vigorously, until it has dissolved.

Simmer the mixture gently for
about 15 minutes, stirring from
time to time, until it is thick. Beat
in the orange blossom water
and pour the mixture into a
bowl or dish for the freezer.

Leave it to cool, then cover and
freeze, beating it at intervals to
break up the crystals. (Or pour
the cooled mixture into an ice-
cream maker and freeze
according to the instructions.)

When ready to serve, spoon the
ice cream into bowls and sprinkle
with chopped pistachio nuts.

PARSLEY

(BAQDOUNIS) *Petroselinum crispum*

Parsley – the flat-leaf variety – is probably the most popular of all herbs in the Middle East. It is sold like big bunches of flowers. Used liberally in cooking throughout the region, it is also served on its own to eat with bread, to cut the spice, to cleanse the palate, to sharpen the appetite, or to freshen the breath. In Roman times, recipes often called for the seeds as well as leaves but nowadays only the leaves are used.

Fresh parsley

HOW IT GROWS

The parsley plant is related to celery and is native to the Mediterranean region. It is a fairly hardy plant and grows wild or cultivated in most places.

APPEARANCE AND TASTE

Flat-leaf parsley looks a bit like coriander, although it has stiffer stems. It is usually a darker green than the curly variety and is packed with that distinctive parsley aroma and taste which are really only released when it is chopped.

BUYING AND STORING

The fresh leaves and stems should be quite crisp and look fresh. They will last for a few days in a plastic bag in the refrigerator, or with the stems dipped in a glass of water. Dried parsley is a waste of time: it smells and tastes like dried grass.

CULINARY USES

Roughly chopped leaves and stalks are added by the handful to numerous salads, such as the Arab *fattush* and the Turkish *çoban salatası*, and to soups, stews, rice dishes and numerous meatball dishes. The leaves, dressed with a little lemon juice, are even sometimes offered as a salad by themselves. In Iran, parsley is one of the main herbs used in egg dishes, such as *kookoo-ye sabzi*, and combined with mint, it is used to thicken the sauce of traditional stews, such as *khoresht-e reevðs* (p173), from the province of Mazandaran. It was the favoured herb in the Ottoman kitchens for meatballs and for meat stuffings. It is used in vast quantities in the Arab cracked wheat salad, *tabbouleh* (*tabbuleh*), and in the Turkish version, *kısır*. The strong, garlicky dips and sauces, made with crushed nuts or *tahini*, are often lightened with chopped parsley. And stalks of leafy parsley are used to garnish most dishes, especially grilled meats and fish.

Traditionally a mountain dish from the eastern Mediterranean, *tabbouleh* (*tabbuleh*) has become one of the most popular Middle Eastern salads, served as a *mezze* dish or with grilled meat. It is believed to have originated from *safsuf*, a meatless stuffing for vine leaves. In the villages, it is still sometimes served with tender vine leaves to scoop it up and, in Turkey, a similar dish, *kısır*, is served in vine or lettuce leaves. The quantities and ingredients vary, but a traditional *tabbouleh* is always packed with parsley.

TABBOULEH
(BULGUR SALAD WITH MINT AND PARSLEY)

Serves 6
Preparation time 35 minutes
Cooking time –

225g (8oz) fine-grained bulgur
1–2 red onions or 6 spring onions, finely chopped
2–3 large tomatoes, skinned and finely chopped
A huge bunch flat-leaf parsley, chopped
A bunch fresh mint, chopped
Roughly 110ml (4fl oz) olive oil
Juice of 2 lemons
Salt and freshly ground black pepper

Rinse the bulgur and soak it in cold water for about 30 minutes, until it is soft but chewy. Drain it thoroughly and tip it into a large bowl with the onions, tomatoes and herbs.

Pour over the olive oil and lemon juice, season generously and mix it all thoroughly. Adjust the flavours to your taste and serve, with vine or lettuce leaves if you like.

Flat-leaf parsley plant

Like the *fatta* (p34) dishes, this salad was most probably conceived as a way of using up stale bread – the Arabic word *fattush* refers to the act of breaking or crumbling bread. Traditionally a peasant salad from Syria, it has become fashionable in the main cities of Egypt, Lebanon and Jordan, where it is usually made with toasted *pitta* (pitta bread) rather than stale bread. In Turkey, there is a similar peasant salad, which sometimes omits the bread, called *çoban salatası*, meaning 'shepherd's salad'. The ingredients may alter a little from family to family, but the salad always contains lots of parsley. Fresh pomegranate seeds or ground *sumac* are sometimes sprinkled over it.

FATTUSH
(SYRIAN BREAD SALAD)

Serves 4–6
Preparation time 20–25 minutes
Cooking time –

1 onion, halved and sliced
1 cucumber, peeled, halved lengthways and sliced
3 tomatoes, skinned and chopped
1 sweet pepper, halved and sliced
2 cloves garlic, chopped
A bunch flat-leaf parsley, chopped
A small bunch mint, chopped
1 flat pitta bread
4–5 tablespoons olive oil
Juice of 1 lemon
Salt and ground black pepper
A little sumac

Put the onion, cucumber, tomatoes, pepper and garlic in a bowl with the chopped herbs.

Open the pitta bread, toast in the oven until crisp, then break into little pieces and add to the bowl.

Toss in the olive oil and lemon juice, season to taste – adding more olive oil or lemon juice if necessary – and serve, sprinkled with a little ground sumac.

Tabbouleh

ALLSPICE

(BAHAR HILU) *Pimenta dioica*

Spanish explorers came across allspice in Jamaica at the beginning of the sixteenth century and from there it would have found its way to the centre of the Ottoman Empire, in the same way that other goods from the New World reached Constantinople, due to the Spanish-Ottoman alliance. Of all the countries in the Middle East, it is most used in Turkey where it is known as *yeni bahar*, meaning 'new spice', or *dolma bahar*, indicating that it is one of the main spices used in the stuffed dishes. In other parts of the Middle East, the spice mixture *baharat* (p162) is often used instead of allspice.

Ground allspice

HOW IT GROWS

Allspice is the dried unripe berry of the tropical tree *Pimenta dioica*, which is mainly cultivated in Jamaica, hence its other name, 'Jamaican pepper'. The handsome, aromatic tree grows to a considerable height and has small white flowers.

APPEARANCE AND TASTE

The unripe berries are round and green but when they dry they become hard and turn a reddish-brown, similar in appearance to a large peppercorn. The ground spice is a dark rust colour. The flavour resembles a mixture of cloves, nutmeg and cinnamon, which is why it is called 'allspice' in English, but as most of its flavour is in the oil, which is mainly made up of eugenol – the main element in cloves – it can be substituted for cloves in some recipes.

Allspice berries

Baskets of dried fruit, herbs and spices

BUYING AND STORING

As always with spices, it is best to buy the whole berries and grind them yourself when you need them. They keep well in an airtight container in a cool, dark place.

CULINARY USES

The berries are used whole in pickles and marinades. In Iran and Turkey, the crushed or ground berries are used in rice dishes and in the aromatic rice fillings for many stuffed fruit, vegetable, poultry and seafood dishes. Allspice is also used in some lamb, chicken and game dishes, such as *tavşan yahnisi* (p204), a spicy rabbit stew, and in some cakes and puddings.

The Persians created some wonderful dishes combining fruit and meat, many of which are popular throughout the Middle East today. The following recipe is used for both quince and apples. The Turks make a similar dish, called *elma dizmesi*, using rice instead of split peas.

DOLMEH SIB

(APPLES STUFFED WITH MINCED MEAT AND YELLOW SPLIT PEAS)

Serves 6
Preparation time 20–25 minutes (plus 25 minutes' cooking of split peas)
Cooking time approximately 50 minutes

50g yellow split peas, rinsed
1 onion, finely chopped
1 tablespoon olive oil
225g (8oz) minced beef
½ teaspoon ground allspice
½ teaspoon ground cinnamon
A small bunch of fresh dill, chopped
Salt and freshly ground black pepper
6 large tart apples, washed
2 tablespoons white wine vinegar
1 tablespoon sugar

Preheat the oven to 180°C/350°F/gas mark 4.

Put the split peas into a pan, cover with plenty of water and boil them for about 25 minutes, until they are soft. Drain and refresh them.

Sauté the onion in the olive oil, until it begins to colour, then stir in the meat. Cook for a minute or two, until the meat has changed colour, then stir in the spices, dill and cooked split peas. Season with salt and pepper and take off the heat.

Remove the cores from the apples, making sure you leave about 1cm (½in) at the bottom, and hollow out some of the pulp to make room for the filling. Chop the pulp and add it to the meat and split-pea mixture, then stuff the apples with it. Place them side by side in a baking dish, dab a bit of butter on top of each one, and pour about 200ml (7fl oz) water into the dish. Cover with foil and bake for 25–30 minutes.

Heat the vinegar and sugar with a little water, roughly 50ml (2fl oz), in a pan and pour it over and around the apples. Continue to bake for a further 15–20 minutes, until the apples are nicely tender. Serve hot or cold.

The following recipe is an Istanbul speciality which is particularly popular as a *mezze* dish, served in restaurants, or from makeshift stalls in the streets. In old wooden boats, families chug up and down the Bosphorus and along the edges of the Sea of Marmara, as they dive for the big mussels in the rocks. The catch is then usually destined to be tossed in a beer batter and deep-fried, as for *midye tavasi*, or stuffed with an aromatic rice and eaten cold.

MİDYE DOLMASI
(STUFFED MUSSELS)

Serves 6
Preparation time roughly 1 hour
Cooking time 15 minutes

Roughly 24 large fresh mussels
2–3 tablespoons olive oil
2 onions, finely chopped
2 tablespoons pine nuts
2 tablespoons currants, soaked in water for about 15 minutes
1 teaspoon ground allspice
½ teaspoon ground cinnamon
2 teaspoons tomato paste
150g (5oz) short-grain rice, rinsed and soaked in water for about 15 minutes
Salt and freshly ground black pepper
A bunch fresh dill and parsley, finely chopped
Lemon wedges to serve

Put the mussels into a bowl of cold water and discard any that open.

Heat the oil in a pan and stir in the onions and pine nuts. Fry them until they begin to take on a little colour, then stir in the currants, spices and tomato paste, followed by the rice.

Cover with just enough water, season with salt and pepper and bring to the boil. Reduce the heat and simmer for 10–15 minutes, until the water is absorbed and the rice is cooked but still firm. Leave the rice to cool in the pan then, using a fork, gently toss in the herbs.

Place a colander or steamer in a large pan and pour in enough water for steaming. Then, using a sharp knife, carefully prise the mussels open widely enough to spoon some of the rice into them. Close the shells and pack them tightly into the steamer, placing a plate, weighed down with a stone, on top of them.

Cover the pan, steam the mussels for about 15 minutes, then leave them to cool. Serve cold with wedges of lemon to squeeze over them.

Midye dolması

ANISEED

(YANSOON) *Pimpinella anisum*

Aniseed is a native of the Levant. The culinary uses of this aromatic seed date as far back as the Pharaohs of Egypt and classical Rome. It has long been used as a digestive and diuretic, often in the form of tea, which is also considered to be soporific. The seeds are chewed on their own as a breath freshener and they are particularly popular coated in sugar and given to children as a treat.

HOW IT GROWS

Dill, fennel, caraway and cumin are all botanical relatives of aniseed. The plant grows to about 60cm (2ft) in height with clusters of yellow white flowers at the top.

APPEARANCE AND TASTE

The leaves and the seeds have an unmistakable bitter-sweet, warming smell and taste. The small seeds are pale brown and ribbed, often sold amongst tiny bits of husk and stalk. The seeds can be dry-roasted to produce a strong, sweet, aromatic flavour.

BUYING AND STORING

Fresh or dried aniseed leaves are available in some Middle Eastern markets, but they lose their flavour and aroma very quickly. The seeds also lose flavour quite quickly and need to be stored in an airtight container and used within months. As for ground aniseed, it loses flavour rapidly so it's best to buy the seeds and grind them yourself as you need them.

CULINARY USES

The fresh and dried leaves are occasionally added to a fish soup or stew, or they are infused to make an aromatic tea to aid the digestion. Combined with other spices, the seeds are used to make a soothing tisane and to flavour some breads, biscuits and cakes. Aniseed marries beautifully with dried figs, and it flavours the ceremonial rice pudding *meghlie*, served to visitors at the birth of a son. It is also the principal flavouring in the Turkish *rakı*, and in *arak* from Syria, Lebanon and Jordan. Both *rakı* and *arak* are distilled from grapes and diluted with ice and water, which turns the alcohol cloudy, and drunk with *mezze* or fish.

Middle Eastern jams and preserves are heavenly – aromatic and spicy. Often using whole or large chunks of fruit and vegetables, they are deliciously syrupy, designed to be dribbled over bread, white cheese, or thick yogurt.

TEEN BI SUKKAR
(DRIED FIG JAM WITH ANISEED AND PINE NUTS)

Makes roughly 1.5 litres (2½ pints)
Preparation time 10 minutes
Cooking time roughly 30 minutes

450ml (16fl oz) water
450g (1lb) sugar
1 tablespoon lemon juice
Roughly 900g (2lb) dried figs, coarsely chopped
3–4 fresh rose geranium leaves
1 teaspoon ground aniseed
3 tablespoons pine nuts
A tiny piece of mastic (p186 – ¼ teaspoon), ground with a little sugar

Put the water, sugar and lemon juice into a large pan and bring to the boil, stirring all the time. Reduce the heat and simmer for about 5 minutes.

Stir in the figs and geranium leaves and continue to simmer gently for about 15 minutes, until the figs are tender.

Add the aniseed and pine nuts, simmer for a further 5 minutes,

Rakı

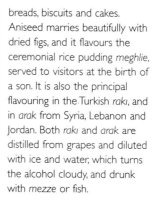

then stir in the mastic. Leave to cool in the pan, then spoon the preserve into sterilised jars and store in a cool, dry place.

In Syria and Lebanon, the following pudding was traditionally made to celebrate the birth of a son. A drummer, followed by villagers playing reed flutes, would lead well-wishers to the family's door and large amounts of *meghlie* would be made to serve the flow of visitors. The arrival of a newborn daughter was not usually met with such ceremony, although a humble offering of *meghlie* tea (or *miglee*) was occasionally served to visitors. Nowadays, daughters, who are often

Aniseed

referred to as 'the flower of the house', are usually cherished as much as sons, so in many Arab communities this spicy rice pudding is made to celebrate the birth of any child.

MEGHLIE
(RICE PUDDING WITH ANISEED)

Serves 8–10
Preparation time 35 minutes
Cooking time approximately 25 minutes

1 piece of fresh ginger (about 2½cm/1in) long, peeled and grated
1.5 litres (2½ pints) water
50g (2oz) ground rice or rice flour
Roughly 8 tablespoons sugar
1 teaspoon ground aniseed
1 teaspoon ground caraway seed
1 teaspoon ground cinnamon
½ teaspoon ground cloves
A handful of chopped blanched almonds, toasted pine nuts or pistachios for the top
Grated fresh coconut

Put the ginger into a small pan with half the water and bring it to the boil. Reduce the heat, cover the pan and simmer for about 25 minutes. Drain it, keeping the ginger water – a basic *meghlie* tea – and leave it to cool.

In a bowl, mix the ground rice to a loose paste with the cooled ginger water. Add the sugar and spices and mix well.

In a heavy-based saucepan, bring the remaining water to the boil.

Gradually add the ground rice mixture, stirring vigorously with a wooden spoon. Bring the mixture to the boil again, then reduce the heat and simmer gently, stirring from time to time, for about 45 minutes, until it thickens and coats the back of the spoon.

Pour it into individual bowls, leave it to cool, then cover and chill. Just before serving, sprinkle a few nuts and some grated coconut over the top.

Meghlie

MASTIC

(MASTAKA) *Pistacia lentiscus*

This aromatic gum is obtained from the *Pistacia lentiscus,* a tree that grows wild in the Mediterranean region. Mastic has such a strong taste of the tree that it was used as a spice in medieval Islamic stews. Today, it is rarely used as a spice in savoury dishes but is coveted for the chewy twang and delicious resinous flavour it imparts to sweet dishes and breads. Softened with a little candle wax, it is sold as chewing gum. It should not be confused with gum arabic, the resin of acacia trees, which is used as glue.

HOW IT GROWS

The *Pistacia lentiscus* is a small, bushy, evergreen tree which grows wild on the hillsides of Lebanon, Jordan, Syria and Turkey. To obtain the mastic, a vertical cut is made on the thin trunk from which a teardrop of the clear, sticky resin will exude. Some of the blobs of resin are scraped off with a knife, others have to be collected from the ground, where ants may have stuck to them.

APPEARANCE AND TASTE

Mastic is sold in the form of hard, transparent crystals, sometimes complete with ants.

They should smell of the tree, an aroma that is intensified when they are crushed. To cook with, the crystals must first be pulverised with a little sugar in a pestle and mortar. In its natural form, mastic is chewed for pleasure like chewing gum. It has a fresh, resinous aroma and taste.

BUYING AND STORING

Two grades of mastic are available: the perfect, clear crystals which have been scraped off the tree and are, therefore, more expensive; and the cheaper ones which have been collected off the ground and may contain some passing wildlife. In my experience, both taste the same and store well in airtight containers away from direct sunlight, which turns them yellow over time.

CULINARY USES

With its rich resinous flavour and chewy texture, mastic is fabulous stuff. In Turkey it is what gives a punch to the famous snowy-white, chewy ice cream and the glorious milk pudding from the Ottoman kitchens. It is occasionally added to *rakı* to give it an interesting, chewy dimension. There is also a mastic-flavoured Turkish Delight. In Egypt it is still added to some stews and, in some parts of the Middle East, it is added to some sweet bread doughs for flavour, as well as to make them more elastic.

Mastic is sometimes added to the potent *rakı*

Mastic

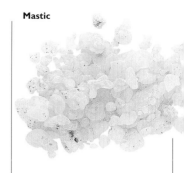

The following deep-fried fritters, which vary in shape and size in the different regions, are usually associated with religious feasting, such as the breaking of the fast of Ramadan. In Turkey, they are believed to represent the Prophet's seal and are served during the celebrations of *Kandil*, when the minarets are illuminated throughout the country. They are delicious flavoured with mastic and *rakı* and soaked in a honey or lemon syrup.

SARAY LOKMASI
(MASTIC-FLAVOURED PUFFS IN HONEY)

Serves 6
Preparation time approximately 5 hours
Cooking time 20 minutes

For the batter:
I teaspoon dried yeast
200ml (7fl oz) lukewarm water
225g (8oz) strong plain flour
A good pinch salt
I mastic crystal, ground with I teaspoon sugar
2–3 tablespoons rakı

For the syrup:
110g (4oz) sugar
110ml (4fl oz) water
About 4 tablespoons honey of your choice

Sunflower oil for deep-frying
Ground cinnamon or nutmeg for sprinkling

Dissolve the yeast in a little lukewarm water.

In a large bowl, sift the flour with the salt. Make a well in the middle and pour in the yeast, mastic, rakı and some of the water. Use a wooden spoon to draw in the flour from the sides and gradually add the rest of the water until you have a smooth, loose batter.

Cover the bowl with a damp tea towel and leave to stand for 4–6 hours until the batter thickens and becomes quite elastic.

To make the syrup, put the sugar and water into a heavy-based saucepan and bring to the boil, stirring all the time. Reduce the heat, stir in the honey, and simmer for 10 minutes. Put aside.

When the batter is ready, heat enough oil in a shallow, or curved, pan for deep-frying.

Muhallabia

Drop little spoonfuls (you might find it easier to use two spoons, one for scooping up the elastic batter, the other for scraping it off that spoon) into the oil and watch them puff up and rise to the surface. Fry in batches until golden brown, fishing them out with a perforated spoon and drain on kitchen paper.

Pop the puffs onto a serving dish, heat up the syrup, and pour it over them. Use a spoon to coat them well in the syrup and serve warm or at room temperature with a little ground cinnamon or nutmeg sprinkled on top.

This classic milk pudding, common throughout the Middle East, can be made as plain or as grand as you like. Served plain, it is usually sprinkled with icing sugar. For a more elaborate presentation, it is served floating in rose water, garnished with fresh or crystallised petals. Some people decorate the pudding with almonds and pistachios, others flavour it with chocolate or vanilla, but to my mind the most exquisite of all is the taste of mastic.

MUHALLABIA
(MASTIC-FLAVOURED MILK PUDDING)

Serves 4–6
Preparation time 5 minutes
Cooking time 35–40 minutes

50g (2oz) rice flour
850ml (1½ pints) milk
110g (4oz) sugar
I piece of mastic (the size of a fingernail), pounded with I teaspoon sugar
Icing sugar

In a small bowl, mix the rice flour to a loose paste with a little of the milk and put it aside.

Put the rest of the milk into a saucepan with the sugar and bring it to the boil, stirring all the time.

Stir a little of the hot milk into the rice flour, then tip the rice flour into the pan. Stirring vigorously, bring the liquid back to the boil, then add the mastic. Reduce the heat and simmer gently for 25–30 minutes, stirring from time to time, until it thickens.

Pour the mixture into a serving bowl, or individual bowls, and leave to cool and form a skin on top.

Chill before serving and sprinkle the top with a little icing sugar.

SUMAC

(SUMAK) *Rhus coriaria*

Sumac berries

Long before the arrival of lemons in the Middle East, sumac and the juice of sour pomegranates were the only souring agents and still are in parts of Syria and northern Iraq, where lemons are rare. Sumac was used by the Romans and is mentioned in medieval Arab cookbooks. Mixed with water, ground sumac was believed to aid digestion and prevent diarrhoea, but now, in Lebanon, Syria, Turkey and Iran, it is commonly used as a condiment for grilled fish and kebabs.

HOW IT GROWS

Various species of the genus *Rhus* grow wild in the Middle East and Mediterranean regions but it is the fruits of the *Rhus coriaria* that are used in Middle Eastern cooking. The shrub grows in the wild and bears dark red berries which are dried for use.

APPEARANCE AND TASTE

The hard, dried berries are brick-red, tinged with purple, with a lemony, woody taste. They can be used whole, crushed, or ground into a coarse powder.

BUYING AND STORING

Whole or ground berries are available in Middle Eastern stores and some wholefood shops. The whole berries keep for months in an airtight container but the ground berries tend to lose colour and flavour quite quickly.

Ground sumac

CULINARY USES

Sumac is used to give a citrus lift to some salads, such as *fattush* (p181), to *pilafs*, eggs, *kibbeh* (p126), flat breads and to grilled fish and meat dishes. It is one of the key flavourings in the Palestinian country dish *musakhan*, which consists of chicken sautéed in olive oil, spices and lemon juice, then stuffed into pitta bread. The crushed berries can be steeped in water to extract their flavour and the strained liquid can then be drunk or used like lemon juice in a variety of dishes. Ground sumac is sprinkled over soups and grilled meat and is also one of the spices in the Arabic spice mix *zaatar* (p196), which includes sesame seeds, salt and thyme. In some restaurants and kebab houses in the Middle East, sumac will be one of the condiments on the table, along with dried mint, oregano or thyme and Middle Eastern red pepper (p152) or paprika, for sprinkling over soups and kebabs.

These excellent Arab-style pizzas make wonderful snack food as well as a meal. Called *lahmacun* in Turkish and *missahatz* by the Armenians, they are enjoyed by all. The Armenians were at one time responsible for the bread and pastry trade in Syria and Lebanon and they are still known for their delicious *lahma bi ajeen*. Generally, they are made very thin and served with chopped parsley, sumac and lemon to squeeze over them. If they are bought in the street, they are usually rolled up and eaten in the hands.

LAHMA BI AJEEN
(SAVOURY FLAT BREADS)

Serves 4–8 people (depending on size and how greedy people are!)
Preparation time approximately 3 hours
Cooking time 8–10 minutes for each batch

For the dough:
10g (½oz) fresh yeast or 5g (¼oz) dried yeast
½ teaspoon sugar
Roughly 300ml (½ pint) lukewarm water
450g (1lb) strong white flour
½ teaspoon salt
2 tablespoons sunflower or olive oil

For the filling:
2 tablespoons olive oil
2 onions, finely chopped
2 cloves garlic, finely chopped
450g (1lb) minced lamb
2 tomatoes, skinned and finely chopped
2 teaspoons tomato paste
1 teaspoon sugar
1–2 teaspoons Middle Eastern red pepper (p152)
Juice of ½ lemon
A small bunch parsley, finely chopped
Salt

For the top:
1–2 tablespoons sumac
A small bunch parsley, roughly chopped
1 lemon cut into wedges

First, dissolve the yeast with the sugar in a little of the lukewarm water.

Sift the flour with the salt into a big bowl and make a well in the centre. Pour the yeast, the rest of the water and the oil into the well, then, using your hands, draw in the flour and work the mixture into a dough.

Turn the dough onto a floured surface and knead it for about

10 minutes, until it is smooth and elastic. Put a few drops of oil into the base of the bowl and roll the dough in it. Cover the bowl with a damp cloth and leave the dough to rise for about 2 hours, until it has doubled in size.

Meanwhile, preheat the oven to 240°C/475°F/gas mark 9.

Heat the oil in a frying pan and soften the onions and garlic. Turn off the heat before they brown, leaving them to cool in the pan.

In a bowl, mix the minced lamb, the tomatoes (drained of excess juice) and the tomato paste. Add the sugar, red pepper, lemon juice, parsley and salt, and knead the mixture with your hands. Drain the onions and garlic of oil and add them to the mixture, kneading well.

When the dough has risen, knock it back and divide into 8 balls, or lots of walnut-sized ones. On a floured surface, roll each ball into a thin, flat circle or oval, stretching it a little with your hands. Spread the meat filling generously in a smooth layer over each flat dough, right up to the edges, and transfer them to lightly oiled baking sheets.

Pop them into the oven for about 8–10 minutes, depending on the size of the flat dough. (If cooking in batches, the oven temperature may drop – try not to let it go below 230°C/450°F/gas mark 8.) The meat should be cooked but the flat bread should remain soft enough to roll up.

Sprinkle each one with sumac and parsley, and a squeeze of lemon juice if you like, and eat it flat off a plate, or roll it up and eat it with your hands.

Lahma bi ajeen

A Palestinian country dish, *musakhan* is popular in Jordan, where a large proportion of the population is Palestinian. The chicken, flavoured with sumac and other spices, is traditionally baked on thick, spongy *tabun* bread, which is similar to Turkish *pide* – ordinary pitta bread is often used as a substitute.

MUSAKHAN
(PALESTINIAN BREAD WITH CHICKEN AND SUMAC)

Serves 4 as a meal, 8 as a snack
Preparation time 10 minutes
Cooking time 25–30 minutes

3 tablespoons olive oil and a little butter
3–4 onions, chopped
450g (1lb) boned chicken breasts, cut into bite-size pieces
2 teaspoons ground sumac
1 teaspoon ground cinnamon
½ teaspoon ground cardamom
Juice of 1 lime
Salt and ground black pepper
4 pitta breads, halved to form 8 pockets

Preheat the oven to 180°C/350°F/gas mark 4.

Heat the oil and butter in a heavy-based pan and stir in the onions.

Cook until they just begin to colour and add the chicken and sumac. Cook for a few minutes to seal the chicken pieces, then reduce the heat and stir in the spices and lime juice. Cook gently for about 10 minutes until the chicken is tender.

Season to taste, then fill the *pitta* pockets with the chicken mixture. Arrange them on a baking sheet and pop them in the oven for about 10 minutes, to toast through.

Serve with strained yogurt, either spooned into the pocket or on top, and a salad.

ROSE

(WARD) *Rosa*

Dried roses in spice shop

The origins and uses of the rose can be traced back to ancient Egypt, Persia and Babylon. In the days before soap, the Egyptians bathed in water scented with rose petals as a perfumed body was believed to give sensual pleasure. The Romans, who associated the rose with Venus, scented their water and wine with roses and celebrated their victories by scattering rose petals in the streets. By the ninth century, the Persians were making wine from rose petals and distilling rose water on a large scale, but the discovery of rose water has been attributed to the eleventh-century Persian physician, Ibn Sina, known as Avicenna in the West, as it was in his time that the scented water was used as a food flavouring in the sumptuous Arab dishes. During the Ottoman period, it became one of the favourite flavourings of the Palace kitchens, where it was used in many syrupy pastries and milk puddings. As the Ottoman Empire expanded, roses were introduced to Bulgaria, where the Valley of the Roses is famous for its roses and rose products.

HOW IT GROWS

There are numerous species and hybrids which have edible petals and from which rose water can be made. The most common types used for culinary purposes in the Middle East are the *Rosa centifolia* (cabbage rose), *Rosa damascena* (damask rose) and *Rosa moschata* (musk rose). They grow well in Azerbaijan and around the desert city of Kashan in Iran, and they grow in the lake district of central Anatolia and in the plains and hillsides around Isparta in Turkey. The roses are planted in January and don't produce a crop of flowers until their third year, but the plants live for twenty to thirty years. The flowers are gathered in the early morning before they are exposed to the hot sun and lose their essential oils.

APPEARANCE AND TASTE

Most of the rose petals used for culinary purposes are candy pink, lilac, or red. They must be in full bloom and richly scented to impart their sweet smell to a dish. Fresh rose petals can be used for culinary purposes but generally they are dried first. Rose water is colourless with a light, fresh smell of roses.

BUYING AND STORING

If you have your own garden, you can harvest petals from your own roses, otherwise you will have to choose fresh, fragrant roses from a flower shop and dry them yourself. Bags of dried rose petals are available in Middle Eastern stores. Rose water and rose oil are sold in wholefood and Indian shops, as well as Middle Eastern stores. The petals will lose their fragrance over time, as they do in pot-pourri if they are not kept in an airtight container. Rose water will last for a couple of years and the oil will keep no longer than five years.

OTHER USES

Attar of roses (from Persian *atr*), also known as otto of roses or rose oil, is made by soaking or steaming the petals to extract their fragrance. Attar of roses distilled from the *Rosa damascena* is an essential oil used in many fine perfumes. It takes three to four tons of fresh rose petals to produce 1 kg (2¼ lb) of oil, which makes its value comparable to its weight in gold. Turkey produces 60 per cent of the world's attar of roses and it also produces a refreshing, fragrant rose cologne.

Rose- and lemon-flavoured Turkish Delight

CULINARY USES

To capture their delightful, sweet fragrance, rose petals have been infused in sugar, wine, honey, oil, vinegar, syrup, milk and water since ancient times. In Iran and Turkey, rose petals are used to make a heavenly scented jam and a refreshing, floral sorbet. In those parts of the Middle East influenced by the Ottoman Empire, rose water is used to flavour chilled fruit and nut compotes, such as *khoshaf* (p145), and traditional milk puddings such as *muhallabia* (p187). It flavours the plain or milky syrups used in sweet pastries, such as the Turkish pudding *güllaç*, made with starch wafers and most commonly associated with *Ramazan*, and in puddings such as *belila* (p126), a Jewish grain pudding served to commemorate happy occasions such as the cutting of a baby's first tooth in Sephardic communities. It is also used to flavour *aşure* (p109), which according to legend was made with all the grains, fruit and nuts on Noah's Ark when supplies ran low, and it is the favourite flavouring in the famous Turkish Delight, *güllü lokum*. In Iran, the dried petals or dried rose buds are added to a mild version of the spice mixture *advieh* (p169), to give it a fragrant lift. And in Azerbaijan, the dried petals are ground to a powder to give a fragrant lift to some sweet and savoury rice dishes, and to sprinkle over chicken. The fruits (rose hips) are occasionally used for tea or for flavouring syrup.

This exquisite, scented jam is one of the ancient delights of the Middle East. Packed with delicate rose petals and runny like thick syrup, it is delicious spooned onto bread or over

Gül reçeli

ataif (p143), the Middle Eastern pancakes. Any scented rose petals will do, even the old-fashioned cottage garden rose. Sometimes rose petals are soaked in lime water, or slaked lime, to render them almost transparent before adding them to the syrup.

GÜL REÇELİ
(ROSE PETAL JAM)

Makes approximately 700ml (1¼ pints) jam
Preparation time 5 minutes
Cooking time 40 minutes

450g (1lb) fresh or dried, scented pink or lilac rose petals
300ml (10fl oz) water
450g (1lb) sugar
Juice of 1 lemon

Trim the petals, rinse them if necessary, and drain them.

Pour the water into a deep, heavy-based pan, add the petals and bring it to the boil. Then strain the petals, put them aside and pour the rose-scented water back into the pan.

Stir in the sugar and bring the water to the boil, stirring all the time. Reduce the heat and simmer for about 10 minutes.

Stir in the lemon juice and the rose petals and simmer for a further 10–15 minutes, until the syrup thickens. Leave the jam to cool in the pan, then spoon it into sterilised jars.

Sweets play a big part in the social life of the Middle East. Special sweets are eaten on religious holidays and festive days. Sweets are distributed at celebrations such as births, weddings and circumcisions. In the home, sweet pastries or cakes are offered to guests with tea, coffee, or a cool sherbet drink. Guest don't come empty-handed either, arriving with wrapped boxes of sweet pastries such as *baklava* (p137) or Turkish Delight, *lokum*. Rose-flavoured Turkish Delight is one of the all-time favourites, often tinged pink with a little red food colouring. Home-made Turkish Delight is much softer than its commercially made cousin and melts deliciously in the mouth.

GÜLLÜ LOKUM
(ROSE-FLAVOURED TURKISH DELIGHT)

Makes 30–35 pieces
Preparation time 5 minutes
Cooking time approximately 2 hours

700g (1½ lb) sugar
600ml (1 pint) water
110g (4oz) cornflour (plus extra for lining the mould)
2–3 tablespoons rose water
Icing sugar

Prepare a square mould, roughly 18–20cm (7–8in) wide, by lining it with a piece of muslin covered with a layer of cornflour.

Put the sugar and water into a heavy-based pan and bring it to the boil, stirring all the time. Put the cornflour into another pan with about 225ml (8fl oz) water. Mix it well and bring it to the boil, stirring all the time, until it is smooth and creamy.

Gradually, add the cornflour mixture to the hot syrup, stirring vigorously to prevent lumps from forming. Keep stirring while you bring the mixture to the boil, then reduce the heat to very low and cook, uncovered, for about 1½ hours, with frequent stirs to prevent sticking and caramelising. The mixture should be so thick, it barely drips off the spoon.

Add the rose water and a few drops colouring, if you wish, then test the mixture by dropping a little into a cup of cold water and seeing if it forms a soft jelly.

Pour the mixture into the mould and leave it to cool and set. Spread a thick layer of icing sugar on a flat surface and invert the *lokum* onto it. Remove the muslin, brush off the excess cornflour, then cut the block into small squares. Roll each one in the icing sugar until well coated.

CLOVE

(MASAMIR QARANFUL) *Syzygium aromaticum*

The name clove derives from the Latin *clavus*, meaning 'nail', which is also reflected in the Arabic, *masamir qaranful*, which translates as 'nails of clove'. Used in China as early as the third century BC, cloves are thought to have originated in the Moluccas, the Spice Islands. The Dutch, who occupied the islands in 1605, cultivated cloves and controlled the monopoly until the French smuggled seeds to Mauritius, from where the spice reached Madagascar and Tanzania. Cloves first entered the Middle East through Egypt, from India, and made their way to the Mediterranean regions.

HOW IT GROWS

Cloves are the dried, unopened flower bud of a small evergreen tree which belongs to the myrtle family and only grows in tropical, maritime climates, so it thrives in Indonesia, Madagascar and Tanzania. It flowers twice a year and the fully grown, unopened buds which grow in clusters are harvested by hand, just at the moment they develop a pink flush. Once the buds have been picked, they are dried in the sun until they become woody and turn brown. It is the four petals of the flower, with the stamens inside, that form the nail-like head of the clove.

APPEARANCE AND TASTE

The shape of the clove is similar to a small nail, which is reflected in the Arabic name, as well as in French, Spanish and Portuguese. Freshly dried cloves should be dark brown in colour with a strong, almost sharp, bitter taste on the tongue when chewed on their own. They leave the mouth feeling quite warm and numb, as well as refreshed. It is the eugenol, which is also present in cinnamon, that gives cloves their distinctive flavour.

BUYING AND STORING

Look for whole cloves with a definite brown colour, not grey or dusty ones. If they have been recently dried they will be slightly oily when you press or crush them. Whole cloves keep well if stored in dry, airtight containers, but ground cloves lose their flavour quickly so it is best to grind them when you need to.

CULINARY USES

Whole cloves are used to flavour some rice dishes, festive biscuits, puddings and jams, such as the Turkish plum-tomato jam. They are also used to cut the fat in heavy meat stews, or to purify the meat in some offal dishes, such as the Turkish dish of stewed brains *beyin salatısı*, and the Arab dish of calf's feet and chickpeas, *kawareh bi hummus*, found all over the Middle East. Whole cloves are also infused with cinnamon, ginger and aniseed to make the Arab spiced drink *miglee* (*meghlie*), which is served to visitors when a baby is born. Cloves feature in the Arab spice mixture, *baharat* (p162), which also includes black pepper corns, coriander seeds, cinnamon, cumin, cardamom, nutmeg and paprika. With their cleansing, spicy aroma and sensation, whole cloves are often chewed to freshen the breath after strong tastes such as garlic and mint.

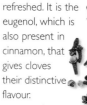

Whole cloves

The cooked feet of lambs and calves are very popular in the Middle East. Traditional soups and stews are made with them when an animal is slaughtered, particularly during *Eid-el-Kurban*, the festival to mark the near-sacrifice of Isma'il (p69). The calf's feet in the following dish, which is enjoyed in the Balkans, Portugal and Spain too, are sometimes substituted with pig's trotters by some Jewish and Christian communities.

KAWAREH BI HUMMUS

(CALF'S FEET WITH CHICKPEAS)

Serves 4
Preparation time 20 minutes
 (plus 8 hours' soaking)
Cooking time approximately 4
 hours

*2–3 tablespoons clarified butter
 (ghee), or olive oil with a little
 butter*
*2 calf's feet, thoroughly cleaned
 and blanched in boiling water*
*225 (8oz) chickpeas, soaked for 8
 hours, or overnight, and drained*
1–2 teaspoons ground turmeric
6 cloves
2 dried bay leaves
*Salt and freshly ground black
 pepper*
4 eggs, well scrubbed

Heat the clarified butter, or oil, in a heavy-based pan and brown the feet all over.

Add the chickpeas, turmeric, cloves and bay leaves, and cover with water. Season with salt and pepper and carefully slip in the whole eggs.

Bring the liquid to the boil, then turn the heat down very low and simmer for 3–4 hours, adding more water if necessary, until the meat is almost falling off the bones. Cut the meat off the bones, if you like, and serve hot with flat bread and pickles.

This delightful jam comes from Turkey, where the plum tomatoes are first dipped into a lime-water solution to stabilise the firm texture. It is more of a conserve than a jam, ideal for spooning onto bread or yogurt. To prepare the tomatoes, first submerge them in boiling water for a few seconds, then plunge them into a bowl of cold water and peel off the skins.

Domates reçeli

DOMATES REÇELİ
(PLUM-TOMATO AND ALMOND JAM)

Makes 3–4 jars
Preparation time 15–20 minutes
Cooking time approximately 30 minutes

1.8kg (4lb) firm plum tomatoes, skinned
About 300ml (10fl oz) water
900g (2lb) sugar
175g (6oz) whole, blanched almonds
8–10 whole cloves

If the tomatoes vary in size, halve some of the larger ones, but keep most of them whole.

Put the water and sugar into a pan and bring it to the boil, stirring all the time.

Pop in the tomatoes and boil vigorously for a few minutes, skimming some of the froth off the top. Reduce the heat and simmer for 5 minutes, then stir in the blanched almonds and cloves.

Bring to the boil once more, then simmer for 10–15 minutes, until the syrup coats the back of a spoon. Turn off the heat and leave to cool completely. Spoon the jam into sterilised jars and store in a cool place.

TAMARIND

(TAMER HINDI) *Tamarindus indica*

Tamarind pods

Native to tropical Africa, the large evergreen tamarind tree spread to India in prehistoric times and now grows in the tropical and subtropical regions of the world. It would have been the Arabs who first brought tamarind across the Persian Gulf from India, influencing the cooking of the south-east of Iran, the Gulf region and Egypt. Some of the best recipes using tamarind are found in the coastal regions of the Gulf, where it is often married with fenugreek, turmeric or curry powder, echoing the flavours of India, in delicious fish dishes. Reflecting its origins, the Arabic for tamarind translates as 'Indian date'.

HOW IT GROWS

With strong, bending branches and an extensive root system, the tree can survive in dry soil and high winds. The cinnamon-coloured pods, which are the fruit of the tree, grow in clusters and contain very small beans, which are surrounded by a sour, fruity pulp. When the pods have fully ripened, it is the pulp that is extracted for culinary use.

APPEARANCE AND TASTE

The bean-shaped pods and small seeds are inedible but the fresh tamarind fruit pulp, which is light brown in colour, is dried and compressed into sticky blocks that look like a mass of fruit, fibres and seeds. It is also pressed and strained to make a smooth, concentrated paste. Both the blocks and paste are dark, almost black, a colour similar to dried dates, and have a taste akin to a sour prune.

BUYING AND STORING

Fresh tamarind pods are available only in some Asian markets, but both the blocks of compressed tamarind pulp and the jars or tubs of paste are available in Middle Eastern, Asian and wholefood stores, and in some supermarkets. They both keep for a long time but, once opened, the block should be stored in an airtight container; the paste keeps better in the fridge. A prepared syrup, ready to be diluted as a drink, can also be found in some of the same stores.

CULINARY USES

The tamarind pulp needs to be soaked in water, then strained to extract the dark brown juice, before use. The concentrated paste can be diluted with hot water or added directly to a dish, often balanced with sugar or honey to give a sour-sweet flavour. A teaspoon of the concentrated paste, sweetened with sugar and diluted with boiling water, is sometimes served as a drink. The tamarind syrup is also added to dishes for its sweet-sour flavour and it is used to make an instant, refreshing drink by just adding chilled water. Tamarind is used for its unique flavour in a number of meat and vegetable dishes. It works very well as a sauce with stuffed or sautéed onions, leeks, potatoes and aubergines, or in a dressing for shellfish. In Iran and the Gulf region, it is a popular flavour in fish and shellfish dishes.

This delicious dish from the Persian Gulf represents a history of trade between the Arabs and Indians, who stopped off at the Persian ports. It is one of many such dishes from that area using local fish and large prawns.

GHALIYEH MÂHI
(FISH STEW WITH TAMARIND AND GARLIC)

Serves 6
Preparation time 20–25 minutes
Cooking time 45 minutes

110g (4oz) tamarind pulp, soaked in 350ml (12fl oz) water for about 15 minutes
2 tablespoons plain flour
2 tablespoons olive oil
1 teaspoon curry powder
1 teaspoon ground fenugreek
½ teaspoon ground turmeric
½ teaspoon red chilli powder
3–4 cloves garlic, chopped
A big bunch flat-leaf parsley, chopped
1kg (2¼ lb) fresh white fish, such as sea bream or haddock, cut into steaks
Salt

Squeeze the tamarind paste in your fingers to separate the pulp from the seeds and stalks, then strain the pulp through a sieve and reserve the tamarind water.

Brown the flour in a heavy-based pan. Add a little oil and stir in the curry powder, turmeric, chilli powder and fenugreek, working them into a paste.

Add the garlic and parsley and toss them about in the pan for a few minutes, making sure that the spices don't burn. Stir in the tamarind water, cover the pan, and simmer gently for 15–20 minutes.

Slip in the fish steaks and simmer for a further 15–20 minutes, until the fish is tender. Season with salt and serve with rice.

Tamarind paste

As you travel inland, tamarind tends to be combined with vegetables in sweet and sour dishes, a taste that Arabs have enjoyed since medieval times. The preferred vegetables are leeks, aubergines and onions, which are sometimes stuffed before being cooked in tamarind juice. The following simple dish can be made with small onions, shallots, spring onions trimmed down to the white stalk and bulb, or leeks.

BASAL BI TAMER HINDI
(SWEET AND SOUR ONIONS WITH TAMARIND)

Serves 4–6
Preparation time 15 minutes
Cooking time 25–30 minutes

2–3 tablespoons olive oil
450g (1lb) small onions or shallots, peeled and left whole
1 tablespoon tamarind paste
1 tablespoon sugar
Salt
A small bunch fresh coriander, finely chopped

Heat the oil in a heavy-based flat pan and add the onions. Toss them about the pan until they are golden brown all over.

Stir in the tamarind and sugar with enough water to cover the base of the pan and create a sauce, then reduce the heat and put on a lid.

Simmer gently until the onions are soft and the sauce has reduced. Season with salt, sprinkle with coriander and serve hot or cold.

Basal bi tamer hindi

THYME

(ZAATAR) *Thymus vulgaris*

Thyme grows wild in the hills and Mediterranean regions of the Middle East, where it is also known as 'mountain oregano' because of its similar appearance and aroma. Although there are many types of thyme, there is one (*Thymus capitatus*) which is particularly associated with the Middle East. In Arabic it is called *zaatar farsi*, meaning 'Persian thyme', and it this species which is usually used in the spice mixture *zaatar*.

Fresh thyme

HOW IT GROWS

Thyme is a hardy and aromatic plant with small lilac flowers that produce a lovely pungent honey. The leaves are usually picked and dried in the sun. *T. capitatus* (Middle Eastern thyme) is one of the species which provides us with oregano and marjoram.

APPEARANCE AND TASTE

Fresh thyme has a lovely, warm, dry and spicy aroma which is intensified when it grows under a hot sun. The thin stems are quite woody and the small, green leaves are usually oval and pointed, or rounded, covered in minute hairs. The herb tastes exactly as it smells: warm, dry and aromatic. Thyme dries well, turning a darker shade of green but retaining its flavour and aroma.

BUYING AND STORING

Fresh thyme is available in most supermarkets and keeps quite well in plastic bags in the refrigerator. The best dried thyme comes from the Middle East, as the leaves are picked from wild plants and dried in the sun. It's available in Middle Eastern and wholefood shops and should be stored in an airtight container.

CULINARY USES

Zaatar (or *za'atar/zahtar*) is the Arabic name for wild thyme but also the name for the Arab spice mixture which consists of dried wild thyme, ground sumac, salt and occasionally toasted sesame seeds. In the markets and streets, this spice mixture is sold in paper cornets, ready to dip hot, fresh bread into. Thyme is the herb used in the ancient dish *mefarka*, a cold dish of minced meat and broad beans, which is enjoyed by Jewish communities. Used in much the same way as oregano, which is popular in Turkey, Azerbaijan and other parts of north-west Iran, thyme is sprinkled over bread, white cheese, fish, tomatoes, thick yogurt and fried eggs, and it can be mixed to a paste with olive oil and spread over bread dough before it is baked, to make *fatayer bi zahtar*. Dried thyme is also used to make an aromatic tea which is believed to be an aphrodisiac. Fresh thyme, which is thought to aid the digestion, is used to flavour game and heavy lamb dishes containing sheep's-tail fat.

A dish of ancient origin, *mefarka* is prepared by Jews on feast days, often for the men returning from the synagogue. It is an unusual, aromatic dish that is served cold.

MEFARKA
(BROAD BEANS WITH MINCED BEEF AND THYME)

Serve 4–6
Preparation time 15 minutes
Cooking time 25–30 minutes

450g (1lb) fresh broad beans, shelled
1 teaspoon dried thyme
Salt and pepper
2 tablespoons olive oil (plus 1 extra tablespoon for beans)
350g (12 oz) lean beef, minced
1 teaspoon baharat (p162)
2 eggs
Juice of ½ lemon

Put the broad beans into a pan with the thyme, some salt and pepper and a tablespoon of olive oil mixed with about 150ml (5fl oz) water. Simmer gently, topping up with a little more water as it is absorbed, until the beans are tender.

Meanwhile, heat the olive oil in a heavy-based pan and add the beef. Stir in the spice mixture and add enough water to just cover the meat. Simmer until the meat is cooked but still moist, and with *baharat* season to taste.

Dried thyme and dried oregano

Zaatar

Add the beans to the pan and mix well with the beef, crushing the mixture lightly with a fork. Break the eggs into the pan and stir them into the mixture until they have set.

Turn the the contents of the pan onto a serving dish and leave to cool. Taste to check the flavours, adding more salt or thyme if necessary, and serve with a splash of lemon juice.

These little spice breads are popular breakfast and snack food, sold in cafés, bakers' shops and in the street.

FATAYER BI ZAATAR
(THYME AND SUMAC BREADS)

Makes 20
Preparation time approximately
  2½ hours
Cooking time 10 minutes for
  each batch

For the dough:
10g (½oz) fresh yeast or 5g (¼oz)
  dried yeast
½ teaspoon sugar
300ml (½ pint) lukewarm water
450g (1lb) strong white flour
½ teaspoon salt
2 tablespoons olive oil

For the paste:
4 tablespoons dried thyme
2 tablespoons ground sumac
4 tablespoons olive oil
Salt

Fatayer bi zaatar

Dissolve the yeast with the sugar in a little of the water, until it froths. Sift the flour with the salt in a big bowl and make a well in the centre. Pour in the yeast, the rest of the water and the oil. Draw in the flour from the sides and work the mixture into a dough.

Turn the dough onto a lightly floured surface and knead for about 10 minutes, until it is smooth and elastic. Pour a few drops of oil into the base of the bowl and roll the dough in it. Cover with a damp cloth and leave the dough to rise for about 2 hours, until it has doubled in size.

Meanwhile, preheat the oven to 230°C/450°F/gas mark 8.

In a bowl, mix together the thyme, sumac, olive oil and salt to form a paste.

When the dough has risen, punch it back and divide it into roughly 20 pieces. Flatten the pieces out in the palm of your hand, stretching with your fingers. Place them on lightly oiled baking sheets and, using your fingers, spread some of the paste evenly over each one.

Pop them in the oven for about 10 minutes, until lightly browned. Serve hot or at room temperature.

Fenugreek seeds

FENUGREEK

(HILBEH) *Trigonella foenumgraecum*

The botanical name of fenugreek means 'Greek hay', as the plant used to be cultivated in the Mediterranean region for animal fodder, although the seeds were reserved for medicinal purposes. The ancient Egyptians were known to plaster their bodies in a paste made from ground fenugreek seeds to reduce fever. Fenugreek greens are a staple food in Yemen and the seeds, which are rich in vitamins and sugar, are used in a number of Arab dishes. Ground fenugreek, which is more often associated with commercial Indian curry powder, features in the cooking of the Arabian Gulf.

The best *pastırma* is said to be made by the Armenians, who have been involved in its manufacture since the height of the Ottoman Empire. Finely sliced, this dry, flavoursome delicacy is often served as *mezze*, along with olives and white cheese, or it is cooked with spinach, eggs, or beans. The following Anatolian peasant dish, in which the *pastırma* lends its deliciously pungent flavour and aroma to the other ingredients, is traditionally cooked in a flat earthenware dish, or curved tile, called a *kiremit*. Turkish *pastırma* and Arab *basterma/bastirma* are available in some Middle Eastern stores.

Pastırma (or basterma in Arabic)

HOW IT GROWS

Related to clover, fenugreek is cultivated in the Mediterranean region, Yemen and Egypt. It is an annual plant that grows to about 60cm (2ft) tall. The oval leaves grow in clusters with slender pods which contain the seeds.

APPEARANCE AND TASTE

Fenugreek seeds are like small, golden pebbles. They are extremely bitter to taste and need to be dry-roasted to bring out their warm, spicy, celery-like aroma, which is both pleasant and pungent. Ground fenugreek should be the colour of golden sand.

Ground fenugreek

BUYING AND STORING

Whole seeds and ground fenugreek are available in most Middle Eastern and Indian stores. Sometimes the fresh and dried leaves are available too. The seeds store well in an airtight container and are easy to roast and crush or grind to a powder.

MEDICINAL AND OTHER USES

Ancient herbalists believed that fenugreek reduced fever and aided digestion. In the eleventh century, the Persian physician Ibn Sina (Avicenna) recommended fenugreek for diabetes and today, too, fenugreek is used in medicines for diabetics and in the manufacture of some oral contraceptives. Crushed or ground fenugreek yields a yellow dye which is used in fabrics and to colour wool for carpet-making.

CULINARY USES

Fenugreek greens are cooked like spinach in Yemen. In the Arab kitchen, the seeds are often used to flavour spinach, vegetable stews, lentils and a sweet rice dish called *shola-e-olba*. The seeds are also used in pickles. Ground fenugreek is used in some sauces for meat, poultry or fish, and in the fenugreek dip *hilbeh*, which is popular in Yemen and the Arabian Gulf. Ground fenugreek is also the principal flavouring in *çemen*, the red pepper and garlic paste that coats *pastırma*, the Turkish air-dried fillet of beef (called *basterma/bastirma* in the Arab world). The fresh leaves, seeds and powder also give some of the Iranian and eastern Anatolian herb omelettes and vegetable stews their distinctive flavour and pungency.

KIREMİTTE PASTIRMA

(*PASTIRMA* BAKED WITH ONIONS AND PEPPERS)

Serves 4–6
Preparation time 15 minutes
Cooking time 45 minutes

225g (8oz) finely sliced pastırma, *cut into small pieces*
2 bell peppers, roughly chopped
2 onions, roughly chopped
2 cloves garlic, roughly chopped
Olive oil
Salt and freshly ground black pepper
A small bunch of fresh flat-leaf parsley or coriander, chopped

Preheat the oven to 200°C/400°F/gas mark 6.

Put the *pastırma*, peppers, onions and garlic into a shallow baking dish and drizzle over a generous amount of olive oil. Cover the dish with foil and pop it in the oven for about 25 minutes.

Remove the foil and return the dish to the oven for 20 minutes.

Season the mixture and toss in the fresh herbs. Serve hot with flat bread.

The flavour of fenugreek is one of the distinctive features of the cooking of Yemen and the Arabian Gulf. *Hilbeh*, a paste made with fenugreek seeds and fresh coriander, is one of the household condiments, like *zhug* (p169), that is used as a dip for bread or added to stews. Bound with the pulp of fresh tomatoes, it is served as a *mezze* dish, also called *hilbeh*.

HILBEH
(FENUGREEK RELISH)

Serves 4
Preparation time about 25 minutes (plus 18 hours' soaking)
Cooking time –

2 teaspoons fenugreek seeds, soaked in water for about 18 hours until they have softened and formed a jelly-like coating, drained
2 cloves garlic, chopped
1 fresh chilli, chopped
A good-sized bunch fresh coriander, chopped
2–3 big tomatoes, skinned and chopped to a pulp
½ teaspoon sugar
Juice of ½ lemon
Salt

Using a pestle and mortar, grind the fenugreek seeds, garlic, chilli and coriander to a coarse paste. Tip it into a bowl and bind it with the pulped tomatoes.

Beat in the sugar and lemon juice and season it with salt to taste. Serve with flat bread to scoop it up.

Kiremitte pastırma

VEGETABLES

ONION

(BASAL) *Allium cepa*

Onions

HOW IT GROWS

Different varieties of onion grow in the Middle East – some are harvested in the spring, others in the autumn, so they are always available. Spring onions and the long, thick onion tops are also popular. Scallions, named after the ancient Palestinian port of Ascalon, are grown as salad onions.

BUYING AND STORING

All onions should be hard and firm when bought. Don't buy them if they are soft or sprouting little green shoots. In theory, onions should store well through the winter if they are kept in a cool, dry place.

APPEARANCE AND TASTE

The most common varieties of onion in the Middle East are the big, round, white-skinned ones which are mild in taste, the elongated pinky-gold or purple ones which are sweet and strong with a pinkish flesh, and the pale golden-skinned ones which can be quite strong. The spring onions are quite sweet and juicy, usually munched on like a celery stick, and the onion tops are quite sharp-tasting, like leeks, so they are often mellowed in butter or cooked in an Arab *eggah* (p219).

CULINARY USES

As a simple *mezze* dish to be eaten with bread, onions are sometimes chopped and mixed with fresh, sour pomegranate seeds and a squeeze of lemon juice, or marinated in a little vinegar and chopped fresh mint. One of their principal roles in Middle Eastern cooking is in the form of onion juice, used as a marinade for grilled fish or lamb, such as the Turkish dish *çöp şiş*. (p73). To make onion juice, the onions are grated or chopped to a pulp, sprinkled with salt and left to weep. The pulp is then pressed through a sieve to extract the juice.

Originally native to central Asia, various members of the onion family have been cultivated and eaten since prehistoric times. They appeared in the tomb paintings of ancient Egypt and onion bulbs were placed inside the bandages of mummies to encourage the dead to breathe again. In the Bible (Numbers 11:5), the Israelites are said to have longed for onions and garlic in the wilderness. In ancient Greece and Rome, onions were eaten by the common people and shunned by the nobility because of their lingering, pungent smell. Like garlic, onions gave men courage and strength but bad breath too. The Prophet Muhammad is said to have liked eating onions but disliked their odour, so he asked people not to smell of onion or garlic when they came to the mosque. Today in the Middle East, onions are used liberally and daily, raw and cooked. In Iran, fried onions play such an important role that it's said a girl is ready for marriage when she can get her onions crispy and golden.

Freshly harvested onions drying on a mesh top

Raw onions often form part of a salad, such as the Syrian and Turkish ones made with oranges, lemons, onions and olives, or the gypsy and peasant ones made with fresh herbs and onions, often with a little crumbled cheese tossed through them. They are also used in numerous bean salads and the bulgur and herb salads *tabbouleh* (p180) and *kısır*, so popular in Turkey, Syria and Lebanon. The large, sweeter onions are often hollowed out, stuffed with a meat or rice filling, and baked. Whole sweet onions are also baked in their skins, often in the bread ovens or ashes of a fire, and then the mellow, cooked flesh is roughly chopped and dressed with olive oil, lemon juice and parsley. The smaller onions are often cooked whole in stews or grilled in kebabs. And the little button or pearl onions are delicious cooked in a sweet and sour dish with sultanas and mint.

Onions are chopped or sliced and added to stews, such as the Turkish *yahni* dishes, and to soups, particularly the Iranian soup *eshkeneh*, an onion and egg soup with broken, dried bread, said to have been fed to the Ashkani foot soldiers during King Arsaces' reign. Crispy, fried onions are an important component of many Iranian dishes, where they are used for flavour, for thickening sauces, for stuffings and for a garnish.

Spring onions are mostly eaten raw in salads and the long, fresh onion tops are popular fried in butter and cooked in a type of omelette. Onion seed, *shamar* in Arabic, is often mixed with sesame seeds and sprinkled on bread or on savoury biscuits such as *kahk*, (p163) which are shaped like bracelets.

Such is the stigma with onions that some Muslims stay clear of them on Fridays, the day of prayer at the mosque. But there is a saying that 'He who eats onions for forty-one days will become a *hadji* [pilgrim] to Mecca.' As Mecca is in Saudi Arabia, here is a delicious onion dish from there.

MAHSHI BASAL
(SAUDI ARABIAN STUFFED ONIONS)

Serves 4
Preparation time 35–40 minutes
Cooking time 1¼ hours

2 large onions, peeled and left whole
225g (8oz) lean minced lamb
75g (3oz) long-grain rice, washed and drained
2 teaspoons tomato paste
1 teaspoon ground cinnamon
A small bunch fresh parsley, finely chopped
Salt and freshly ground black pepper
2 tablespoons olive oil
1–2 tablespoons vinegar
1 teaspoon sugar

Bring a pan of water to the boil. Using a sharp knife, make a cut in each onion, from top to bottom, down one side, then toss them into the boiling water for about 10 minutes, until they are soft and begin to unwrap. Drain and refresh the onions, then separate each layer.

Put the minced lamb in a bowl and knead it for a minute or two, slapping it down into the bowl. Add the rice, tomato paste, cinnamon, parsley and some seasoning, and knead for about 10 minutes to make sure it is mixed together well.

Place roughly a tablespoon of the filling into the hollow of each onion layer, and then roll it up tightly.

Put the stuffed onions in a wide, heavy-based pan, packed together closely, and pour over the olive oil, vinegar, a sprinkling of sugar and enough water to just cover. Put the lid on and cook gently for about 50 minutes, until the rice and meat are well cooked.

Meanwhile, preheat the oven to 200°C/400°F/gas mark 6.

When the stuffed onions are cooked, quickly transfer them to a baking tray and put them in the oven for about 15 minutes to dry them out a little and wrinkle them. Serve hot with lemon to squeeze over them.

Wild game, such as rabbit, hare and deer, have featured in Middle Eastern recipes since medieval times but they are nowadays seldom found in the cities. In the rural areas, where people can rarely afford to buy meat, wild rabbit and other creatures often end up in a stew. The following Turkish recipe, one of the few to use wine, is for a tasty hunter's stew, served on a winter's day, with lots of bread to mop up the aromatic juices. The word *yahni* in Turkish always denotes a stew made with onions.

TAVŞAN YAHNİSİ
(AROMATIC RABBIT STEW WITH ONIONS, SULTANAS AND FIGS)

Serves 2–3
Preparation time 20 minutes
Cooking time approximately 1¼ hours

2–3 tablespoons clarified butter (ghee)
1 rabbit, cleaned and jointed into 4 or 6 portions
10 shallots or small onions, peeled and left whole
6–8 cloves garlic, peeled and left whole
6–8 allspice berries, crushed
4–6 cloves
1 cinnamon stick
1 whole dried chilli or 1 teaspoon roasted Middle Eastern red pepper (p152)
2 tablespoons sultanas
A handful of dried figs, halved
1 tablespoon honey
A sprinkling of fresh or dried thyme
1 tablespoon red or white wine vinegar
Roughly 200ml (7fl oz) red wine

Heat the clarified butter in a wide, heavy-based pan. Pop in the rabbit joints, brown the meat on all sides, then transfer the joints to a dish.

Add the shallots, garlic, spices and chilli to the pan and cook for a few minutes, until the shallots and garlic begin to colour. Stir in the sultanas, figs, honey and thyme, and return the rabbit joints to the pan.

Quickly, pour in the vinegar to de-glaze the pan, then pour in the wine. Bring the liquid to the boil, then reduce the heat, cover the pan and simmer gently for about 1 hour, until the rabbit is tender. Serve immediately with lots of bread.

Selling freshly cut onion tops, Eastern Turkey

Robust, traditional soups, padded out with dried or stale bread, are generally regarded as peasant fare but have become fashionable in the cities of the Middle East too. According to legend, this soup dates back to the ancient Persian Arsacid dynasty, the Ashkanians. Like *işkembe çorbası* (p208), the traditional Turkish tripe soup, *eshkeneh* is usually served with vinegar or pickles.

ESHKENEH
(PERSIAN ONION SOUP)

Serves 6
Preparation time 10 minutes
Cooking time 1 hour and 10 minutes

3 onions, sliced
1–2 tablespoons clarified butter, or 1 tablespoon olive oil with a little butter
2 tablespoons flour
1 tablespoon dried fenugreek leaves
1 teaspoon turmeric
Roughly 2 litres (3 pints) chicken stock or water
Salt and freshly ground black pepper
3 eggs, beaten
Dried or stale flat breads, broken into pieces

In a deep, heavy-based pan, cook the onions in the clarified butter until golden brown.

Stir in the flour, dried fenugreek leaves and turmeric, and pour in the stock. Bring the liquid to the boil, stirring all the time, then reduce the heat and simmer for about 1 hour.

Season the soup to taste and, just before serving, bring the soup back to the boil and stir in the beaten eggs.

Toss in the pieces of stale bread and serve immediately with a splash of vinegar or pickles and fresh bread.

Tavşan yahnisi

GARLIC

(TOM) *Allium sativum*

Garlic, which is one of the most powerfully flavoured vegetables, probably originated in central Asia or the eastern Mediterranean. It was an important ingredient in the diet of the ancient Egyptians, helping to keep up the strength of the labourers as they built the Great Pyramid, and it was left as an offering in the tombs. As they began their exodus, the Israelites looked back longingly at the garlic of Egypt (Numbers 11:5). The ancient Greeks and Romans also regarded garlic as a strengthening food, good for soldiers and oarsmen but not necessarily for the nobility. Horace, the Roman poet, complained that the smell from garlic could make one's lover refuse a kiss and move over to the far side of the bed. In most regions of the Middle East, where garlic is used fairly liberally, bowls of fresh parsley or basil and mint are passed around to sweeten the breath. In Iran, garlic is really only used in the dishes of the coastal regions, and in the Ottoman Palace dishes of Istanbul, it is used with a light touch. Because of its pungency and the 'magical' powers attributed to it, strings of garlic bulbs are hung in doorways to ward off the evil eye.

Garlic bulbs

The pyramids, built by labourers whose strength was fortified with garlic

HOW IT GROWS

A variety of wild and cultivated garlic grows in the Middle East. It is a hardy, perennial herb from the onion family and easy to grow. With long, reed-like leaves, garlic resembles the onion above the ground but, unlike the onion, the harvested bulb is divided into segments.

APPEARANCE AND TASTE

Garlic is an onion-shaped bulb, made up of individual moon-shaped segments. The bulb is encased in a white or a pinky-purple papery sheath, as is each creamy-coloured segment, called a 'clove'. Bulbs and their cloves vary in size and strength. Generally fresh garlic, or wet garlic, is milder in flavour than the ubiquitous dried bulbs of garlic, which are generally pungent and quite sharp. A larger variety of garlic, *Allium ampeloprasum*, aptly named elephant garlic or Levant garlic, after its place of origin, has a much milder flavour, so it is often baked whole in its skin, threaded whole onto kebabs, or sliced raw and added to salads and flat-bread fillings.

BUYING AND STORING

Dried bulbs of garlic can be found almost everywhere, all year round. Look for plump, firm bulbs with bright, healthy-looking sheaths. They are often sold individually or on strings. Fresh garlic, which is usually sold on the stalk, is available in the spring and the autumn. Both fresh and dried garlic keep well if stored in a dry, cool place.

MEDICINAL AND OTHER USES

Pickled garlic

CULINARY USES

Garlic is the 'bulb of life'. It has been used medicinally, or therapeutically, since ancient times, although it has not always been understood why. It is rich in minerals, including high amounts of sulphur compounds, and garlic is famous for its antibacterial, anti-fungal, anti-rheumatic and anti-thrombotic qualities. With its antiseptic qualities, strings of garlic are hung around children's necks to guard them during infectious disease epidemics. Garlic is also rich in vitamins B₁ and C and it contains iron and calcium.

Garlic is such a useful ingredient, it is used as a herb, a condiment, a vegetable, and even as a treat on its own, tossed into the ashes of a fire and left to soften to a mellow cream. It is a popular pickle, preserved whole or in individual cloves, and it is added to other pickles for flavour. Its strong flavour puts a punch in the nut-based *tarator* sauce, a popular accompaniment to fish and shellfish in Turkey, Syria, Lebanon and Egypt. It is often crushed and rubbed over small fish and poultry, such as red mullet and quails, before they are grilled or fried, and it is an essential part of the hot, spicy sauce in the Arab fish dish *samak harra*. It is used in a number of spice mixtures, such as the North African *harissa* (p155), which makes an appearance in some parts of the

Garlic seller, United Arab Emirates

Middle East, and the fiery Yemeni paste *zhug* (p169).

In Iran, its role is sparse, but it is essential in the Caspian broad bean stew *khoresht Gol dar*

Chaman. Numerous marinades, meat, vegetable and poultry stews, meatballs, and egg dishes include a clove or two of garlic. *Mezze* dips, such as *hummus* and the Turkish *ezme* dishes, are flavoured with garlic. Garlic cloves are stuffed into green olives or marinated and crushed with them. Whole heads of garlic are grilled with sheeps-tail fat in eastern Anatolia, as in the famous kebabs from Amasya and Tokat. But perhaps its most unique role, and definitely my favourite way of eating garlic, is in the sublime combination of yogurt and garlic, so often served with grilled or fried vegetables, or bound with their pounded or grated flesh, particularly in the *meze* dishes of Turkey.

Tying garlic

A lesser-known feature of the Middle Eastern kitchen is the number (and variety) of egg dishes. Whether they are cooked in their shells to an ancient recipe, *beid hamine*, bound with vegetables and fried in an Arab *eggah*, or simply fried with garlic, *beid bi tom*, they can be transformed from the ugly duckling into the swan – a street snack to an elegant dish at an elaborate feast.

BEID BI TOM
(FRIED EGGS WITH GARLIC)

Serves 3–6
Preparation time 5 minutes
Cooking time 5–10 minutes

6 eggs
2 tablespoons butter
3 cloves garlic, crushed with salt
1 teaspoon ground sumac (p188)
A fingerful dried mint
Salt

Break the eggs into a bowl. Melt the butter in a large frying pan and stir in the garlic and sumac. As soon as the garlic begins to colour, carefully slip in the eggs. Fry gently and sprinkle the dried mint over the top.

Cover the pan with a lid for a minute or two to help the eggs set, then serve them lightly sprinkled with salt.

Associated with *Kurban Bayramı*, when every part of the sacrificed sheep is used, this Turkish soup is also a great favourite for late-night workers, travellers, and drinkers, as it is renowned for its sobering qualities. A particular feature of this very traditional soup is the sharp, tangy accompaniment of garlic-flavoured vinegar and garlicky pickles.

Fruit, nut and garlic stall, Syria

Dried garlic in baskets

İŞKEMBE ÇORBASI
(TRIPE SOUP)

Serves 4–6
Preparation time 30 minutes
Cooking time 20 minutes

225g (8oz) lamb tripe, well
* washed*
1.2 litres (2 pints) water
1 tablespoon clarified butter
2 tablespoons plain flour
1 egg yolk
Juice of lemon
Salt and freshly ground black
* pepper*

To serve:
2-3 cloves garlic, crushed
Salt
4 tablespoon white-wine vinegar
Sharp, garlicky pickles (p55) or
* pickled garlic*

For the top:
2 tablespoons ordinary butter
1 teaspoon flaked Middle Eastern
* red pepper (p152)*

Put the tripe into a pan and cover it with water. Bring it to the boil, skim off any froth from the top, and continue to boil for 20–25 minutes, until the tripe is tender. Drain and keep the cooking liquid, then cut the tripe into fine slices.

Melt the clarified butter in a deep heavy-based pan. Stir in the flour to make a roux and pour in the cooking liquid, stirring until it thickens a little. Add the tripe and simmer gently for about 15 minutes.

In a bowl beat the egg yolk with the lemon juice. Add a little of the hot soup to it, then tip it into the pan, stirring vigorously to make sure it is well blended. Season the soup to taste and keep it simmering gently while you make the final preparations.

In a bowl, stir the crushed garlic with a little salt into the vinegar and put it aside. In a small pan, melt the butter and stir in the red pepper. Pour the soup into individual bowls, spoon a little of spiked butter over each one, and serve with the garlicky vinegar and pickles.

This is a wonderful garlicky sauce, popular in Egypt, Syria, Lebanon and Turkey. It can be used as a dip, but it is more commonly used as a sauce for fish or shellfish, particularly in the Arab dish *samak tarator*. This is a large baked fish, such as sea bass, garnished with fried nuts and black olives, and in the Turkish dish *midye tavası*, mussels deep-fried in a beer batter. The sauce is usually made with walnuts, almonds or pine nuts and the quantity of garlic used varies from hand to hand.

TARATOR
(GARLIC AND NUT SAUCE)

Serves 4 – as a dip or sauce
Preparation time 20 minutes if pounding by hand (2 minutes in the mixer)
Cooking time –

1 head of garlic, peeled and crushed to pulp
3–4 slices day-old or stale bread, soaked in water and then squeezed out
Juice of 1 lemon
50g (2oz) walnuts, roughly ground
4–5 tablespoons olive oil
Salt and freshly ground black pepper

Pound the ingredients together with a big pestle and mortar, adding the olive oil gradually as you would to make mayonnaise, and beat the mixture until it is thick and pulpy. Alternatively, whiz the ingredients in an electric mixer, still adding the oil gradually.

Season the sauce to your taste and garnish with crushed nuts or parsley.

Tarator

CAPSICUM PEPPER

(FILFIL HILU) *Capsicum annum*

Immature capsicum peppers

Like the hot red pepper, tomatoes and potatoes, the plump, bell-shaped capsicum entered the Middle East in the sixteenth century when the Ottomans and the Spanish dominated the political stage, resulting in a great deal of trade with the New World.

Red capsicum

Another name for this mild capsicum fruit is pimento. There is also a delightful bright green, long, tapering pepper which comes from the same family and is called *çarliston biber* in Turkish, which may indicate its place of origin. In the Mediterranean regions of the Middle East, the red bell peppers are ground to a pulp with a few hot peppers, olive oil and salt. This pulp is then spread out in shallow pans and left to dry in the sun until it resembles a thick paste. Buckets of this paste are often sold in the markets. Dried red peppers are often ground to a powder, which we know as paprika.

Paprika

HOW IT GROWS

All capsicums are native to the Americas and are related to the tomato and potato. Despite its botanical name, it is a perennial plant in its native habitat, but everywhere else it is an annual plant which bears fruit within a couple of months of sowing.

APPEARANCE AND TASTE

The large sweet peppers of the Middle East range in colour from a deep olive green to bright red and yellow, all slightly sweet, crunchy and juicy. Immature green peppers are picked when they are small, light green and thin-skinned as they are slightly piquant and, ideal for stuffing. The long, green *çarliston* peppers are delicately perfumed and can be quite fiery.

BUYING AND STORING

All fresh peppers should feel hard and crisp with glossy skins. Unless you are planning to dry them, fresh peppers should be used within ten days before they start to go soft, dull and wrinkly. Red pepper paste and paprika are available in Middle Eastern stores and some supermarkets. Both keep quite well in a cool, dry place.

CULINARY USES

Peppers, particularly the *çarliston* variety, are added to salads or they are grilled and skinned, then tossed in olive oil and lemon juice, or fried and served with garlicky yogurt. Peppers are often stuffed with a meat or rice filling and baked or poached. In Iran, the filling is

Sacks of red capsicum peppers at a depot, Turkey

Çarliston peppers

sometimes made with yellow split peas, and in Turkey, Syria and Lebanon, the young, thin-skinned peppers are stuffed and served cold with an aromatic rice filling. Chunks of pepper are often threaded onto skewers for meat, chicken, or fish kebabs, or they are cooked with vegetables such as aubergines and tomatoes in dishes that are served hot or cold. All peppers are popular pickled, whole or stuffed.

Like aubergines, red peppers are hollowed out and left to dry in the sun. Then they are hung on strings and used through the winter to stuff or add to stews. The red pepper paste is used to flavour dips, sauces, stews, meatballs and stuffings. It is also spread on bread with olive oil, crushed garlic or chopped onions and parsley as a snack. A similar paste can be made by chopping to a pulp roasted peppers with a few hot red peppers, or by whizzing them to a purée in a food processor, then heating the purée with olive oil and salt in saucepan and leaving it to simmer until it has reduced to a paste. Like the slightly hot Middle Eastern ground red pepper (p152), paprika is sprinkled liberally over smooth *mezze* dishes, such as *hummus*, and kebabs. It is also one of the ingredients in the Arab spice mix *baharat* (p162).

This salad is from northern Cyprus and, given the history of the island, it could be of Greek origin. However, the refreshing combination of grilled peppers and soft, juicy fruit is quite common in the Mediterranean regions of southern Turkey, Syria and Lebanon. Peaches, melons, and plums are all delicious with the soft grilled or roasted flesh of sweet bell peppers.

KIBRIS SALATASI
(GRILLED PEPPER AND PEACH SALAD)

Serves 3–4
Preparation time 25 minutes
Cooking time –

2 red bell peppers
2 large ripe peaches, skinned and stoned
2 tablespoons olive oil
Juice of 1 lime
Salt

Place the peppers over charcoal, directly over a gas flame, or under a conventional grill. Keep turning them until they buckle and blister all over. Pop them into a plastic bag to sweat for a few minutes, then hold them under running cold water and peel off the skin.

Halve the peppers lengthways, remove the stalks and seeds, and cut them into thick slices. Slice the peaches into similar-sized pieces, then place them and the peppers in a shallow bowl.

Pour over the olive oil and lime juice, season with salt, and toss lightly before serving.

Stuffed peppers are one of the most popular dishes throughout the Middle East. They are a particular favourite in the Mediterranean regions, where the immature, thin-skinned peppers are often filled with an aromatic rice and served cold as a *mezze* dish. They are also often stuffed with a minced meat filling and served hot, usually accompanied by stuffed tomatoes, stuffed courgettes, and stuffed aubergines.

MAHSHI FILFIL HILU
(STUFFED GREEN PEPPERS)

Serves 4
Preparation time 40 minutes
Cooking time 30–40 minutes

6–8 small green peppers
2 tablespoons olive oil
1 onion, finely chopped
½ teaspoon sugar plus some to sprinkle
3 tablespoons pine nuts
2 tablespoons currants
1–2 teaspoons dried mint
1 teaspoon ground cinnamon
½ teaspoon ground allspice
175g (6oz) short-grain rice, washed and drained
Salt and freshly ground black pepper
2–3 tomatoes
Juice of a lemon mixed with 50ml (2fl oz) olive oil
2 lemons cut into wedges

Cut the stalks off the green peppers and remove any seeds and pith from inside the bell. Wash them inside and out and put aside.

In a heavy-based pan, heat 2 tablespoons of olive oil and stir in the onion and ½ teaspoon of sugar. As the onion begins to colour, stir in the pine nuts and currants. When the currants plump up and the nuts begin to brown, stir in the mint. Add the spices, followed by the rice, and pour in enough water to just cover. Stir in the seasoning, bring the water to the boil, and simmer until the water has been absorbed.

Cut the sides off the tomatoes to make lids for the peppers. Spoon some of the rice mixture into each pepper, fit them with the tomato lids, and place them upright, side by side, in a heavy-based pan.

Mix together roughly 250ml (9fl oz) water with the olive oil and lemon juice mixture and pour over the peppers. Sprinkle with a little sugar, cover the pan and cook gently for approximately 30 minutes, until the peppers are tender.

Leave to cool in the pan. Serve cold with wedges of lemon to squeeze over them.

Mahshi filfil hilu

MELOKHIA

(MELOKHIA) *Corchorus olitorius*

Field workers tilling the soil, Cairo, Egypt

The leaves of the melokhia plant are eaten as a vegetable in parts of the Middle East, North Africa, the Caribbean, and South-East Asia, but it is in Egypt that they have the greatest culinary importance. In fact, one of Egypt's national dishes is an ancient peasant soup called *melokhia*. Prepared in exactly the same way as depicted in some of the Pharaonic tomb paintings, the soup is made almost daily by the peasant women, who carry large pots of it on their heads to the men working in the fields. The word *melokhia* means mallow in Arabic, and the vegetable is often referred to as Jew's mallow.

Dried melokhia

HOW IT GROWS

Related to the mallow, melokhia belongs to the same genus as the jute plant, which is grown all over the world as a source of fibre. In the summer, most Egyptian peasants reserve a small patch of ground to grow melokhia.

APPEARANCE AND TASTE

The leaves of the plant are dark green with serrated edges. They taste a bit like sorrel and, in a similar way to okra, they impart a mucilaginous quality to the dish.

BUYING AND STORING

In the markets of the Middle East, the leaves are sold fresh. They are also dried for storing, which is how they are usually sold outside the Middle East.

CULINARY USES

Generally, melokhia leaves are cooked and eaten like spinach or purslane, another leafy, mucilaginous vegetable. In Egypt, where they are used the most, the leaves are made into the glutinous, peasant soup called *melokhia*, which in medieval times was much more of a meal because fried meatballs were added to it. In Syria and Lebanon, the Egyptian *melokhia* soup is very thick and is made from chicken stock. It is then used as a sauce for the chicken that has been boiled for the stock and is served with rice.

This is such a popular soup amongst the hard-working Egyptian peasants that some of them eat it at midday and again in the evening. As it is eaten so often, the leaves are usually cooked in a simple vegetable stock, water that other vegetables have been boiled in. In this recipe, I am using dried melokhia leaves, but if you can find fresh leaves, they need to be washed and dried first, then chopped to a pulp, added to the boiling stock and cooked for about 10 minutes.

MELOKHIA
(EGYPTIAN MELOKHIA SOUP)

Serves 4–6
Preparation time 20 minutes' soaking
Cooking time 30 minutes

Melokhia

450g (1lb) dried melokhia leaves
1.2 litres (2 pints) vegetable or chicken stock
2 cloves garlic
Salt and ground black pepper
1 tablespoon clarified butter (ghee)
1–2 teaspoons ground coriander
1 scant teaspoon ground red pepper

Crush the dried melokhia leaves with your hands and soak them in a little boiled water until they have doubled in bulk.

Heat the stock in a large saucepan and bring it the boil. Stir in the melokhia and boil for about 25 minutes.

Crush the garlic with a little salt and fry it in the *ghee*. When it begins to brown, stir in the coriander and ground red pepper and mix to a paste.

Stir this paste into the soup and simmer for a few minutes. Season it to your taste and serve hot.

CUCUMBER

(KHIYAR) *Cucumis sativus*

The cucumber, which probably originated in India, is one of the oldest cultivated vegetables. In the Middle East, they have been known since classical times. As they are 96 per cent water, fresh cucumbers are very refreshing. In fact, their most important role in the Middle East is to quench the thirst. Street sellers peel and salt them for thirsty passers-by in hot weather.

Cucumbers

HOW IT GROWS

A member of the squash family, the cucumber is cultivated throughout the Middle East, both indoors and outdoors. It is in season from March to December.

APPEARANCE AND TASTE

Middle Eastern cucumbers can be short and stubby, almost seedless with slightly pimply skins, or long and slender with smooth skins. Most are sweet and juicy but some, like their ancestors, are quite bitter and require salting before use. There are also tiny cucumbers which are used for pickling.

Left: Growing cucumbers in the desert, Egypt

Right: Cucumber seller, Gaza Strip

BUYING AND STORING

When buying cucumbers, the main thing to look out for is that they are firm to the touch. They store well in warm and cool places but they will just turn to water if you freeze them. The Middle Eastern cucumbers can be found in some Indian and Italian stores as well as Middle Eastern outlets.

CULINARY USES

Peeled, salted strips of fresh cucumber are a delight, often served as a *mezze*. They are added to salads for their refreshing bite, usually married with warming herbs such as dill, mint and parsley, and dressed with lemon juice or orange blossom water. In Egypt, diced cucumber is added to a mixture of onion, lemon juice, olive oil, and a crumbly white cheese, like feta, to make the wonderful dish *michoteta*. Throughout the Middle East, cucumber is combined with yogurt in a light salad, such as the Iranian *mâst-o khiyâr*, an extremely decorative and delicious dish with walnuts and sultanas. Similarly, cucumbers and yogurt are combined in the Turkish dish *cacık*, which can be served as a *mezze* dish, as an accompaniment to meat or *pilafs*, or as a chilled soup.

Occasionally, cucumbers are added to summer stews in place of aubergines or courgettes, and they are sometimes added to the famous Lebanese and Syrian dish of bulgur and herbs, *tabbouleh* (p181). In Turkey and Iran, they are tossed with pomegranate seeds in a simple, juicy salad. And in Iran, they are soaked in lime water for a few days, until they are transparent, and then they are boiled with sugar to make a delicious, delicate-looking jam, *morabbâ-ye balang*.

Dips made with mashed or pulped ingredients are some of the most popular *mezze* dishes, ideal for scooping up with flat bread. The following Egyptian dish, made with crumbly white cheese, is sometimes served as an accompaniment to the great national favourite, *ful medames* (p116). A similar *mezze* dish, called *peynir ezmesi*, is popular in Turkey.

Mâst-o khiyâr

MICHOTETA
(CHEESE AND CUCMBER SALAD)

Serves 3–4 (as part of *mezze* spread)
Preparation time 15 minutes
Cooking time –

225g (8oz) crumbly white cheese (or feta)
2 tablespoons olive oil
Juice of 1 lemon
1 red onion, finely chopped
1 small cucumber (½ a large one), peeled and diced
Salt and freshly ground black pepper
A few mint leaves, finely chopped

Using a fork, mash the cheese in a bowl, then work in the olive oil and lemon juice. Mix in the onion and cucumber and season.

Spoon into a serving bowl, drizzle a little olive oil over the top and sprinkle with fresh mint.

Yogurt and cucumber make a very refreshing combination. On this theme, the two dishes that stand out are *cacik*, a Turkish dish enjoyed all over the Middle East, and *mâst-o khiyar*, the following Iranian dish which is characteristically exotic and flamboyant with its garnish of dried rose petals.

MÂST-O KHIYÂR
(YOGURT AND CUCMBER SALAD WITH WALNUTS AND SULTANAS)

Serves 4 (as part of *mezze* spread)
Preparation time 20 minutes
Cooking time –

1 long cucumber, peeled, deseeded and finely chopped
Salt
225g (8fl oz) strained yogurt
2–3 tablespoons sultanas, halved
1–2 tablespoons walnuts, coarsely chopped
A small bunch chives, finely chopped
A small bunch fresh dill and mint, finely chopped
Salt and freshly ground black pepper
A few dried rose petals
Two pinches dried mint

Sprinkle the cucumber with salt to draw out the water.

Beat the strained yogurt in a bowl, and stir in the sultanas, walnuts, chives and herbs. Add the weeping cucumber and season to taste.

Chill for an hour before serving, and garnish with the rose petals and dried mint.

PUMPKIN

(QAR'AT) *Cucurbita pepo*

The pumpkin is another vegetable that came to the Middle East from the New World. Perhaps more than any other vegetable, the pumpkin is linked with the cooking of various peoples rather than countries. The Armenians and the Kurds, in particular, are known for their sumptuous pumpkin dishes. Invariably the flesh is flavoured with strong, aromatic spices such as cinnamon and cloves, and it is sweetened with honey or sultanas.

HOW IT GROWS

Pumpkins are the gourd-like fruits from an annual plant that grows in temperate and tropical climates. From the same genus as melons, it is a rapid-growing plant that spreads itself wildly along the ground, producing large fruits that expand at a fast rate.

APPEARANCE AND TASTE

Middle Eastern pumpkins are generally orange in colour, large, and round or oval-shaped. Eaten when they are fully ripe, their bright orange or yellow flesh is fibrous and delicately perfumed when cooked. Generally, the more vibrant the flesh, the tastier it is, and the larger the pumpkin, the less flavoursome the flesh.

Pumpkins

CULINARY USES

Pumpkins are used in both savoury and sweet dishes. Cooked pumpkin flesh is used as a filling for some sweet, syrupy pastries and it is mashed with spices, herbs or onions and bulgur to fill savoury pastries. In Armenian communities cooked pumpkin is often layered with rice in a sweet, spicy, homely dish. The Armenians, the Kurds, the Turks, and the Jews all have their own version of a syrupy pumpkin jam or preserve, a thick, hearty pumpkin soup, and whole pumpkins stuffed with an aromatic lamb, rice and pine nut filling. The Turks and the Kurds poach cubes of pumpkin flesh in syrup to make the sumptuous, golden, winter dessert, *bal kabağı tatlısı* or *shirini*. And, like melon seeds, roasted and salted pumpkin seeds make a popular snack.

In Turkey the following winter dessert is called *bal kabağı tatlısı*, but in other parts of the Middle East it is known as *shirini*, a classic Kurdish speciality. Although the Kurds are Muslims, they are not Arabs, and possess their own language, customs and dishes. One of the most famous Kurds in history was Saladin, who, in the twelfth century became the sultan of Egypt and Syria.

Shelled pumpkin seeds

SHIRINI
(PUMPKIN POACHED IN SYRUP)

Serves 4–6
Preparation time 20 minutes
Cooking time approximately 2 hours

450g (1lb) sugar
200ml (7fl oz) water
Juice of ½ lemon
3–4 cloves
900g (2lb) pumpkin flesh, cut into 5cm (2in) cubes or rectangular blocks

Put the sugar, water and lemon juice into a heavy-based pan, and bring the liquid to the boil, stirring all the time, until the sugar has dissolved. Toss in the cloves and add the pumpkin pieces, then cover the pan with a lid and bring the liquid back to the boil.

Reduce the heat and leave the pumpkin pieces to poach gently, turning them over from time to time (until they are tender and gleaming) – depending on the size of your pumpkin pieces, this should take 1½–2 hours. Leave the pumpkin to cool in the pan, then place the pieces on a dish and spoon the syrup over them. Serve chilled, or at room temperature, with clotted cream.

Pumpkin seeds

Throughout their history, the Armenians have been invaded, conquered and dispersed. In the pre-Ottoman era, when Byzantium was at its peak, many Armenians were based in Constantinople, where their culinary culture merged with that of the city and the Greek community to create a cuisine that would later influence the Turks. Still residing in Istanbul and beyond, the Armenian communities, being Christian, drink wine and eat pork, unlike their Muslim neighbours. This recipe is for one of their homely dishes, usually served with pork.

ERMENİ PİLAVI
(ARMENIAN RICE WITH PUMPKIN, CINNAMON AND HONEY)

Serves 4–6
Preparation time 35–40 minutes
Cooking time 30 minutes

Roughly 700g (1½lb) pumpkin flesh, finely sliced
1 tablespoon clarified butter (ghee)
1 onion, chopped
1 teaspoon sugar
2 tablespoons sultanas
1 teaspoon cardamom seeds
1 teaspoon ground cinnamon
225g (8oz) long-grain rice, washed and drained
Salt and freshly ground black pepper
4 heaped tablespoons honey
2 tablespoons ordinary butter

'Turk's Turban' pumpkins

Preheat oven to 200°C/400°F/ gas mark 6.

Bring a pan of water to the boil. Toss in the pumpkin slices for a couple of minutes, then drain and refresh under cold water, and put aside.

In a heavy-based pan, melt the clarified butter and stir in the onion with the sugar. When the onion begins to colour, add the sultanas and cardamom seeds, followed by the cinnamon. Stir in the rice and pour in enough water to just cover. Stir in the seasoning and bring the water to the boil, then reduce the heat and simmer until it has all been absorbed.

Meanwhile, melt the honey in a pan and grease an oven-proof dish with a generous amount of the butter. Dribble some of the honey into the base, then line it with half the pumpkin slices, overlapping each other. Dribble a little more honey over the slices and tip the rice on top. Arrange the remaining pumpkin slices, pressed down firmly over the rice.

Return the pan of honey to the heat, melt the rest of the butter in it, and pour over the pumpkin. Place the dish in the oven for about 30 minutes, until the pumpkin is tender and slightly caramelised. Serve hot with roasted or grilled meat.

Shirini

COURGETTE

Courgette in flower

(KOUSA) *Cucurbita pepo*

ourgettes, or zucchini are an offspring of the marrow, which has been used in Mediterranean cooking for a long time. The wealthy Romans indulged in outrageous feasts which featured the tongues of flamingos and nightingales and vast quantities of marrows. The Byzantine emperors enjoyed marrows stewed with grape juice, a dish that Mehmet the Conqueror served at banquets in the fifteenth century. In the parts of the Middle East where culinary trends were influenced by the Ottomans, marrows are still believed to be cooling to the blood, so they are balanced by warming herbs such as dill and mint.

HOW IT GROWS

The large marrow (or squash, in America) is a member of the *Cucurbita* family, which is a creeping plant with serrated leaves, large, papery, yellow flowers, and an elongated fruit. When picked young and slim (10–20cm/4–8in long), the fruit are known as courgettes, or zucchini.

APPEARANCE AND TASTE

Very fresh, tender courgettes should have a delicate, almost perfumed flavour. They can be eaten raw or lightly cooked. They shouldn't be watery.

BUYING AND STORING

Look for the bright green, slim and firm courgettes, preferably still with a flower attached – they really will be fresh. Courgettes have a tendency to go limp and rubbery quite quickly, even if they are kept in a cool, dry place, so don't store them for long.

CULINARY USES

As courgettes have such a delicate flavour, they should be lightly cooked. Raw, grilled, lightly steamed or fried young courgettes are often added to salads, such as the Turkish dish *bostancı*, with lamb's lettuce, or they are lightly fried with sultanas, roasted pine nuts, and a little lemon juice. They are delicious steamed and served with a *tarator* sauce made with crushed hazelnuts (p133) or pine nuts. In the fashion of all stuffed vegetable dishes, *mahshi khodar* (*dolma* in Turkey, *dolmeh* in Iran), they are often filled with aromatic rice or bulgur, or a minced lamb and rice mixture, and then poached or baked. At the beginning of the season, the courgette flowers as well are stuffed with similar fillings. There is an ancient dish that calls for courgettes to be filled with rice and minced lamb, then layered in a pan with soaked, dried apricots, which may have Persian origins.

Like carrots and aubergines, courgettes are fried, or deep-fried in batter, and served with yogurt, particularly in Turkey. Courgettes are also grated and fried and added to an egg and cheese mixture to make lovely, light patties; they can also be combined with cheese and egg in savoury pastries, or baked with cheese and egg. On the egg and cheese theme, they are a popular vegetable in the Arab *eggah* (Persian *kookoo*) dishes, which are a bit like thick Spanish omelettes, packed with flavour. Cooked with tomatoes and dill, they appear in a number of vegetable, pulse or meat stews, in which they are interchangeable with aubergines. Similarly, steamed or fried courgettes or aubergines are added to minced meat to make tasty meatballs. And a mock *İmam bayıldı* (p51), using courgettes, has become popular in recent years. In Iraq, there is a special dish called *koubba helwa*, (p79) which is a type of *kibbeh* in a semolina shell cooked in a tomato and courgette sauce. In Turkey, they are used make a delightful *helva*, flavoured with cardamom, which has echoes of Iran or India.

Throughout the Middle East, the roasted and salted seeds of mature marrows are a nutritious and tasty snack – the seeds of courgettes are far too small, of course.

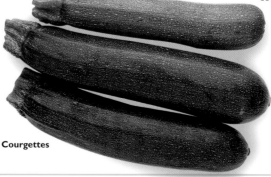

Courgettes

Vegetable stall with cucumbers and young marrows

The Arab omelette *eggah* is thick, firm and full of character, rather like a Spanish omelette. It can be made on top of the stove, or in the oven, and is eaten hot or cold, cut into rectangular portions. Often packed with ingredients, the most common *eggah* dishes include broad beans, aubergines, leeks, spinach, minced meat, and chicken.

EGGAH BI EISH WA KOUSA

(ARAB BREAD AND COURGETTE OMELETTE)

Serves 6
Preparation time 25–30 minutes
Cooking time 25 minutes

2–3 courgettes, sliced
1 onion, sliced
2–3 tablespoons ordinary or clarified butter
A small bunch fresh mint, chopped
6 eggs
3 slices bread, with the crusts removed, soaked in a little milk
Salt and freshly ground black pepper

Sprinkle the courgettes with a little salt to draw out the water, rinse them and pat dry.

In a heavy-based pan, soften the onion in half the butter, then add the courgettes. Fry until soft and golden, and stir in the mint. Leave to cool.

Beat the eggs in a bowl. Squeeze the bread dry and crumble it into the beaten eggs. Add the courgette and onions, and season with salt and pepper.

Heat the rest of the butter in a heavy-based frying pan. Tip the egg mixture into the hot butter and cook gently over a low heat, until the eggs are set. Cover the pan with a large plate and invert it, so that the *eggah* lands on the plate upside down, then carefully slip it back into the pan to brown the other side. Flip the eggah onto a serving dish and cut it into segments, like a cake.

Generally, vegetable stews are made with a little meat, but in the hot months a meatless stew is often favoured. In rural communities, these stews are cooked in earthenware pots which are placed in the cooling bread ovens to bake. A summer stew will always include courgettes, aubergines and peppers, to which beans and artichokes are sometimes added, and plenty of herbs.

KHUDRA BIL FURN

(MIXED VEGETABLE STEW)

Serves 6
Preparation time 25 minutes
Cooking time approximately 1 hour

3–4 courgettes, cut into slices roughly 2½cm (1in) wide
2 long, slim aubergines, or 1 fat one, cut into quarters length-ways, then into 2½cm (1in) chunks
2 green or red peppers, with stalk and seeds removed, cut into similar-sized pieces
2–3 onions, peeled and quartered
4 tomatoes, skinned
4 cloves garlic, finely chopped
1 teaspoon ground fenugreek
1 teaspoon sugar
A bunch fresh flat leaf parsley, dill and mint, chopped
Salt and freshly ground black pepper
125ml (4fl oz) olive oil
Juice of 1 lemon

Preheat the oven to 200°C/400°F/gas mark 6.

Place the courgettes, aubergines, peppers, and onions in an earthenware pot or oven dish.

Chop 3 of the tomatoes and add them to the pot, along with the garlic, fenugreek, sugar and herbs. Mix it all together well, then season generously with salt and pepper.

Mix the olive oil and lemon juice together, add enough water to increase the volume to about 300ml (½ pint), and pour it all over the vegetables. Slice the remaining tomato finely and lay the slices over the top of the vegetables (if using a wide oven dish, you will need an extra tomato), then pop the vegetables into the oven for about 1 hour, or until they are tender, stirring them once after the first 30 minutes.

Serve the hot stew either on its own with rice, or as an accompaniment to meat or poultry.

Khudra bil furn

ARTICHOKE

(KHURSHUF) *Cynara scolymus*

Dedicated to Venus and believed to be an aphrodisiac, it was no wonder that the globe artichoke became a regular feature in the diet of wealthy Romans. In fact, Pliny described the vegetable as a luxury fit only for the wealthy and noble. The globe artichoke is just a glorious thistle, a superior version of the ancient cardoon that grows wild in the Mediterranean region, but it is regarded as a delicacy in the Middle East. The old Arabic name for artichoke, *al-khurshuf*, means prickle or thorn.

Artichokes

HOW IT GROWS

The globe artichoke is a tall, majestic plant with serrated leaves and when the purple flowers are in full bloom it is a splendid sight. The globe artichoke are harvested in the early summer, but there is a cone-shaped, smooth-edged variety that is harvested in the winter. They are picked to eat before the flower blooms, although some are left to provide seeds for the next year's crop.

APPEARANCE AND TASTE

The artichoke globe is usually spherical in shape and mossy green or purplish in colour. It is made up of sharp-pointed, layered scales which encase the flower and the nectarous calix. The flesh on the scales is eaten in southern Europe, but in the Middle East, the scales are usually fed to the animals and only the heart is consumed. Healthy and full of goodness, the gently cooked heart is delicate and sweet to taste, with a firm but soft texture.

BUYING AND STORING

Artichokes were expensive for the Romans and they still are today. Usually, they are not weighed by the kilo or pound, but individually. When selecting them yourself, choose large heads with tightly closed, fresh-looking, juicy scales. They go brown and dry out very quickly. If you hold them by their thick stems, the heads should nod. If they are stiff, like maracas, then the stem and heart will be woody. Fresh artichokes should be stood in fresh water, like a bunch of flowers, until you are ready to use them. Frozen ready-prepared hearts are also available in Middle Eastern stores and some supermarkets.

MEDICINAL USES

The artichoke has been used for medicinal purposes since early times, mainly because it contains cynarin, which is understood to be beneficial to the liver. The tonic properties of the artichoke are believed to improve the body's metabolism and a person's complexion, as well as giving an overall feeling of well-being. They are also said to have aphrodisiac qualities.

CULINARY USES

In parts of the Middle East, ready-prepared artichoke hearts are sold in the streets, which makes life easy, as preparing them yourself can take time. Once you have removed the stalk, scales, flower and hairy choke, you must rub lemon

Selling bundles of artichokes

juice over the exposed heart before it discolours and then plunge it into a bowl of salted cold water with a little lemon juice. In the early summer, the hearts are much sought after. They are particularly popular in Turkey and Egypt. They can be stuffed with minced meat and served in an egg and lemon sauce, or they can be stuffed with a mixture of diced carrot and potato, and poached in olive oil and lemon juice. A classic Middle Eastern dish consists of artichoke hearts stuffed with fresh, green broad beans, sometimes with almonds or pine nuts, and poached in olive oil and lemon juice. At their simplest, the hearts are poached alone in olive oil and lemon juice with a little fresh dill for flavouring. The cooked hearts are pounded to a paste with minced meat to make an Egyptian meatball dish. The boiled or steamed hearts, chopped and dressed in olive oil, crushed garlic and lemon juice, or with preserved lemon, make a lovely salad or *mezze*. And the raw hearts are pickled in oil and lemon juice.

Globe artichokes growing in a field

Of all the Turkish *zeytinyağlı* dishes, this one is king. Cooked gently in olive oil, flavoured with lemon and dill, and served cold, it is one of the nicest ways to appreciate the subtle taste and texture of the creamy artichoke hearts.

Zeytinyağlı enginar

ZEYTİNYAĞLI ENGİNAR
(ARTICHOKE HEARTS IN OLIVE OIL)

Serves 4
Preparation time 20–25 minutes
Cooking time roughly 30 minutes

4 fresh globe artichokes, trimmed
  down to the hearts, rubbed with
  lemon juice, and kept in a bowl
  of salted cold water with a little
  lemon juice, until ready to use
110ml (4fl oz) olive oil
Juice of ½ a lemon
Roughly 50ml (2fl oz) water
Salt
A small bunch dill, chopped
1 lemon, cut into wedges

Place the artichoke hearts in a heavy-based pan with the olive oil, lemon juice, and water. Cover with the lid and poach gently for 15–20 minutes. Add salt to taste and continue to poach for a further 10 minutes, until the hearts are tender. Leave to cool in the pan.

Place them on a serving dish, spoon the flavoured olive oil over them, sprinkle with the dill, and serve with wedges of lemon to squeeze over them.

In some parts of the Middle East, the artichokes are known by the more modern Arabic name, *ardishawki*, and are frequently stuffed with meat or, as in the following Lebanese dish, combined with broad beans.

ARDISHAWKI WA FUL AKHDAR
(ARTICHOKES WITH BROAD BEANS AND ALMONDS)

Serves 4
Preparation time about 30 minutes
Cooking time 35–40 minutes

1 tablespoon flour
300ml (½ pint) water
2 teaspoons sugar
Juice of 1 lemon
2 cloves garlic, crushed
A small bunch of dill
Salt and ground black pepper
2–3 tablespoons olive oil
6–8 fresh globe artichokes,
  trimmed down to the hearts,
  rubbed with lemon juice, and kept
  in a bowl of salted cold water
  with a little lemon juice, until
  ready to use
200g (7oz) fresh broad beans,
  shelled and, if necessary, skinned
50g (2oz) blanched almonds

Mix the flour to a loose paste with a couple of tablespoons of the water, then pour it and the rest of the water into a heavy-based pan.

Add the sugar, lemon juice, garlic, dill and salt (about ½ teaspoon) and bring the liquid to the boil, stirring all the time so that the flour doesn't become lumpy. Simmer the liquid for about 10 minutes, then stir in the olive oil.

Add the artichoke hearts, broad beans, and almonds, and cook gently for about 20 minutes, until they are tender.

Check the seasoning and serve hot or cold, with the broad beans and almonds spooned into the cupped hearts.

CARROT

(JAZRA) *Daucus carota*

The carrot is believed to have originated in Afghanistan, where wild red and purple varieties have grown since ancient times. It appeared on the list of aromatic herbs, rather than vegetables, grown in the royal gardens of Babylon in the eighth century BC, indicating that the carrot leaves and seeds, both of which have a carrot flavour, were used instead of the roots. In fact, it took a long time for the carrot root to be cultivated and consumed, as there is no mention of the Greeks or Romans eating carrots. When he conquered the Persian Empire, Alexander the Great took the dark purple carrot as one of the spoils of war, but it wasn't until somewhere between the eighth and tenth centuries AD that the carrot travelled westwards with the Arabs, across the north of Africa and into Spain. One of the earliest descriptions of the carrot was by an Arab writer who talked about a red variety that was tasty and juicy and a yellow one that had an inferior flavour. At some point on its journey in western Europe in the seventeenth century, the carrot changed colour to orange, and was depicted in the Dutch paintings of the period. Both red and yellow varieties still grow in the Middle East and purple carrots are cultivated in the south of Turkey.

HOW IT GROWS

The wild carrot still grows in its natural habitat in western Asia, particularly Afghanistan. The cultivated orange carrot grows well throughout the Middle East and keeps for a long time in the soil.

APPEARANCE AND TASTE

Most carrots are orange, due to the presence of beta carotene. They are long and slim with tapered ends. They contain quite a lot of natural sugar, so they are generally sweet and juicy to the taste. The purple and red varieties are slightly sharper, as you would imagine a radish crossed with a carrot might taste.

BUYING AND STORING

The conventional orange carrot should be firm and juicy-looking when fresh, not rubbery or woody. If stored in a cool, dry place, or in sand, carrots keep for a long time.

Purple carrots, Turkey

CULINARY USES

The natural sweetness and vibrant colour of the carrot are exploited to the full in the Middle East. Shredded raw or cooked carrot is often added to a *pilaf* or salad for a splash of colour. In Iranian rice dishes, it is often married with blanched almonds and bitter orange peel for flavour and texture. And a glorious-looking, syrupy jam is made with thinly sliced or shredded carrot in Iran and Turkey. Carrot slices are pickled in salt and vinegar, often with one of its umbelliferous relatives, such as celery or fennel seeds, to accentuate the flavour. Carrots are grated raw and served as a simple salad, dressed with lemon juice, and they can be fried in olive oil, or deep-fried in batter, and served with yogurt as a *mezze*. As you would expect, carrots appear in many stews, soups, pulse dishes, and *pilaf*s.

I've eaten this delicious carrot jam in a number of places but only the Persian version uses cardamom seeds. You can shred or slice

Carrots

the carrot into any shape or size you like but I prefer thin rounds so that it looks like carrot jam rather than orange marmalade. As with most Middle Eastern jams, the consistency is more like a syrupy conserve than a solid, easy-to-spread jam.

MORABBÂ-YE HAVEEJ
(CARROT JAM WITH ORANGE AND CARDAMOM)

Makes enough for 2–3 small jars
Preparation time 30 minutes
Cooking time 20–25 minutes

700g (1½lb) sugar
425ml (¾ pint) water
900g (2lb) carrots, peeled and sliced into fine rounds
Juice of 2 small oranges, and the rind, cut into slivers
Juice of ½ lemon
2 tablespoons rose water
Seeds of 5–6 green cardamom pods
50g (2oz) blanched almonds, cut into slivers

Gently dissolve the sugar in the water in a deep, wide, heavy-based pan and bring the liquid to the boil, stirring all the time.

Stir in the carrots and orange rind and, once again, bring the liquid to the boil. Continue to boil the liquid, stirring from time to time, until it begins to thicken a little and become syrupy.

Stir in the rose water, orange and lemon juice, cardamom seeds and almond slivers, and gently boil the syrup for a further 5 minutes, until the carrots are tender and the syrup is just right (test it by spooning a little onto a plate and leaving it to cool – it should be quite thick and dribble slowly, not run, from your finger). Leave the jam to cool completely, then spoon into sterilised jars.

In the summer months, families congregate outdoors as much as possible, eating on balconies, terraces, in gardens, and in any space in the countryside.

Morabbâ-ye haveej

Weekends are peppered with picnics, often consisting of olives, white cheese, fruit, a rice dish, and *kibbeh* or *köfte*. The following Turkish *köfte* are delicious hot or cold, so they are ideal for country picnics.

HAVUÇ KÖFTESI
(CARROT ROLLS WITH APRICOTS AND PINE NUTS)

Serves 4–6
Preparation time 40 minutes
Cooking time 5–10 minutes

10 medium-sized carrots, peeled, steamed until soft, and drained
2–3 slices day-old bread, rubbed into crumbs
8–10 dried apricots, finely chopped
4 spring onions, finely sliced
3 tablespoons pine nuts
2–3 cloves garlic, crushed
1 teaspoon Middle Eastern red pepper (p152), or paprika
A bunch of fresh flat-leaf parsley, mint and dill
1 egg

Salt and ground black pepper
Flour
Sunflower oil for frying
Some lemon wedges

Put the cooked carrots into a bowl and mash with a fork. Add the rest of the ingredients except the flour, oil and lemon wedges, and knead well. The mixture should be moist and sticky – if it is too wet and sticky, add extra breadcrumbs. Tip a small heap of flour onto a flat surface, then take an apricot-sized portion of the mixture in your hands and mould it into a sticky oblong roll. Dip the roll in the flour to coat it, pat into shape and put on a plate. Repeat with the rest of the mixture.

Heat a thin layer of sunflower oil in a heavy-based frying pan. Place the carrot rolls in it and fry over a moderate heat, until they are nicely browned on all sides. Drain them on kitchen paper and serve hot or cold with lemon wedges, or with garlic-flavoured yogurt.

Carrots sold from a donkey cart, Egypt

OKRA

(BAMIA) *Hibiscus esculentus*

Okra is thought to be native to Africa but there is no trace of it in the Middle East until the thirteenth century, when it was recorded growing beside the Nile in Egypt. In some parts of the Middle East, immature okra is picked while still small and hung on strings to dry.

Fresh okra

A field of okra

HOW IT GROWS

Another member of the mallow family, the *Hibiscus esculentus* is an annual plant which grows in tropical and subtropical regions. Although they are eaten as a vegetable, okra are the pods of this plant. It is cultivated extensively in Egypt.

APPEARANCE AND TASTE

Generally the pods are ridged, dark or light green, and long and tapering, hence their other name, 'ladies' fingers'. Some varieties though are stubby and fat, while others are almost red in colour. They range in size from about 2½cm (1in) to 20cm (8in). Each pod has compartments filled with seeds and a gummy substance which gives okra its particular character. If left whole and cooked lightly they remain crunchy and pod-like, but if they are cut before cooking, they become slimy, a texture that some people like. The tiny dried pods are grey-green in colour and quite hairy. When they are added to soups and stews, they impart a tart flavour.

Dried okra

BUYING AND STORING

Fresh green okra should be firm and free of black markings. They are available in Asian stores and in some supermarkets, but don't keep for very long. Dried okra, on the other hand, are available only in Middle Eastern and wholefood stores. They keep for a year in a dry place.

CULINARY USES

When preparing okra, some cooks toss them in lemon juice before cooking so they retain their colour. Lightly fried with a little sugar and lemon juice is quite a popular way of cooking fresh okra quickly to eat with rice, or as a *mezze* dish; they can also be dipped in batter and deep-fried. They are sometimes used instead of courgettes in the sauce for the Iraqi speciality *koubba helwa* (p79).

And throughout the Middle East, apart from in Iran, okra are cooked with beef, lamb, or chicken in a stew, or with tomatoes and onions in a simple ragout, sometimes flavoured with garlic, sour pomegranate juice, dill or fresh coriander. In Iran, they are relatively new and don't make an appearance in the traditional dishes, but their Persian name, *bamieh*, is borrowed by sweet pastries which are shaped like okra and bathed in syrup. The dried okra beads are used solely for stews and soups, such as the Anatolian dish, *kuru bamya çorbası*.

In parts of the Middle East, it is quite common to cook vegetables with a little sugar and lemon juice, especially if the dish is going to be eaten cold. Okra are particularly good done this way, as are leeks, shallots, and aubergines. In this simple Arab recipe, the okra are kept whole and eaten like deep-fried anchovies, from head to tail. The whole sweet and sour pods are popped into the mouth, complete with stalk, as they are deliciously tender with a crunchy bite to them.

BAMIA
(SWEET AND SOUR OKRA)

Serves 4
Preparation time 5 minutes
Cooking time 10–15 minutes

350g (12oz) fresh okra, washed
*   and left whole*
Juice of 1 lemon
3 tablespoons olive oil
1 tablespoon sugar
Salt and freshly ground black
*   pepper*

Put the okra into a bowl and toss in the lemon juice. Leave them for 5 minutes, then lift them out onto a plate, leaving most of the lemon juice behind.

Heat the olive oil in a wide, heavy-based pan and add the okra. Sauté them for about 5 minutes, tossing them gently about in the pan. Sprinkle the sugar over them and toss them again, then add the lemon juice.

Season the okra with salt and pepper, and pour in a little water to just cover the base of the pan. Cook for a further 5 minutes, adding a splash more water if necessary, until the pan juices are almost caramelised and the okra are beautifully tender.

Serve hot, or leave to cool in the pan and serve cold, dipped in the sweet and sour juices.

The strings of small, sour-tasting dried okra hanging in the markets are usually destined for a lamb or chicken stew, or for this traditional Anatolian soup, which is served to refresh the palate between courses at ceremonial feasts.

KURU BAMYA ÇORBASI
(DRIED OKRA SOUP)

Serves 4–6
Preparation time 10 minutes
Cooking time 50 minutes

50g (2oz) mutton, cut into small
*   pieces*
2 onions, finely chopped
1 teaspoon coriander seeds
1–2 tablespoons sheep's-tail fat or
*   clarified butter (ghee)*
2 tablespoons tomato paste
1.2 litres (2 pints) lamb stock
50g (2oz) small dried okra
Juice of 1 lemon
Salt and freshly ground black
*   pepper*

In a heavy-based pan, fry the meat and onions with the coriander seeds in the fat or butter. When they begin to brown, stir in the tomato paste, followed by the stock. Bring the liquid to the boil, then reduce the heat and simmer for about 20 minutes, until the meat is tender.

Meanwhile, rub the dried okra in a clean towel to remove the dust and hairs. Rinse them, toss them in half the lemon juice, and place them in a pan. Cover with just enough water and boil them for about 10 minutes. Drain and refresh them and, if they are on strings, slip them off at this stage, then add them to the soup with the rest of the lemon juice.

Bring the soup to the boil once more, season it to taste, then cover the pan, reduce the heat, and simmer for a further 15–20 minutes. Serve the soup hot, by itself with bread, or spoon it over plain rice.

Bamia

TOMATO

(BANADURA) *Lycopersicon lycopersicum*

Covered vegetable market, Turkey

In spite of its ubiquitous use, the tomato is relatively new to the Middle East. The Aztec cultivated it long before it ever arrived on

Plum tomatoes

the Mediterranean shores, where it was treated with suspicion as it came from the family that contained deadly nightshade. Along with potatoes, maize, capsicum and chilli peppers, tomatoes reached the Ottoman Empire from the New World, via Spain, in the sixteenth century, when Madrid and Constantinople dominated the political stage. Considering how ancient the Middle Eastern culinary tradition is, it is amazing that the influence of this relatively recent fruit is so great in the food of the Middle East. It sits so perfectly in practically every dish, as if it has always been there. The most descriptive name for tomato is the Persian *gojeh farangi*, which means 'foreign plum'. The flat roofs of rural dwellings throughout the Middle East are used for reducing and thickening fresh tomato pulp in the hot sun, to be used by each household in winter.

Vine tomatoes

HOW IT GROWS

The tomato plant, which is a member of the *Solanaceae* family, to which capsicum peppers, potatoes and aubergines belong, grows well in a Mediterranean climate, often in poor soil. Generally, the fruit (it is only termed a vegetable because of its culinary use) of the plant is harvested from late summer to early autumn.

APPEARANCE AND TASTE

The tomatoes of the Middle East are usually large and long, or fat and round. They range in colour from greenish red to brilliant crimson and, because they grow in the right conditions, they are all tasty, juicy and sweet.

MANUFACTURING

Turkey is one of the biggest producers of tomatoes. Tons of fresh tomatoes are exported every year. Many are preserved in tins or turned into a commercial tomato paste, and they are dried for export too.

BUYING AND STORING

Freshly plucked tomatoes that still smell of the vine are the best, but most tomatoes for sale have been kept refrigerated for days. No matter what shape, colour or size, choose firm, taut-skinned tomatoes and keep them in a cool place. Tinned tomatoes and tomato paste keep for a long time if unopened. Once opened, they must be used within days. Dried tomatoes keep well in an airtight container or in olive oil.

CULINARY USES

The culinary role of the tomato is infinite. It marries well with herbs, onions, garlic, aubergines, peppers, pulses, grains, meat and fish. The list goes on. It provides the colour, pulp and juice in many vegetable, meat, and fish stews and soups, such as *âbgoosht* (p115), a substantial working man's lamb soup in Iran. It binds together onions, garlic and peppers in stuffings and fillings, as in the famous Turkish dish *İmam bayıldı* (p51) and *khandrajo*, a Jewish tomato and aubergine filling for pastries. It binds together similar ingredients in egg dishes, such as *menemen* or the Arab *eggah* dishes. Various tomato-based rice dishes, some with herbs, others with potatoes or aubergines, are served with grilled or roasted meat and poultry.

The big, juicy, round tomatoes are often baked or poached whole, stuffed with an aromatic rice or minced meat mixture. Slices of tomato provide a moist cap for many other stuffed vegetables and chunks of tomato are often threaded onto

Weighing carrots and tomatoes

kebabs for a burst of juice. Raw tomatoes are so sweet and refreshing, they are often added to vegetable, grain or pulse salads. They are pulped and used to make a sauce for *rishta* (noodles, p126), *mantı* (an ancient form of pasta), and for some meatballs. Sometimes the sauce is spiced with chilli, garlic, coriander and cumin, with a touch of fruitiness from the sour pomegranate or grape molasses.

Tomato paste is added to stews and pulse and rice dishes, and it binds the spices in the raw meat and bulgur balls called *çiğ köfte* in the Turkish and *kibbeh nayya* in Arabic. Tomato paste is also used for the delicious Arab flat breads, *lahma bi ajeen* (p188), which are a bit like a thin pizza with a tasty, minced lamb topping. Unripe green tomatoes are pickled in salt and vinegar, and really ripe, freshly picked tomatoes are often eaten like a fruit to quench the thirst.

One of the characteristics of Yemeni cooking is the use of hot spices. *Zhug* (p169), which is one of the fieriest pastes in the Middle East, and *hilbeh* (p199), a hot fenugreek and coriander paste, both come from Yemen. Even this simple salad is lit up with a hot chilli.

BANADURA SALATA BIL KIZBARA
(TOMATO SALAD WITH CHILLI AND CORIANDER)

Serves 4
Preparation time 20 minutes
Cooking time —

6 plump, fresh tomatoes, skinned and coarsely chopped
1 hot green chilli, with stalk and seeds removed, and finely chopped
2 cloves garlic, finely chopped
A bunch of fresh coriander leaves, finely chopped
A little sugar
2–3 tablespoons olive oil
Juice of ½ lime or lemon
Salt

Put the chopped tomatoes into a bowl.

Add the chilli, garlic and coriander. Sprinkle with a little sugar and mix it all together.

Pour in the olive oil and lime or lemon juice, season with salt, and give it another toss before serving.

Tomato-based stews featuring a single vegetable are common throughout the Middle East. Particularly popular are the ones made with okra, courgettes, green beans, and Jerusalem artichokes. This dish can be served either hot or cold as a side dish, or on its own with rice.

TARTOUFA
(JERUSALEM ARTICHOKE AND TOMATO STEW)

Serves 3–4
Preparation time 15minutes
Cooking time 35–40 minutes

2–3 tablespoons olive oil
1 onion, finely chopped
1–2 cloves garlic, smashed
500g (1lb 2oz) Jerusalem artichokes, washed, peeled, and cut into thumb-length pieces
2–3 tomatoes, skinned and chopped
1 tablespoon concentrated tomato paste
1 teaspoon sugar
A small bunch of fresh parsley and dill, chopped
Salt and freshly ground black pepper
1 lemon, cut into wedges

In a heavy-based pan, fry the onion in the olive oil until it begins to brown.

Stir in the garlic, then add the artichokes and cook for a minute or two, rolling them about in the pan.

Add the tomatoes, the tomato paste, sugar, and most of the herbs (reserve some for serving). Pour in just enough water to cover, then simmer gently for about 30 minutes until the artichokes are tender and the sauce has reduced.

Season well to taste, sprinkle with the remaining herbs and serve with lemon to squeeze over it.

Harvesting tomatoes in the Jordan valley

The following Turkish dish is often cooked in ports and bus stations, while passengers wait for transport. Large, slightly curved, shallow pans are set over a fire, or gas flame, and the dish is cooked in minutes. As street and station food, the eggs are usually scrambled through the tomatoes and peppers, but when the dish is cooked at home, the eggs are often set on top. It is delicious served with a dollop of garlic-flavoured yogurt.

MENEMEN
(TOMATOES AND PEPPERS WITH EGGS)

Serves 4
Preparation time 15 minutes
Cooking time approximately 20 minutes

2 onions, sliced
2 green peppers, sliced
2 tablespoons olive oil plus a little butter
1 teaspoon Middle Eastern red pepper (p152) or 1 chilli, finely sliced
1–2 teaspoons sugar
5–6 tomatoes, skinned and chopped or 1 tin of chopped tomatoes
Salt and freshly ground black pepper
4 eggs
5 tablespoons thick, set yogurt
1–2 cloves garlic, crushed

In a wide frying pan, fry the onions and green peppers in the olive oil and butter, until they take on a bit of colour. Then stir in the Middle Eastern red pepper, or chilli, and add the tomatoes and sugar. Cook for a few minutes until the liquid has reduced.

Season to taste, then crack the eggs over the top of the tomato mixture, positioning them around the pan. Cover and leave to cook gently until the eggs are just cooked.

Meanwhile, beat the yogurt with the garlic in a bowl and season to taste. Serve the *menemen* directly from the pan and enjoy it with the cool yogurt.

AUBERGINE

(BADINJAN) *Solanum melongena*

Originally from India, the aubergine plays such a leading role in the culinary cultures of the Middle East, one would think it had always been there, yet it was only introduced in the seventh and eighth centuries. The Arabs fell under its spell when they conquered Iran in the seventh century, and adopted the Old Persian name, *badin-gan*, changing the hard 'g' to *al-badinjan*. From there, the Arabs spread the aubergine through the rest of the Middle East and North Africa, where it is now considered a staple food, often referred to as 'poor man's meat'. In Iran, it is called 'poor man's caviar'. The aubergine is also known as *betingan* in parts of the Middle East, and as *patlıcan* in Turkey, where it is considered to be the king of vegetables. As there are said to be two hundred dishes using aubergines in Turkey and they appear so frequently on the table, there is a saying: '*Patlıcansız tarafından olsun!*' ('Let it be from the part without an aubergine'), meaning, 'For goodness sake let's have a change!'

Aubergine jam

HOW IT GROWS

Aubergines need warmth to grow, so the Mediterranean climate suits them well. They are grown throughout the Middle East.

APPEARANCE AND TASTE

There are many different kinds of aubergine. In the Middle East, the most common varieties are long and slender, ideal for stuffing, or large and bulbous, which are delicious smoked over a flame or fried. Their shiny skins vary in colour from violet to deep purple and blue-black. Aubergines have their own distinct taste but, when they are cooked with spices, herbs and other ingredients, their sponge-like flesh takes on the flavours of the dish. Aubergines cooked whole over a naked flame or fire have a sharp, smoky flavour that blends beautifully with yogurt and olive oil.

BUYING AND STORING

Regardless of colour or size, fresh aubergines should be firm and glossy. If they are soft, spongy, or turning brown, they are too old. Generally, supermarkets sell fat or thin aubergines, with little variation on colour and size. Italian, Greek, Middle Eastern and Asian stores sell a variety of shapes and sizes, including the tiny aubergines (sometimes from Kenya), that are ideal for jam and the classic Persian stew *khoresht-e bâdenjân*. Fresh aubergines keep for about two weeks stored in a cool, dry place, or in the fridge. Dried aubergine shells, used for stuffing and aubergine pickles and jams, are available in some Middle Eastern stores.

Dried aubergine skins

CULINARY USES

Aubergines have a sponge-like ability to soak up oil and cooking juices. Rather than being a drawback, this is one of the delights of aubergines, except when they are fried. To prevent them from absorbing too much oil in the frying pan, Middle Eastern cooks soak the sliced or diced aubergines in salted water and then drain them before using. Otherwise, the succulent aubergine flesh should be left

Aubergine

to absorb all the garlicky, tasty goodness of the dish.

Perhaps the most famous aubergine dish in the Middle East is the Turkish *İmam bayıldı* (p51), the sumptuous stuffed aubergine dish over which the Imam was said to have fainted with pleasure at the quantity of olive oil used. Aubergines are frequently smoked over a naked flame and then the cooked pulp is used in numerous olive oil- or yogurt-based salads and dips, such as the Turkish *patlıcan ezmesi* and the great Lebanese and Syrian favourite, *baba ghanoush* (p82, also known as *moutabal*). In Turkey, the famous dish, *Hünkâr beğendi* (p46), meaning 'Sultan's delight', consists of the smoked pulp combined with a cheese sauce and served as a bed for meatballs cooked in a tomato sauce. The long, thin varieties are stuffed with an aromatic rice and the plumper ones are split open and stuffed with meat,

such as the Turkish *karnıyarık*. Throughout the Middle East, they are fried or grilled and served with plain or garlic-flavoured yogurt, or a fresh, piquant tomato sauce; they can also be served with a dressing made with olive oil, garlic and pomegranate or grape molasses. In recipes for which we can also use courgettes, fried aubergine slices or chunks are added to meatballs and patty mixtures and are baked with *rishta* (p125) in a tomato sauce.

Aubergines are a popular ingredient in bulgur or rice *pilafs*, such as the Istanbul *patlicanlı pilav*, in pulse and vegetable dishes, such as the Iranian aubergine and pomegranate stew *sheeshandâz*, which is just an aubergine *fesenjân*, in savoury pastries, and in lamb stews. They are delicious in an Arab *fatta* dish, particularly favoured in Egypt and Syria, where a bed of toasted pitta bread is layered with cooked lamb and fried

aubergine, and topped with a garlic and *tahini*-flavoured yogurt. A rather splendid-looking mould of aubergine, lamb and rice, *makloub* (*maqlubi*, p131), meaning 'turned over', is Palestinian in origin but can be found in Jordan, Lebanon, and Syria.

In the south of Turkey, Iran and Syria, a delicious jam is made with young, small, seedless aubergines, which are dipped in lime water to preserve their colour and shape before cooking. Pickled aubergine is also a great favourite, often stuffed with walnuts or peppers and wrapped in celery leaves, or the aubergine slices are wrapped around garlic.

The pulped, smoked flesh of grilled aubergines is mixed with a variety of ingredients throughout the Middle East to create tasty, soothing *mezze* dishes. The following recipe is particularly popular in Turkey.

PATLICAN EZMESİ
(SMOKED AUBERGINE PURÉE)

Serves 4
Preparation time 5 minutes + 15 minutes' grilling and peeling aubergines
Cooking time –

2 big aubergines
2–3 tablespoons olive oil
2 tablespoons white wine vinegar
3–4 cloves garlic, crushed
4–5 heaped tablespoons creamy set yogurt
Salt and freshly ground black pepper

Place the aubergines directly onto a gas flame or, if cooking outdoors, over a charcoal grill. Turn them occasionally until they are well smoked and soft. (If you are using a gas flame the aubergine skin will become charred and papery, whereas the charcoal grill lightens and toughens the skin.)

Take the aubergines by the stalks and hold them under cold running water to gently remove the skin, taking care to leave behind as much of the flesh as possible. Still holding the aubergines by the stems, gently squeeze the softened pulp to drain off the excess water, then lay them on a board.

Cut the stems off the aubergines and chop the flesh to a pulp. Put the flesh into a bowl and beat in the olive oil, vinegar and garlic, followed by the yogurt and seasoning. (All of these ingredients can easily be adjusted to your own taste.)

Spoon the mixture onto a serving dish and splash a little olive oil over it to keep it moist. Serve with plenty of fresh bread.

Patlıcan ezmesi

Wherever they conquered, the Arabs spread the aubergine and its many dishes, like the following classic Persian stew. Many variations of it can be found in the path of the Arab conquests. Traditionally, small whole aubergines and tiny, sour grapes should be used for this dish. To substitute, large aubergines could be cut into long strips and sultanas could be used, but the sourness will come only from unripe grapes.

KHORESHT-E BÂDENJÂN
(PERSIAN AUBERGINE STEW)

Serves 4
Preparation time 15–20 minutes
Cooking time approximately 1 hour

3–4 tablespoons olive oil (you may need more if using strips of aubergine as they will absorb more oil)
1kg (2¼lb) small aubergines
1 onion, halved and sliced
225g (8oz) lamb, trimmed of fat and cut into 2½cm (1in) cubes
1 teaspoon ground turmeric
2 tablespoons tomato paste
2 tomatoes, skinned and chopped
75g (3oz) small, unripe grapes
Juice of ½ lemon
Salt and freshly ground black pepper

Heat the olive oil in a heavy-based pan and fry the whole aubergines until they have softened (if using long strips of aubergine, fry them until golden). Remove from the pan and drain.

Add the onion to the pan and fry until golden. Add the lamb and brown it on both sides, then stir in the turmeric. Add the tomato paste, chopped tomatoes, sour grapes and lemon juice, with enough water to cover. Put on the lid and simmer gently for approximately 30 minutes.

Strings of dried aubergines and capsicum peppers for sale

Pop the aubergines back into the pan, add a little water to cover, season with salt and pepper, and simmer for a further 20 minutes, until the meat is tender.

Spoon the stew onto a serving dish, placing the aubergines around the edge with the rest in the middle. Serve hot with rice.

A classic dish from the Ottoman Palace kitchens, *karnıyarık* literally translates as 'split stomach' as the whole aubergines are slit open and filled. The dish can be made with fat or thin aubergines and served hot or cold.

KARNIYARIK
(AUBERGINE STUFFED WITH MINCED LAMB)

Serves 4
Preparation time 25–30 minutes
Cooking time approximately 1 hour

225g (8oz) minced lamb
1 onion, finely chopped
2 tomatoes, skinned and chopped
1 tablespoon tomato purée
2 tablespoons pine nuts
1 teaspoon ground cinnamon
1 teaspoon ground allspice
a bunch of fresh parsley and dill, chopped
salt and freshly ground black pepper
4 aubergines, partially peeled like the stripes of a zebra and soaked in salted water for 1 hour
Sunflower oil
1 tomato, sliced
Green bell pepper, cut into 4 strips
4 tablespoons olive oil
Juice of ½ lemon
Roughly 4 tablespoons water
1 teaspoon sugar

Preheat the oven to 200°C/ 400°F/Gas mark 6.

Put the minced lamb in a bowl with the onion, tomatoes, tomato purée, nuts, spices, herbs and seasoning, and mix well. Knead the mixture with your hands, lifting it up and slapping it down into the bowl, until it resembles a paste.

Drain the aubergines and pat dry. Heat up some sunflower oil in a shallow pan and roll the aubergine in it until they are lightly browned and softened. Lift the aubergines out of the oil and place them in a oven-proof dish. Use a knife or tongs to slit each aubergine open, down the middle from top to botto, taking care not to cut through the bottom and to leave the ends intact. Prise each slit open and stuff them with the meat mixture. Place a slice of tomato at the head of the meat stuffing and a strip of pepper below it, as if it is the stem and the tomato is the flower. Mix together the olive oil, lemon juice and water with the sugar and pour over the stuffed aubergines. Cover the dish with foil, pop it in the oven for 20 minutes, then remove the foil and put it back in the oven for a further 40 minutes, until the meat and aubergines are very tender and almost all the liquid has gone. Serve hot or cold.

SPINACH

(SABANIKH) *Spinacia oleracea*

Fresh spinach

According to the twelfth-century Arab writer, Ibn al-Awam, spinach is the 'prince of vegetables'. It originated in Persia, where it was cultivated as early as the fourth century AD and was used as a herb. The word spinach derives from the old Persian name, *aspanakh*. Once the Arabs had incorporated spinach into their cuisine, it spread across the Middle East and into Europe, via the Moorish occupation of Spain. There are medieval recipes of Arab origin that use spinach in sweet dishes, combined with ingredients such as honey, almonds and spices, but the spinach dishes of the Middle East today are all savoury.

HOW IT GROWS

Spinach is a member of the beet family, which grows in temperate climates, often near the sea. It can be grown all year round but it is best picked small while the leaves are still tender.

APPEARANCE AND TASTE

Fresh spinach leaves vary in size and tenderness but all are dark green in colour. When cooked, spinach becomes soft-textured with a strong flavour, which marries well with spices and creamy substances such as yogurt and soft cheese.

BUYING AND STORING

You have to buy a lot of fresh spinach to make a reasonable-sized dish – the leaves reduce greatly when cooked. If you can, buy spinach on the stalk while it's still springy. Fresh spinach doesn't keep for long but it can be cooked and frozen, or bought frozen, which is useful for soups and stews.

MEDICINAL AND OTHER USES

Spinach has a mild laxative effect. It is rich in vitamins and minerals and is regarded as a source of iron and calcium. Spinach juice is such a strong green colour, it is used as a vegetable dye.

CULINARY USES

Spinach combines well with cheese and eggs in the Arab-style omelette, *eggah*, and in fillings for thin savoury pastries and flat breads, such as *fatayer bi sabanikh*, a bread-dough pie filled with a mixture of spinach, raisins and walnuts. In Iran, spinach is layered with rice and meat in a rather grand inverted dish called *tahcheen-o esfenâj*. Throughout the Middle East, spinach is added to *pilafs* or partnered with beans or chickpeas, for colour and texture, such as *aloo sfenaj*, a Persian dish of black-eyed beans, spinach and prunes. It forms a thick sauce in a variety of lamb stews with almonds, sultanas, apricots and prunes, or with tart yellow plums in the Iranian dish *khoresht-e esfenâj-o aloo*. It is often cooked on its own, softened in a little butter with prunes or almonds, or it is sautéed with onions and blended with yogurt in the Iranian dish *boorâni-ye esfenâj*, and in a similar Turkish dish, *ıspanak ezmesi*. In Iran and the Gulf, a piquant, sour-tasting soup is made with spinach and split peas, and in Egypt, the yogurt soup *labaneya*, can be made with spinach or beet leaves. Chopped spinach is added to meatballs, or it is cooked in an ancient, hearty manner with meatballs and chickpeas, and it also appears with brown lentils in a medieval Persian dish, *shula kalambar*, which was believed to cure the sick.

Masjid-I-Jomeh, Isfahan, Iran

Baskets of spinach leaves in a marketplace

A popular way of cooking spinach in the Middle East is to sauté it with onions, or with pine nuts and raisins, toasted almonds or prunes. Simple and delicious, the following recipe is from Iraq.

SABANIKH BI KHAWKH
(SPINACH WITH PRUNES AND TOMATOES)

Serves 3–4
Preparation time 5–10 minutes
Cooking time 10 minutes

450g (1lb) fresh spinach
2 tablespoons olive oil plus a little
*   butter*
1 onion, halved and sliced
2 tomatoes, skinned and chopped
110g (4oz) soft, pitted prunes
*   (soak in water if not soft)*
½–1 teaspoon ground coriander
A scant teaspoon sugar
Salt and freshly ground black
*   pepper*

Wash the spinach well and remove any tough-looking leaves or stems. Put it into a pan, cover with the lid, and cook for a few minutes over a low heat, until the leaves soften and droop. Drain off any excess water and chop the spinach coarsely.

Heat the olive oil and butter in a shallow pan, stir in the onion, and fry until golden.

Add the tomatoes, prunes, coriander and sugar, and cook for a few minutes, until the mixture has reduced a little. Mix in the spinach, season to taste, and serve hot.

According to legend, the origins of the Persian *boorâni* dishes are attributed to Queen Poorandokht, a monarch of the Sassanian dynasty in AD 626. She was said to be so fond of yogurt dishes that the chefs of the royal kitchens created some

Sabanikh bi khawkh

specifically for her, calling them *Poorâni* after the queen herself. Later, the conquering Arabs adopted these dishes, changing the 'p' to a 'b' to suit their alphabet. The most popular *boorâni* dish is made with spinach, and variations of it are found throughout the Middle East. Traditionally, it is served as an accompaniment to a main course. In Turkey, where the dish is known by its Persian name in two of the Islamic strongholds, Bursa and Konya, it is served as a *meze*.

BOORÂNI-YE ESFENÂJ
(SPINACH WITH YOGURT)

Serves 4
Preparation time 5–10 minutes
*   (plus overnight straining of*
*   yogurt if necessary)*
Cooking time 10–15 minutes

2 tablespoons olive oil plus butter
2 onions, halved and sliced
½ teaspoon ground turmeric
1kg (2¼ lb) fresh spinach, washed,
*   drained and chopped*
225g (8fl oz) strained yogurt
Salt and freshly ground pepper

In a heavy-based pan, heat up the oil and butter. Stir in the onions and fry until golden. Stir in the turmeric and add the spinach.

Cover the pan and cook gently until the spinach is soft. Mix well and leave to cool.

Beat the strained yogurt in a bowl and add the spinach. Mix well and season to taste.

Serve cold, or chilled, with bread.

GLOSSARY

Advieh An Iranian spice mixture which varies from region to region, sometimes with pistachio nuts or rose petals, but always including cardamom.

Alya The fat rendered from the podgy tail of the Asian sheep bred in the Middle East. Called *kuyrukyağı* in Turkish and *roghan-e donbeh* in Farsi, it is mainly used in the meat and grain dishes of rural areas.

Arak A clear alcoholic drink, distilled from grapes and flavoured with aniseed, that turns cloudy when diluted with water. In Turkey, where it is particularly popular with *meze* and fish, it is called *rakı*.

Baharat A ground spice mixture used throughout the Arab world. It varies from region to region, but generally includes black pepper, coriander seeds, cumin, cinnamon, cardamom, cloves, nutmeg and paprika.

Bastirma Air-dried fillet of cured beef in a fenugreek and garlic paste, called *pastırma* in Turkish and sometimes spelled *basterma* in Arabic.

Börek Turkish savoury pastries from the Ottoman period. They can be baked, steamed or fried.

Chelow Persian steamed white rice which is first parboiled.

Dibs A thick molasses from a variety of pressed fruits, used as a sweetener or for its fruity flavour. Called *robb* in Iran and *pekmez* in Turkey.

Dolma Any Turkish dish that is stuffed, such as peppers, tomatoes, courgette flowers, vine leaves, and baby squid. Even the stuffed taxis in the cities are called *dolmuş*. In Iraq stuffed vegetables are known as *yapraq* from the Turkish word for leaf, *yaprak*.

Eggah Arab omelettes packed full of ingredients, akin to a Spanish omelette. Similar omelettes in Iran are called *kookoo*.

Eid-el-Kurban An Islamic festival that marks Ibrahim's near-sacrifice of Isma'il (p69) . A sheep is slaughtered and almost every part of it is consumed. In Turkey, the same festival is called *Kurban Bayramı*.

Eishta Thick clotted cream, usually made from water-buffalo milk, known as *gaymar* in Iraq and *kaymak* in Turkey.

Ezme A Turkish meze dish of pounded, pulped, or puréed ingredients, often with olive oil or yogurt, that can be scooped up easily with bread.

Fatta A traditional dish of toasted, or stale, bread soaked in broth. The word *fatta* describes the breaking or crumbling of bread into pieces.

Fesenjân An ancient Persian dish of fowl or fish stewed with walnuts and sour pomegranate juice, known as *fisinjan* in Iraq.

Fila Paper-thin sheets of flat bread dough, used for sweet and savoury deep-fried and layered pastries. Similar flat breads are called *yufka* in Turkey and *lavash* in Iran.

Furn communal oven used for leavened and unleavened breads, called *firin* in Turkish.

Halwa A sweetmeat made with wheat or *tahini* and nuts or spices, called *helva* in Turkey.

Hawayij A peppery spice mixture from Yemen, combining black peppercorns, caraway, cardamom and turmeric.

Kanaka The small, tin-lined, brass or copper pot with a long handle for brewing coffee, called a *cezve* in Turkish.

Khoresht A thin Persian stew which is traditionally used as a sauce for rice.

Kibbeh Savoury balls or patties made with pounded meat and bulgur, a speciality of Lebanon and Syria.

Kishk A dried and fermented mixture of wheat and yogurt used to flavour and thicken stews and soups, known as *tarkhina* in Iraq and *tarhana* in Turkey.

Laban The thick and creamy yogurt, made from the milk of cows, sheep, or goats. In Farsi it is *mâst* and the Turkish word is *yoğurt*, from which the word 'yogurt' derives. *Laban* is also a popular yogurt drink, which is sometimes called *abdug* and is known as *doogh* in Farsi and *ayran* in Turkish. When yogurt is strained to the consistency of cream cheese, it is called *labna* in Arabic.

Lime water Slaked lime powder diluted with water used for bleaching and preserving young fruits and vegetables in jams.

Mansaf The national dish of Jordan and Arabia, consisting of a whole sheep or baby camel served on a bed of rice.

Mezze Literally translated as a 'pleasant taste' *mezze* can either be served as an appetiser to a meal, or as a nibble with a drink. The key to *mezze* dishes is to keep the quantities small, the colours vibrant, and the textures and tastes varied. In some parts of the Arab world *mezze* are called *mazza* and, in Turkey, the spelling is *meze*.

Polow A Persian method of cooking rice by parboiling it and then steaming it with vegetables, fruit, nuts and spices.

Ramadan The ninth month of the Muslim lunar calendar during which the devout fast from sunrise to sunset. It is called *Ramazan* in Turkey.

Rishta Middle Eastern noodles which are boiled or baked like pasta. The word derives from the Persian, *reshteh*.

Samna Clarified butter (or ghee), made from the churned milk of sheep, goats or buffalo. With its distinctive taste and good keeping qualities, it is the preferred cooking fat amongst the nomadic and peasant communities.

Sujuk Air-dried lamb or beef sausages with lots of spices, particularly cumin, called *sucuk* in Turkish.

Tahdeeg The golden-brown crust that forms at the bottom of the rice pot, a traditional feature of Persian rice.

Tahini A thick sesame paste made from crushed sesame seeds, used most in the cuisines of Syria and Lebanon. It is called *tahin* in Turkish and *rashi* in Iran and Iraq.

Tandoor A traditional outdoor clay oven for bread, called a *tandır* in Turkish.

Tarator A nut and garlic sauce commonly served with fish.

Zaatar An Arab spice mixture which includes sesame seeds, sumac, salt and dried thyme.

Zeytinyağlı Vegetable dishes cooked in olive oil and served cold, a legacy of the Ottoman Palace kitchens.

Zhug A fiery paste from Yemen, made with chillies, cardamom and garlic.

BIBLIOGRAPHY

For further reading on the food and culinary cultures of the Middle East, here's a list of books that proved invaluable to me when researching this one:

Miriam Al Hashimi, *Traditional Arabic Cooking* (Garnet Publishing: 1993)
Ghillie Başan, *Classic Turkish Cookery* (I.B. Tauris: 1997)
Alan Davidson, *The Oxford Companion to Food* (Oxford: 1999)
Halil Inalcık, *The Ottoman Empire* (Phoenix: 1994)
Tess Mallos, *The Complete Middle East Cookbook* (Grub Street: 1995)
Middle East (Lonely Planet, third edition: 2000)
Claudia Roden, *A New Book of Middle Eastern Food* (Penguin Books: 1986)
Margaret Shaida, *The Legendary Cuisine of Persia* (Penguin Books: 1994)
Wilfred Thesiger, *Arabian Sands* (Penguin Books: 1964)
Wilfred Thesiger, *The Marsh Arabs* (Penguin Books: 1967)
Sonia Uvezian, *Recipes and Remembrances from an Eastern Mediterranean Kitchen* (University of Texas Press: 1999)
Sami Zubaida and Richard Tapper (eds), *Culinary Cultures of the Middle East* (I.B. Tauris: 1994)

INDEX

ACKNOWLEDGEMENTS

We would like to thank everyone, here and abroad, who has been involved in this book. It has been a delightfully aromatic journey from beginning to end and we are indebted to many. In particular, we would like to mention Sally Little of the Jordan Tourism Board and Lana Harmaneh in Amman, Bärbel Kirchner of the Government of Dubai, Dubai Department of Tourism and Commerce Marketing, Turkish Airlines (THY) and the Turkish Tourist Board. We would also like to thank the Fry family of Frys of Chelsea for supplying fruit and vegetables for photography, particularly Maureen who went out of her way to send them to us in our remote location. And Mrs Shahla Suleiman and Lel Scobie in the Department of Islamic and Middle Eastern Studies at Edinburgh University who gave up their time to assist with some of the Arabic words.

We would like to mention our agent, Giles Gordon, who is always an encouraging voice at the end of the phone. We take our hats off to Kyle Cathie, herself, both for taking us on in the first place and for bearing with us under frustrating circumstances. Robina Pelham-Burn, the copy-editor, was a star for meticulously editing the text between children, Christmas parties and nativity plays. Georgina Burns worked hard and long, patiently sourcing photographs. And Sheila Davies, the editor, deserves a medal for her mammoth task of laboriously checking details and photographs against the clock. Where others would have torn their hair out, she never lost her charm or her cool.

On a more personal note, we salute Emin and Sibel Iren for all their help on the ground and for extending their warm hospitality in their sumptuous apartment to include our boisterous children. Similarly, Ali and Tess Erginsoy kindly leant us props and dishes but, more importantly, they frequently and uncomplainingly looked after our children. To both sets of friends, we owe a big thank you.

All photography by Jonathan Başan except the following:
Bridgeman Art Library p13, 15 (Rouargue brothers), p138 (Lemoine engraving) & 232; **Garden Picture Library:** Christi Carter p180, Christopher Fairweather p80 (bottom); Lamontagne p97 (bottom), 217; Marie O'Hara p202; **Hayes Archive:** p86 (top), 138, 150, 170, 172, 176 & 221; **Impact Colour Library:** Christopher Bluntzer p39, 69 & 81; Mark Cator p64 & 80 (top); Rupert Conant p25; Alex Dufort p26, 56 & 212; Ben Edwards p23 & 126; Paul Forster p53; Michael Good p33 (top), 38, 49 (top), 60 (bottom) & 168; Mark Henley p16, 18, 72 (top), 86 (bottom), 101 & 208x2; Colin Jones p240; Alan Keohane p11, 14, 17, 19, 22, 30/1, 34 (top), 36, 45, 46x2, 49 (bottom), 51, 62, 65x2, 66, 68, 72 (bottom), 84 (bottom), 93 (top), 190 (top), 214 (bottom left); Toby Key p83 & 84 (top) Robin Laurance p5 & 27; Alain le Garsmeur p52 (top); Wendy Levine p158; W. Louvet/Visa p210; Bill Lyons p107 & 227 (bottom); Farzin Malaki p42, 61 (top), 76 & 121 (top); Gary John Norman p24; Caroline Penn p20, 28, 33 (bottom), 52 (bottom), 61 (bottom), 122, 124, 134, 164, 207 (top) & 219; Dominic Sansoni p148/9; Simon Shepheard p34 (bottom), 71 (bottom), 90 & 206; Paul Simmons p12; Bruce Stephens p214 (bottom right); Pamela Toler p99 (top) & 174; Alexis Wallerstein p224; **Lonely Planet:** Greg Elms p44 (top), 103 (top), 130, 132 (bottom); Eddie Gerald p60; Thomas Hartwell p110/1; Matthew Kurrian p93 (bottom); Chris Mellor p58/9 & 94; Tony Wheeler p117; **Still Picture Library:** Jack Mikrut p8/9